Living Liminal
A Slice of Pandemic Life

LINDA HOYE

ALSO BY LINDA HOYE

Two Hearts: An Adoptee's Journey Through Grief to Gratitude

The Presence of Absence: A Story About Busyness, Brokenness, and Being Beloved

LINDA HOYE

LIVING LIMINAL: A SLICE OF PANDEMIC LIFE

BENSON

Living Liminal: A Slice of Pandemic Life
By Linda Hoye

Copyright © 2023 Linda Hoye
All rights reserved

No part of this book may be reproduced in any form, except for brief quotations in printed reviews, without prior written permission from the author.

Benson Books
Moose Jaw, Saskatchewan

Contact the author at linda@lindahoye.com
www.lindahoye.com

ISBN: 978-0-9937303-4-4

DEDICATION

For those who will follow.

The grace of God means something like: "Here is your life. You might never have been, but you *are*, because the party wouldn't have been complete without you. Here is the world. Beautiful and terrible things will happen. Don't be afraid. I am with you. Nothing can ever separate us. It's for you I created the universe. I love you."

Frederick Buechner

INTRODUCTION

In 2020, memes on social media reminded us that while we were weathering the same storm, we were doing so in different boats. COVID-19 affected every person in every place in the world, but we live in different places, belong to different demographic groups, and dealt with different regulations according to varying timelines. Our experiences were not the same. In British Columbia, Canada, we learned to live in the liminality of waiting for a semblance of pre-pandemic life to return while weathering an unprecedented fire season in 2021—the third worst on record in terms of area burned—followed by flooding and mudslides. The term "post-apocalyptic" has been overused, but it's what it felt like as we grew wearier and wearier.

This book chronicles 2020 and 2021, describing quotidian days, in times that were anything but, by way of snippets of blog posts from *A Slice of Life* (https://www.lindahoye.com), social media posts, poetry, and journal entries.

Interspersed throughout these pages are orders put into place by British Columbia's medical officer, Dr. Bonnie Henry. It is not a comprehensive list and is included to only to provide context. You'll also find statements from B.C.'s Health Minister, Adrian Dix and Premier, John Horgan. The wildfires mentioned during the summer of 2021 are those deemed "wildfires of note" in the Thompson-Nicola and Columbia-Shuswap regional districts which are closest to Kamloops. It is, by no means, a comprehensive list of fires.

The picture we are left with when the world settles into whatever the After looks like should not be the one presented solely through the filter of the mainstream media. To understand the human cost these years demanded of us, we must consider the experience of ordinary people in the culture and context of the time. *Living Liminal* is my contribution to that story.

(This book was not professionally edited. I set the work aside in early summer of 2022 and, upon returning it, felt the trauma of those years settle in my gut like a brick. Maybe it was still too soon. I didn't think I could go back there, and I didn't want to go back there, but felt it important to do so. This is a chronicle for the benefit of those who will follow—our grandchildren, great-grandchildren, and so on—so I moved forward with it, real and raw, much like I, and countless others, felt during 2020 and 2021. I trust you'll forgive mistakes.)

Linda Hoye, 2023

In December 2019, there are news reports of a new infectious coronavirus identified in the city of Wuhan, China in the Hubei province spreading rapidly from person to person.

I don't the give the story more than casual passing notice

YEAR ONE

JANUARY 2020

Saturday, January 18, 2020

Gerry and I arrive home in the wee hours, far, far too late for this old body to still be upright. We stumble around suitcases and fall exhausted into bed. Unpacking will come tomorrow—or later today, depending on how you think about it. We spent the first weeks of 2020 at the Grand Palladium all-inclusive resort in Playa del Carmen, Mexico. It was muggy and hot and windy and rainy and sunny and all the things a vacation should be. I read seven books and started another, sipped lattes, scribbled in my notebook, and stood on the beach before dawn worshipping the Creator, and watching the sunrise. We spent days on the sandy beach and others poolside, at one of the quiet adult pools. We enjoyed good food and conversation. We walked, though not as much as in past years because I'm still recovering from surgery I had in the fall, and rested. It was a grand way to kick off the year.

Now I'm awake after having had too few hours of sleep, sitting in the dark and sipping a soy milky frothy cup of coffee (and missing my Mexican lattes), thinking about things it's time to turn my attention to. The new book I'm birthing in a few months. Laundry. The impressive amount of snow on our deck that Gerry will have to tend to after he picks up our Yorkshire Terrier, Maya, from the dog sitter, and that I'll probably take a nap later.

On January 21, 2020 Adrian Dix, British Columbia's Minister of Health and Dr. Bonnie Henry, the Provincial Health Officer, release a joint statement: "The B.C. Centre for Disease Control and provincial and federal authorities are closely monitoring the

> outbreak of respiratory illness linked to a novel coronavirus. The risk to British Columbians is considered low." [1]

> On January 25, 2020, Adrian Dix and Dr. Henry release a joint statement: "We can confirm that a resident of Ontario is presumed positive for the novel coronavirus that arose late last year in Wuhan, China. To date, there have been no cases of illness caused by the novel coronavirus in British Columbia."[2]

Monday, January 27, 2020

Somewhere along the way, many of us bought in to the myth of "having it all". It's bunk. We realize that now. All one has to do is pay attention to nature to see that there's a reason for different seasons. Each one is unique, each with its own beauty and wisdom. Today, piles of snow from the big storm that blew in while we were on vacation get smaller every day and rivers of snowmelt flow down the streets. A few days ago, I spotted a hyacinth poking up in my flower bed. A hyacinth. In January. What a delight.

Last year I set aside my photography hobby in favor of finishing writing a new book. I missed the world I became part of behind the lens of my camera, but chose to dwell in a season of words instead, knowing I'd return to photography in a different season. Two days ago, Gerry and I drove all over town looking for cut tulips I could photograph. We finally walked through the doors at the local garden shop where fragrant pots of hyacinths in bloom chased residual winter blues from my mind. A rack filled with seed packets greeted us. I opened the door of the cooler where cut flowers were kept and stepped inside. There were cheery yellow daffodils and pink tulips among the more traditional bouquets—not many, but enough to entice.

"It's so good to be here again!" I told the clerk when we paid for an overpriced bunch of the tulips that was worth every penny we pay.

Later, I spent an hour or so in the good company of my camera and those tulips, reminding myself of the gift photography gives me. I'm rusty, and it will take time to get my groove back, but I enjoy the practice. The slow, meditative process of moving around, leaning in, and looking at pockets and

---

[1] https://news.gov.bc.ca/releases/2020HLTH0010-000102
[2] https://news.gov.bc.ca/releases/2020HLTH0011-000129

curls of waxy petals you don't see unless you pause, pay attention, and look closely, all combine to create pure magic.

The season is changing. Weather forecasters are calling for record-breaking temperatures by the end of the week—record-breaking in the right direction, as opposed to the record-breaking deep freeze that settled over the province a few weeks ago when we were still in Mexico. But it's still early and I've been fooled before, thinking winter was over, then been surprised by a late-season storm. It could happen again. Whether winter raises her head with one last blustery blast, or we continue the trajectory toward spring, every day is one day closer to gardening season.

This morning I wake and it's my birthday. I am sixty-one and it feels like a fresh start. I can't imagine what beautiful and terrible things will happen in the coming year; I won't even try. But in tulips and other magical things I plan to examine through my macro lens I'll find both wisdom and wonder. Of that I'm certain.

On January 28, 2020, Adrian Dix and Dr. Henry issue a joint statement: "Late yesterday, our BC Centre for Disease Control public health lab confirmed a positive test for 2019-nCoV. He travels regularly to China for work and was in Wuhan city on his most recent trip. He returned to Vancouver last week and had an onset of symptoms after his return . . . The risk of spread of this virus within British Columbia remains low at this time . . . It is not necessary for the general public to take special precautions beyond the usual measures recommended to prevent other common respiratory viruses during the winter period. Regular handwashing, coughing or sneezing into your elbow sleeve, disposing of tissues appropriately, and avoiding contact with sick people are important ways to prevent the spread of respiratory illness generally." [3]

---

[3] https://news.gov.bc.ca/releases/2020HLTH0015-000151

FEBRUARY 2020

Saturday, February 1, 2020
　　I'm in the den, curled up cozy under a Sherpa blanket with a basketful of books and pens beside me, sipping a mug of soy milky frothy coffee. There's a fierce wind blowing outside. Powerful gusts shake the windows next to the sofa. This wind is different from a January gale that whips whorls of snow into a feverish dance we watch, mesmerized, from the comfort of our homes and offices. This is a working February wind that will get rid of more snow that's been melting and running in rivers these past weeks, making everything dirty and messy. I welcome it.
　　The sound of its fury reminds me that when I'm comfortable somewhere, there's another somewhere where something rages for someone else. Comfort is nothing but a fleeting, often temporary, imagining. As the wind rages, I whisper the names of those on my mind in prayer, releasing the foolish notion that I have answers to their concerns and lifting them toward Love instead. It's windy here. It's dead calm elsewhere. Somewhere a sparrow sings; another shelters from a storm; still another lies cold on the ground. Whenever I think I have things figured out, more questions come. It's in the mystery where I find real answers. And in the wind. Sometimes in the wind.

Sunday, February 2, 2020
　　Gerry brought home a bunch of loud, brash looking tulips a week ago, after the ones I bought at the nursery were finished. I pulled out my camera, affixed my macro lens, and shot a few images, knowing I'd convert them to black and white in post processing because the colours were too much for the calm I hungered for. Now they too are past their prime and there's an uncommon beauty in their wizened petals. I see truth when I look at them and leave them on the table for another day.

Wednesday, February 5, 2020

We're at the walking track one morning and I see a young man I went to high school with on the exercise equipment. It's not him, of course, but it takes a couple of laps before I realize it. The mind plays tricks when it comes to age. It does the same with seasons.

A touch of spring fever took hold when we returned from vacation. I started thinking about what I would do in the garden this year and summer trips we might take. The sunshine and warm weather certainly felt like the start of spring. Then, overnight it changed. Snow and below freezing temperatures returned, and that sweet little hyacinth in the front yard is now tucked away under a blanket of snow. I get fooled every year. But the fever prompted me to order seeds, photograph tulips, and gave me enough of a taste of what's coming to carry me through this short month that always feels so long.

Now, there's that scraping sound of my neighbour's shovel on the driveway. When I glanced out the front window as I waited for the coffeemaker to cough out a cup of elixir earlier, I saw a distinctive glow in the valley below that could only mean one thing: more snow fell overnight. The scrape confirms it.

Sometimes, I try to fool myself into believing I have control over things like aging and seasons, and then wisdom reminds me of my folly. Just be present, it tells me. Wrap your sixty-one-year-old arms around the here and now, hold lightly the gift of the moment, and just say thank you.

Friday, February 7, 2020

I miss the awe of watching the changing eastern sky in the early morning when morning whispers and night tiptoes into obscurity. For many months now, when I wake shortly after 4 a.m., I've chosen to spend the first silent hours under a blanket in the den with a basket of supplies (Bible, notebook, pens, sticky notes) and a cup of soy milky frothy coffee on the table next to me. I do the same thing here that I used to do there. Read scripture. Scribble thoughts. Contemplate. The important work of keeping the wild things away while I fuel up for the day.

This morning I thought about that eastern sky and the wonder of dawn breaking and a holy presence that's just as likely to show up in this room where, in a couple of hours, a little Yorkie will make herself known and I'll open one of the French doors, welcome her into my sanctuary. She'll jump up on one of the sofas and curl up for a couple more hours of sleep.

There's the scrape of our neighbour's snow shovel again and, sure as anything, there's something holy in that sound. Practicing the presence. That's how a 17th century monk described abiding with the Divine in the quotidian. Day begins. Practice resumes.

Monday, February 10, 2020

I pull the KitchenAid from the cupboard where it languishes lonely most of the time, and rummage around looking for the dough hook. Then I dump flour, yeast, kosher salt, and water in the bowl and, after it's kneaded the dough for eight minutes while I putter around doing other things, wonder why I don't do this more often. I form two dough boules, give them a light coating of oil, and leave them to rest under a warm, damp towel for longer than an hour but they seem none the worse for wear for it. Then I make pizza.

Sliced tomatoes from the hydroponic kitchen garden and mozzarella from the grocery store adorn one. I cut up ham and a chunk of pineapple leftover from Friday's dinner for the other. (I know. Hawaiian pizza is oddly more of a Canadian thing.) After the tomato one is baked, I snip fresh basil leaves—also from the hydroponic kitchen garden—for the top, and there's supper. The task seemed daunting when I thought about it but when I get around to it, it's nothing. So many things are like that.

On February 11, 2020, the World Health Organization (WHO) Director-General holds a media briefing announcing an official name for the new respiratory disease caused by the novel coronavirus. Initially referred to as the "Wuhan virus" or "nCoV-2019", the WHO deems it COVID-19. CO for corona, VI for virus, D for disease, and 2019 for the year it was first discovered.

"The development of vaccines and therapeutics is one important part of the research agenda—but it is only one part. They will take time to develop, but in the meantime, we are not defenseless. There are many basic public health interventions that are available to us now, and which can prevent infections now. The first vaccine could be ready in 18 months, so we have to do everything today using the available weapons to fight the virus, while preparing

for the long-term." [4]

Wednesday, February 12, 2020

What if the most important thing I carry with me today is the delight I took in seeing slivers of moonlight reach through the blinds and come to rest on the grey vinyl plank floor in my den? Or the sound my pen makes as it glides across a page in my notebook? Or the comfort of the first sip of soy milky frothy coffee? Or the silence? What if I listen to poets more than politicians? And trust prayer more than the news? And turn off the noise. And sit in silence. What if?

> *On February 14, 2020, Adrian Dix and Dr. Henry issue a joint statement: Today we are announcing a new case of COVID-19 in B.C. A female in her 30s is presumed positive based on local testing . . . She lives in the Interior Health region and recently returned from China . . . Interior Health is actively investigating. Her close contacts have been identified and are being contacted. The patient is in isolation at home . . . The risk of spread of this virus within British Columbia remains low at this time."* [5]

Sunday, February 16, 2020

I meet a young man who mentions he took vacation last month.

"Where did you go?" I ask.

"I visited my family in the Kootenays for a week and spent another week at home."

He tells me how rested he felt when he returned to work, like he had really been on vacation. I think about the staycations I took over the years—how I leaned in to them and appreciated the peace of being at home and doing whatever I wanted, which was usually not very much. I returned to the office

---

[4] https://www.who.int/director-general/speeches/detail/who-director-general-s-remarks-at-the-media-briefing-on-2019-ncov-on-11-february-2020
[5] https://sd38.bc.ca/news/2020-02-14/ministry-health-novel-coronavirus-feb-14-2020

feeling refreshed too. Vacations spent at home were among the best times I spent away from the office. I always felt a little guilty when asked what I was planning to do, or what I did, on my vacation. As if staying home wasn't enough. There's that word again—enough—it's dogged me for much of my life. I'm finally learning to stand face-to-face with it and call it out for what it is. Liar. I am enough. I have enough. I do enough. I believe it most of the time.

Now I'm on permanent staycation and it's a sweet time of life. We vacation away now and then—but not often. It's always been my desire to stay home. Now I can. When I think about that young man who recently returned from his vacation, I sense he is a kindred. As is my daughter, who is beginning a staycation of her own right now too. As are those who are deeply rooted in a place and in their home. It's a gift, this contentment. I grow more certain of it with every day.

Tuesday, February 18, 2020

We're out and about on a sunshiny mid-February afternoon, going about our business and enjoying one another's company, when we encounter a man who has fallen on the ice. He's injured—not seriously—but an ambulance has been called. We're shaken and choose not to go for a walk in this icy area after all. We're subdued. Each of us sitting with our own thoughts until we talk it through and the grip is loosened.

Things change in an instant. The older we get, the more likely one of those instants is to occur. They remind us not to live with dread, but with intention. Not to run hard, squeezing as much as possible for ourselves out of the time we're allotted, but to seek wisdom, enjoy the Divine, and worship with our lives. To make a quiet, lasting difference.

We stop at a park and photograph mallards instead, at the grocery store where we buy a bunch of happy daffodils, then at a coffee shop for a sandwich and a cup of coffee. Later, at home, we enjoy good conversation and a few jujubes (He always gives me the black ones. That's love.). Salmon for a late supper. And Doc Martin. Ordinary stuff that makes life extraordinary.

On February 19, 2020, Adrian Dix and Dr. Henry issue a joint statement. "Today we are announcing the first individual confirmed to have COVID-19 in B.C. has recovered. This is indicated by the resolution of symptoms, followed by two successive negative test results 24 hours apart ... The risk of this virus spreading within British Columbia remains low at this time." [6]

Thursday, February 20, 2020

I have a few questions.
How . . . ?
Is it . . . ?
What . . . ?
I scratch them on a page in my journal. One after another; they keep coming.
Through writing comes understanding. Not answers but illumination.
I scribble prayer.
I wonder if it's okay to use such a common word alongside a holy one.
Then I remember, that's the way this whole thing plays out.

JOURNAL ENTRY – February 24, 2020

Last evening, a blanket of dread or foreboding fell upon me for some unknown reason. This morning I feel a heaviness I can't explain. Maybe I need to release things that aren't serving me well in this season. I don't know.

Tuesday, February 25, 2020

It snows again. The white is startling and pretty. It's not as lovely as it was a couple of months ago because we're sick of it by now, but it makes for a good day to hunker down. I'm grateful for the opportunity. Gerry has a man cold, so he's been hunkering for a few days already. We bring up the 1000-piece jigsaw puzzle that's been languishing unfinished downstairs since we went on vacation and work in companionable quiet on it. It feels like December with no stress and it's nice.

Later I read (I've gotten better at setting busyness aside and doing this in the middle of the day), tend to some book release related work, lose two chess games, and make something different for supper. It's turns out to be a quiet, last-hurrah-of-winter kind of day.

Friday, February 28, 2020

One year ago, I posted a photo of my messy writing desk on social media with these words: "I've been at this pretty much all day and haven't made it

---

[6] https://news.gov.bc.ca/releases/2020HLTH0039-000294

past the second page. Whose idea was it for me to write another book anyway?"

I was buried in revisions of a new book and trying to find the shape of a story in sand I had metaphorically shoveled into a sandbox. It was fifteen months after I first dared to write in my journal that I felt a stirring to write a new book. For fifteen months I had walked a tightrope between inspiration and inability. I kept returning to the idea of writing a spiritual memoir yet felt unqualified. Who was I to think I knew enough of the love of God to write even a paragraph, let alone a book? But I did. I felt as though I had been given a touch of the Divine that surpassed the natural and veered sharply in the direction of the supernatural. I knew that love. I had experienced that love.

I wanted to put this project aside so many times. Even now I wonder if it wouldn't be smarter to toss the whole thing in a drawer, but there's this story about love that keeps wanting to be told. And so I write words that might never go anywhere but that I feel compelled to make note of anyway

MARCH 2020

Sunday, March 1, 2020

Gerry's been sick, so to combat cabin fever we drive across town to the park rather than down the hill to church. We walk in my favourite park—the one where ghosts of boys play baseball and girls wrapped in pink toddle in and out of a building that's no longer there. Worship looks different in a park than it does within four walls, but it's no less genuine. We wander down a trail and Gerry points out fat buds on bushes. Long greening weeping willow branches reach toward the ground. Later, back home, I spy different shades of green in the front flower bed—pale purple and yellow too. That's what I've been waiting for. Flowers.

Sunday unfolds gently with conversation, books, some of this, and a little of that. Gerry comes in from taking our Yorkie, Maya, out before bed and reports that light snow is falling. It's March and I'm not sure if it qualifies as coming in like a lion or a lamb. Either way, this is the month when spring shows up and there will be no stopping it.

JOURNAL ENTRY March 3, 2020

There's this heaviness. I felt it come upon me last night and it hasn't left.

Friday, March 6, 2020

Gerry and I go out for lunch at a little place on Columbia Street, where they serve an Indian buffet. It's become one of our favourite lunchtime treats. Three young people come in while we're feasting on butter chicken, vegetable korma, and naan bread, and sit down at the table behind me. We can tell by their conversation that they're university students and can't help but talk of profs and grades and assignments. They make us smile. It seems like a lifetime since that was our world. It was, I suppose. Many lifetimes, really. I think of myself as a young woman returning to school full time after her youngest started first grade. I had a goal and razor-sharp focus and determination. Those years weren't easy, but in some ways, they were halcyon.

But back to the present and the paneer and a spontaneous lunch out in the middle of the week for no particular reason at all. We'll run an errand on the way home, then Gerry will pull pots from the garage and give whatever is overwintering in them a drink of water. I'll curl up with a book and maybe close my eyes because I'm dead tired after a restless night. Yes, these are the real halcyon days.

JOURNAL ENTRY – March 7, 2020

This morning I am still burdened though I can't say why. I'm having trouble shaking the sense of dread, doom, and fear.

> On March 9, 2020, Adrian Dix and Dr. Henry issue a joint statement announcing the first death in the province attributed to COVID-19. "We are deeply saddened to announce that a resident of the Lynn Valley Care Centre in North Vancouver, a man in his 80s who was previously confirmed positive with COVID-19 (case 27), passed away. We offer our heartfelt condolences to his loved ones, and the staff who provided him care, during this difficult time." [7]

Monday, March 9, 2020

We go to sleep in Standard Time and wake in Daylight Saving Time having lost an hour. Technology makes it almost seamless. There's no longer the need to adjust a multitude of clocks in the house, but our bodies know something screwy is afoot. We get on with the day though, ignoring the foolishness that makes us think we are mighty enough to control time like we

---

[7] https://news.gov.bc.ca/releases/2020HLTH0068-000423

wish we could so many other things wisdom tells us it's best to leave alone. I've been carrying a burden. Last week was a bear for no reason I can pinpoint but there was a battle raging. Now it's Monday. Time to begin again in grace and with love, present, with my eyes and heart open to wonder.

On March 11, 2020, The WHO Director-General issues a media briefing in which the COVID-19 outbreak is declared a global pandemic. [8]

Wednesday, March 11, 2020

It's easier to allow my attention to get caught up in a whirlwind of anxiety about things over which I have little or no control than it is to love well. I wish it wasn't so, but it is. The news cycle is tough right now. We've never been on this path before. I don't know the answers, or even all the questions, but I know there's a human being with a hurting heart who could use a kind word and a prayer offered on her behalf today. We all could. It's easier to speculate and pontificate than to admit that in the quiet place where we're raw and real that we're scared and in pain and could use kindness and a prayer. Maybe tomorrow will be better or maybe it won't. Maybe it will just be different.

There are clumps of tiny purple crocuses in my garden that look a lot like hope, and even though I hear the scrape of my neighbour's snow shovel on his driveway, there are things happening and awakening beneath the surface of the cold soil in my garden that I can't see. In the crocuses I see promise and grace. They remind me to focus more on love than fear today.

On March 12, 2020, Adrian Dix and Dr. Henry issue a joint briefing. "We are recommending against all non-essential travel outside of Canada, including to the United States. Effective today, anyone who chooses to travel outside of Canada will be asked to stay away from work or school for 14 days upon their return. We know that this is a voluntary measure,

---

[8] https://www.who.int/director-general/speeches/detail/who-director-general-s-opening-remarks-at-the-media-briefing-on-covid-19---11-march-2020

but it is our expectation that people will follow this direction as part of their civic duty.

"Effective today, we also directing all event organizers to cancel any gathering larger than 250 people. This includes indoor and outdoor sporting events, conferences, meetings, religious gatherings or other similar events. This threshold has been selected, as it is much easier to maintain important social distancing to prevent transmission of COVID-19 . . . Over spring break the B.C. government will also work with school districts to develop procedures to be implemented with students and staff when classes resume . . . We recognize this will have a significant economic and social impact, and want to reassure British Columbians that these are temporary measures required to protect the health of the public at this critical time of pandemic. We will be reassessing these conditions on an ongoing basis as the pandemic evolves.[9]

The National Hockey League (NHL), the Western Hockey League (WHL), and the British Columbia Hockey League (BCHL) suspend their 2019-2020

---

[9] https://news.gov.bc.ca/releases/2020HLTH0077-000484

seasons. [10] [11] [12]

SOCIAL MEDIA POST

There's a lot of terrible this week. Let's make a point of looking for the beautiful and share it with one another.

Thursday, March 12, 2020
 We wake and check the news and, yes, the world is still in chaos. A low grade *something* simmers within us. We seek what we believe to be reputable news sources and choose not to walk in fear but there's no denying things are churning. We make jokes (some social media memes had Gerry and me chuckling out loud last night before bed) and shake our heads at the craziness. We bump fists and elbows, self-isolate, and socially distance. Feeling like we have no control scares us most of all. So, we lean in hard and listen to the still voice of timeless and eternal truth. We read a poem or write one. Pray. Practice gratitude, pass the peace, and ask for wisdom.
 March is a roaring, raging lion this year. A pandemic, crashing markets, and political chaos—a trifecta of discontent. We could get tangled up in the mess or choose to believe in poetry and prayer and that we've never had the control we like to think we have had.

Friday, March 13, 2020
 I'm on the highway, driving to Prince George to pick up our granddaughter, Makiya, and bring her back to Kamloops to spend spring break with us but it doesn't feel like my usual trip. Today is the last day of school before spring break. There are rumblings on the news that school may not return to status quo after the two-week break but so far, they're just that, rumblings. I was the road early, with a full gas tank and a large caramel macchiato in my cupholder. By the time I get to 100 Mile House I'm ready for a bio-break at my regular spot where I usually grab a breakfast

---

[10] https://www.nhl.com/news/nhl-coronavirus-to-provide-update-on-concerns/c-316131734
[11] https://whl.ca/article/western-hockey-league-pauses-season-until-further-notice.
[12] https://bchl.ca/bchl-season-cancelled

sandwich—but not today because it's closed, as are most fast-food places. If memory serves, there's a rest stop not too far down the road with outhouses so I drive on, hoping I'm right.

I'm in luck, and when I pull the squeaky door open to the smelly bathroom, I spy a roll of toilet paper on a holder. Toilet paper. That's a hot commodity right now. It's hard to find any anywhere. I've heard of single rolls being sold for a few dollars each. I chuckle to myself, hoping word doesn't get out that there's toilet paper here or it'll likely be stolen.

With the necessary things taken care of at the rest stop, I carry on down the highway. My phone rings. It's our financial advisor's administrative assistant. We have a meeting scheduled with our advisor the next and she wants to know if we'd like to postpone.

"No, I think we're okay to come in," I tell her, but I've barely hung up the hands-free when I second-guess myself, pull over, and call her back.

"Maybe we should push it out a couple of weeks," I say. Surely, this thing—whatever it is—will have settled down by then.

I switch on the radio to catch the news and learn that it's confirmed—schools in B.C. will not reopen after spring break and there's no date given for when they will. I arrive in Prince George to a harried daughter who is shaken at the developing story I do my best to keep a positive stance for her sake and that of my granddaughter.

JOURNAL ENTRY – March 13, 2020

The world is in chaos. A pandemic, crashing stock markets, political turmoil. It's hard not to be affected by what's happening. It's a challenge to maintain peace. This is where the rubber hits the road in terms of faith. Now is the time to be prudent but not panic. It's not so complicated when we break it down. Fear will cause us to react unwisely. That, and apathy. It's the time for wisdom and balance and prayer.

On Monday, March 16, many British Columbians begin working from home following directives to stay at home if able.

Monday, March 16, 2020

I saw a meme on social media last night that summed it up: "What a year this week has been." We're all feeling it. I'm struggling to focus and maybe you are too, but we continue to move forward one step at a time and, as best as we can, keep our eyes, minds, and hearts focused on ageless, timeless, and eternal things. Be kind to one another. Wash your hands, don't give in to fear, look to the rock of your faith to keep you strong. Stay home if you can, read good books, have deep conversations, and look for sparks of delight. We'll get through this.

> On March 16, 2020, Adrian Dix and Dr. Henry issue a joint statement. "We are issuing a new order prohibiting all public gatherings of more than 50 people. This includes indoor and outdoor sporting events, conferences, meetings, religious gatherings and other similar events. On the recommendation of the provincial health officer, the attorney general, minister responsible for the British Columbia Lottery Corporation, has ordered all casinos to close until further notice to reduce the risk of COVID-19 transmission." [13]

> On March 18, 2020, the province of British Columbia declares a state of emergency. "Declaring a state of emergency allows the Province, through the minister, to implement any provincial emergency measures required with access to land and human resource assets that may be necessary to prevent, respond to or alleviate the effects of an emergency. This includes securing the critical supply chains to make sure people have access to essential goods and services, and that infrastructure necessary in a

---

[13] https://news.gov.bc.ca/releases/2020HLTH0086-000499

response is readily available.

The state of emergency is initially in effect for 14 days, once issued, and may be extended or rescinded as necessary. The state of emergency applies to the whole province and allows federal, provincial and local resources to be delivered in a co-ordinated effort." [14]

People begin hoarding hand sanitizer and toilet paper and the province prohibits reselling of such items after it is reported that price gouging is occurring. Some stores implement buying limits.

The Government of Canadian announces the closure of the Canada-U.S. border to all non-essential travel.
[15]

SOCIAL MEDIA POST

If there's one thing this season has reminded us of it's that we live in community. There are the communities of our families, work places, where we go to worship, to work out, and to socialize.

But more than that, community is how and who we are as we walk through every day.

Right now, community looks like social distancing,

---

[14] https://news.gov.bc.ca/releases/2020PSSG0017-000511
[15] https://pm.gc.ca/en/news/news-releases/2020/03/20/prime-minister-announces-temporary-border-agreement-united-states#:~:text=The%20Prime%20Minister%2C%20Justin%20Trudeau,take%20effect%20at%20midnight%20tonight.

leaving something in the shop for someone else, delivering groceries, speaking kind words. It manifests in conversations and prayers.

It looks like words, and art, and things being created in a season of staying home that contribute something lovely.

It means focusing on the beautiful more than the terrible. It's the antithesis of fear mongering.

It's admitting we're uncomfortable and that there's an undercurrent stealing our focus, but leaning in to the sheer beauty of voices raised on Italian balconies and a man wearing gloves giving you a cup of coffee and a smile.

Let's live well in our community today, friends. We're in this together

---

On March 20, 2020, Ken Christian, Mayor of the City of Kamloops announces the declaration of a local state of emergency. [16]

Friday, March 20, 2020

The sun shines through the east facing window kissing the bunch of tulips on the dining table. The light is magical. I'd like to put the macro lens on my camera and play but there are other more pressing things to do, so I grab my phone and take a quick shot to mark the moment.

Makiya set up a life-size board game downstairs, complete with good and bad challenges to complete if you land on certain squares. Gerry gets one where he has to drink a bad smoothie mixed with three random ingredients chosen earlier in the game: Zesty Italian salad dressing, banana chips, and

---

[16] https://youtu.be/KehMMMyHIP4

blueberries. It doesn't sound tasty to me but he takes a tentative sip, pronounces it "not bad!", and downs the rest. What a good sport.

We have pancakes for lunch (why not?), then go to the schoolyard and shoot hoops for a while (man, that's fun). I institute an hour of daily afternoon reading time as much for myself as anyone else, and we curl up with books. Spring break looks different this year: a little quieter, a little uncertain, a little more rummaging around in different corners of Grandma's bag of tricks. I never do photograph those tulips, but tomorrow is another day.

SOCIAL MEDIA POST

We're uncomfortable with the opportunities to go and do suddenly taken from us.

We wrestle with being together in closed quarters more than we're accustomed.

The undercurrent of uncertainty is wearing us down.

But we notice light play through the curtains in a way we didn't before.

And we hear the sounds our house makes because we're inhabiting it now.

And we hear ourselves think and make way for a Presence.

And it's beautiful and terrible and it turns out these two live side by side after all.

On March 21, Adrian Dix and Dr. Henry issue a joint update. "Until further notice, personal service establishments — like barbershops, salons, nail estheticians, health spas, massage parlours, tattoo shops and others – are ordered to close."[17]

Saturday, March 21, 2020

I see memes on social media about introversion in the time of self-isolation and social distancing. "Introverts, we've trained for this," they say in some form or another. "This is our time. Let's show them how to do it." I smile because staying home is not a hardship for me. It's what I do. It's kind of my superpower.

There are plenty of other things to be concerned about in a pandemic. You know what they are as well as I do so I won't start listing them. They're the things the grind away in the back of our mind when we're going about our day or wake us in the middle of the night. They punch us in the gut at random times and whirl like funnel clouds threatening to catch us up in the middle of them. People of faith, we have trained for this. This is where the rubber of what we believe hits the road. In time of turmoil, I need something with more substance than platitudes tossed around like confetti. Maybe that's why I like reading the psalms. You won't find platitudes there. You find real and raw emotion. Doubt, fear, and a depth of faith like what I need to lean on in these uncertain times. Yesterday, when the rock in the pit of my stomach felt especially heavy, I thought about how much more difficult it would be for me to walk through these days without faith. It's tough for everyone on all fronts. Fear about the future and the present and the downstream impact of this thing that will stretch years into the future.

I can show by example how to hunker down at home. It's easy and delicious for me. The bigger questions are: can I show by example how to love well? Do my actions reflect what I believe? Does my faith conquer my fear? The answer is sometimes. Probably not as much as I'd like. So, today I begin again doing the best I can.

SOCIAL MEDIA POST

When this is over—one day, it will be over—we'll return to our workplaces and our places of worship and our coffeeshops and we'll be grateful for the opportunity to do ordinary things.

Maybe the pace of our days will change because we

---

[17] https://news.gov.bc.ca/releases/2020HLTH0101-000538

found peace amidst the chaos in the time of imposed stillness. Perhaps quiet will remain a choice.

Meanwhile, children put hearts and rainbows on windows and we reach out virtually to say "hello" and "I see you." We resist fear and seek fact. Things that were once important, suddenly, aren't.

Instead, we delight in the sun shining through windows and a sparrow landing in a nearby tree. The song of a dove who has chosen to sit on the chimney coming in through them fireplace. Fresh bread. Laughter.

The things that remain.

JOURNAL ENTRY – March 21, 2020

Self-isolation. Social distancing. Financial market uncertainty. Diminishing investments. And more. So much more. The pandemic is touching everyone and everyone. Perhaps through this we will begin to have more clarity about what is important and what isn't. I am uneasy as everyone is and struggling to remain at peace. Makiya is here and her presence brings joy and keeps us busy. My early morning devotional time remains intact, thank goodness, because it keeps me connected to my Source. I remind myself over and over again throughout the day that God remains fixed and that love is the thing that will bring us through.

JOURNAL ENTRY – March 22, 2020

I have moments when I'm not okay. My breath catches, the knot in my stomach tightens, and I feel an instant of panic. Let's be real. I'm not calm all the time. I'm afraid like the rest of us. It's the unknown and the lack of perceived control. It's the concern about my family. I really need to cry but I have to remain calm for

Makiya's sake so I come here instead. Scratch that. I'm going to my Bible. Back soon . . .

Wednesday, March 25, 2020

Some mornings I wake up empty, weary before my feet hit the floor and another day in COVID time begins. I think about the jubilation that will come when this nightmare has passed, and wonder about the toll self-isolation is demanding. Looking for delight is more challenging now. That's why we practice looking for gifts in good times—so our vision is attuned to see them in not-so-good times. Especially in unprecedented times like these. Online groups are springing up to help people who need it. "Caremongering," they call it. Shopping, sharing, virtual hands extended to help one another. Encouraging words written on sidewalks in chalk. A legion working to make facemasks for frontline hospital workers. A sense that we're in this together prevails.

Around here we're playing board games and made-up games and doing jigsaw puzzles. We're doing Wii Fit. We bounce a basketball and play 21 in an empty schoolyard where playground equipment is cordoned off with yellow tape. We photograph buttercups and take afternoon drives past houses with construction paper hearts in the windows. I sing the doxology silently while I wash my hands.

My granddaughter and I work together in my writing-room-turned-sewing room making facemasks from my mountain of quilting cotton. It's surreal, this task we've taken on, but the gift of companionable hours spent chatting and working is priceless. One of those beautiful and terrible things that coexist seamlessly.

By evening, we're weary from carrying the weight of it all and we curl up under blankets allowing an hour of light-hearted television to distract us. We turn in early with books, looking back over the past twenty-four hours to take note of delights. We sleep deep. And morning comes and the nightmare plays on and we carry on with the business of walking through another day in COVID time and resume our practice of looking for gifts.

JOURNAL ENTRY – March 23, 2020

Begin again. As always, Monday feels like an opportunity for a fresh start. This week will bring new things related to the pandemic—new anxieties, new delights. There will always be both of these but they are heightened these days.

This morning I am thankful for the first solitary hours of the day. For the opportunity to pray and connect with the Divine. For the signs of caring I see in the community at large. For brave individuals fighting this thing and caring for those affected and, closer to home, preparing for the tsunami they say is on the horizon. For the joy and distraction having Makiya here brings. For hearts and minds turned toward home. For scripture and notebooks and music and creatives who share their work and make this world just a little brighter in doing so.

Have mercy, Lord. Carry us through this day. Give me the ability to love well.

SOCIAL MEDIA POST

I'm not sure how to love well at the best of times. This morning I begin again to try again.

Loving well looks different today than it did a week ago. It's quieter, intentional, close to home. Today we love our larger community well by staying physically away from them.

The gift of technology allows us opportunity to remain connected. For all its downfalls, I'm thankful for social media for that reason today. I see virtual communities springing up, people checking in with one another, and seeds of kindness sprouting.

In our neighbourhood, people have been putting hearts and rainbows in their windows. Today we're writing messages of encouragement on our sidewalks and driveways in chalk.

I don't know how to do this thing we're being called to do. We're all stumbling through day by day. I'm not sure what it's supposed to look like and how it will all play out, but I know loving well is how we'll help each other through it.

Let's check in with one another and find ways to love well

On March 26, 2020, the Government of Canada announces an Emergency Order under the Quarantine Act requiring anyone entering Canada by sea, air, or land to self-isolate for 14 days regardless of whether they have symptoms of COVID-19. Penalties for those refusing to do so include fines up to $750,000 and/or six months imprisonment. [18]

SOCIAL MEDIA POST

If there was ever a time to be intentional about where I set my mind free to wander, that time is now. Wisdom tells me to set limits on how often I check in with the news cycle. It calls me to remember the lovely things and the loved people (hint: that's everyone).

It's hard to wrap my mind around what's happening in the world.

Grocery bags left on front steps, armies of people in their homes sewing fabric facemasks, reports of overwhelmed front-line workers and hospitals nearing capacity, are things I never thought I'd see in my lifetime.

Yet here they are.

---

[18] https://www.canada.ca/en/public-health/news/2020/03/new-order-makes-self-isolation-mandatory-for-individuals-entering-canada.html

A yellow daffodil about to pop. Shared laughter. The warmth of the morning sun through the east facing window. My granddaughter's "mmmmmm" as she bites into a piece of freshly baked and still warm bread.

These things are just as real.

Let's be intentional about filling our minds with beautiful things while, of course, staying informed. Let's choose the garden we dig around in today.

SOCIAL MEDIA POST

It's all been leading up to this. All of our days before have been preparing us for today. The things we have learned, done, and received are all tools we can draw on to make a difference today—in our own lives and in the lives that intersect our own in large and small ways.

Every skill we've honed, every thought we've ruminated upon, every intention we've set to walk with grace and integrity, in love, comes together in these days as an opportunity to serve.

In this time when community is less a gathering together and more a way of being, we reach deep into what we have gathered and offer it with open hands. Let's not squander the opportunity to love well.

It will look different for all of us. The trinkets I've

gathered on my path aren't the same as what you've collected. In the same way our needs are different. It is this diversity that shows us that every offering is as valuable as the other.

Today, friends, let's consider how we've been preparing for such a time as this. Let's use what we've gathered and pour out.

On March 30, teachers in B.C. return to work after spring break and begin planning to teach students virtually.

Monday, March 30, 2020

The round glass vase of tulips has been on the dining table for a couple of topsy-turvy weeks. I push them to one end when I put placemats out before a meal or when we sit down to play a game. We watch them go from tight waxy buds to bright and beautiful flowers and, for the longest time, watch as petals twist and fall to the tabletop. I resist tossing them in the trash. There is still beauty in the fading flowers. Surely, they still serve a purpose. I'm not ready to let them go.

Then, one morning, I spy something on the fabric cushion of the dining chair at the end of the table. I bend, pick it up, and lift it for a closer look. It is a fallen tulip stamen. I brush dried flecks of pollen from the chair and listen as the indigo stamen between my finger's whispers: "it's time". Mid-morning, when I push the vase to the end of the table to make more room for Makiya who is using my laptop to write, she looks up from her work.

"I think it's time to throw those flowers away."

What remained unspoken for so long has been said and there's no denying the truth any longer. Sometimes it takes someone to speak it to incite action. So, I take the vase to the garage, lift the finished flowers from it, and toss them into the trash. They've served us well long past their glorious peak. Later, I lift the empty heavy glass vase and put it back in the cupboard.

SOCIAL MEDIA POST

Another Monday morning and we're all still holding our breath.

We applaud essential workers who brave the non-existent rush hour traffic to serve and care for us. They are our sisters and brothers, our sons and our daughters. We pray for their safety.

Those who stay home wrestle with wild things that having time to think releases. We are learning to tame them in the echo of time we've been given.

We check numbers. They don't tell a complete story, and the piece of the story they tell remains dark, but we can't stop ourselves from checking them anyway. One morning we will see a clear flattening. But not yet. Not just yet.

The light given off by people at grocery store checkouts, in hospitals and care facilities, at home caring for children, and working in our cities and towns to keep things moving shines bright. They are our heroes.

Things fall away. Tides turn. Tears sting. Smiles are genuine. Things we thought most important, suddenly, aren't. Construction paper hearts on windows say "I see you." We greet one another from a distance: "Stay safe." And the slow burn continues.

The week begins and it seems like we're all plodding our way into it shallow breathing.

Here we go. Dare to breathe deep. Let's do this.

JOURNAL ENTRY – March 27, 2020

I'm finding it challenging to focus. There's always a slow burn in the back of my mind with respect to the uncertainty and general awfulness around us right now. Having Makiya here is delightful. She's a bright star in this darkness and yet the uncertainty about her schooling, Laurinda's work, and what that means and how it plays out weighs. I feel as if I'm bearing the weight of two households rather than one.

Things are bad. I expect we have months ahead of us battling this thing before we can begin to piece together a new normal. Meanwhile the world holds its collective breath and waits. The shift that's happening is tangible. Good things will come from this but not without great cost.

Yesterday the first proof copy of my new book arrived. The Presence of Absence *is officially a book! I've been so excited about seeing this book in brick-and-mortar store, but they're shuttered. Surely by the time the book launches in June we will have returned to a semblance of normalcy.*

I don't understand the spiritual implications of what's happening with this pandemic but I know they exist. I know, too, this is the time to lean hard on my faith and read scripture and prayer and meditation but these things are not easy when I struggle to focus. I must choose the better thing. I must focus my mind on the truth.

Some things have not changed. We are as beloved today as we were before this pandemic began as we will be when it ends. And it will end. God walks beside us through it. He is our comfort, our shelter, our lover.

As image bearers we were given this created earth to care for and we have not done a good job of it. We have taken without replenishing. We have sought pleasure above wisdom. We have relied on the things that provide temporary easing of our discomfort rather than peace that is eternal. In the light of eternity how does this play out? In the light of eternity this is a temporary thing that we have an opportunity to learn from. Lord, make us teachable. There will come a shifting—a transition—to a new way of living after this storm passes. Lord may we learn to turn to you and your wisdom above the limited human wisdom we have chosen to value above all else.

JOURNAL ENTRY – March 29, 2020

It's storming. The wind rages and rain is hitting the window. It's only 5:30 am so there is still a chance this storm will blow through so we can go to the garden today as planned. Hope springs eternal.

It's storming, if not literally, for sure figuratively, in the whole world. COVID-19 rages. It has done things we thought impossible a few weeks ago. It has taken lives and it has changed lives. It has sent us to our homes. The world will be different when it finally passes—which, I'm reading, might be many months away.

We three—Gerry, Makiya, and me—have settled into a comfortable routine. Gerry is having the hardest time of all. Long walks help. Makiya is writing a book and working on jigsaw puzzles. I putter and cook and tend to home-based things. We play games. I snitch quiet moments to read.

The uncertainty is hardest to bear. There is a measure of comfort in knowing we're all topsy-turvy as we hold our collective breath. Maybe good things will come of this to our world as a whole. That's little comfort to those who have lost loved ones already, who are sick, facing job loss, economic backlash, the uncertainty about tomorrow, next week and beyond. I suppose we all fall into one or more of those categories.

God promises to be with us in these times. I believe we will see a returning, a turning toward, a dismantling of false gods and systems and a resurgence of genuine faith. God has not abandoned us. Nor did he cause his. Rather, He walks alongside us—our great hope and our great love.

On March 31, 2020, the Canadian Federation of

> *Independent Business reports that 77% of small businesses across Canada are partially or entirely closed due to COVID-19 and, of those, 32 % have closed completely and are unsure if they will ever reopen.* [19]

Tuesday, March 31, 2020

You know that feeling when you're standing in what feels like a precarious place like the top of the Seattle Space Needle or the Capilano Suspension Bridge in Vancouver, BC? That sharp intake of breath, that palpable lump of fear in the pit of your stomach, that heaviness in your chest? I'm having flashes of those same sensations while I'm sitting on my sofa or going about the business of everyday on days that seem far from every day. I wake with two words tumbling around in my mind: And yet. And yet. And yet. And I'm not sure of the message they're trying to deliver.

So we go about our day, grateful. Careful. Grieving for a world in crisis. Lamenting. We consume just enough news to have a sense of current events—The Current Event—and focus the bulk of our attention on the better things instead. We bake bread and do crafts. Piece jigsaw puzzles. Play games. We take drives, because the cheapest thing of all right now is gasoline, past playgrounds cordoned off with yellow tape and empty stores and business with signs in their windows that say "Closed due to COVID-19." We think about the aftermath and the recovery that will take years and a parade of cars driving past a house where a child is celebrating a birthday inside. And a flock of robins on the lawn hunting for worms. And green sprouting in the garden. And rain quenching the thirst of a parched earth.

I stand at the window and watch as the first rays of morning sun kiss bare branches on trees. And yet. And yet. And yet.

JOURNAL ENTRY – March 31, 2020

Pandemic day n. Who knows anymore? Day by day. Hour by hour. Focus on the better things. The timeless and unchangeable things. Let the rest fall away. Now is the time to grasp the truth that we as human beings are not as in control of things as we would like to

---

[19] https://www.cfib-fcei.ca/hubfs/legacy/2020-03/COVID-19-survey-results-March-31.pdf

believe. It is the time to lament and to trust and to turn our attention toward home and toward God. Maybe the one true thing we can do today is to turn things over.

On March 31, 2020, The B.C. government extends the state of emergency for another two weeks. [20]

---

[20] https://news.gov.bc.ca/releases/2020PREM0018-000607

APRIL 2020

SOCIAL MEDIA POST

How are you doing? Are you, like me, overcome by moments of heaviness that stretch into hours? Is doing your level best to stay calm for the sake of those you love, including yourself, becoming more of a challenge? Do you feel like you've had enough, even though you know we're not getting out of this thing anytime soon? Are you feeling the weight of the loss of so many large and small things?

Let go, just a bit, and speak to the awfulness of this thing that has changed and will continue to change our world. Yeah, there are gifts and opportunities, but at the heart of this monster, it just stinks. Sometimes we have to just say it or write it—do something to release it—because if we keep stuffing it down, it will harm us. And we don't want to allow this thing to harm us any more than it already has.

So, speak it, or scribble it, maybe have a good cry. Then take a deep, cleansing breath, and go forward into your day. Pray. Find creative ways to come together. Paint. Sing. Craft something. Lament.

Stay safe. Love well.

Friday, April 3, 2020

I need to get a few groceries, so, for the second time since this craziness began, I venture out from our home as the lone grocery shopper. We decided weeks ago that, when it became necessary to enter a store to pick up a prescription or buy food, I'd be the one to do it. Since then, I've entered the pharmacy where a guard sat by the door of a near-empty store; pharmacists wore gloves, facemasks, and face shields; and tape lines on the floor showed the correct six-foot social distancing space to leave between yourself and the person in front. We've seen people lined up outside grocery stores (again, with the recommended six feet of space between them) waiting for someone to come out so they can go in, as only a select number of shoppers are allowed in the store at a time.

Now, I drive across town, past empty shops with signs on their doors, to the grocery store I favour. Here there is no lineup, just a woman wiping down shopping carts in the entryway.

"Thanks so much," I say, and she smiles as I take a cart and head into the twilight zone.

Tape arrows on the floor show the recommended way to navigate the store. (I never get the hang of how they've got it laid out, and end up fighting the tape lines the entire time.) I glide past the fresh produce. Nope. Not this time. I'm thankful for a freezer stocked with last season's fruit and vegetables. There's lots of eggs where the shelves were empty last time I was here. I reach for a carton. Signs at the meat counter indicate just two items per cusomer are allowed. I glide past that area too, picking up yogurt, butter, and a handful of things I don't ordinarily buy, but we've got an eleven-year-old in residence now. Shoppers dance around one another maintaining a distance, some wearing facemasks. It's awkward and potentially lifesaving. We all look a little bit stunned.

I queue at the checkout, far back from the man in front of me. When he leaves, I move forward to move my items from the cart to the conveyer. A clerk behind a plexiglass barrier smiles, weary. I'm already feeling the heaviness of being in this place for a short time this morning; I can't imagine what it must be like to spend an eight-hour shift here every day.

By the time I load the groceries into the back of my SUV and return the cart, I'm done. I climb into the car and just sit for a few moments. Breathing deep and praying as my eyes well with hot tears before, determined, I drive toward home feeling slightly numb and melting down fast.

There, I carry the first bags into the house where Gerry and Makiya are at the dining table doing geometry.

"It's getting harder and harder to go there," I say.

I try to explain, using an edited version of the experience for the sake of Makiya, how a simple trip to the grocery store has changed. Then, I put the groceries away and arrange a bouquet of tulips in a vase while Grandfather and Granddaughter return to their work and the lump in my gut gets hotter; the weight in my chest, heavier. When I'm finished, I closet myself in the bathroom where I sit on the edge of the bathtub and allow release. I weep silently into a towel, not even sure what I'm crying about. I just need to let some of this whirling emotion out or I'll burst. Then I take some deep breaths, wash my face, and stand tall. I head down the hall toward the kitchen. Makiya meets me halfway and, with no words, wraps her arms around me and leans in. We stand that way for a while, whispering.

"I needed that," I tell her. "How did you know?"

"I saw it in your face," she says.

I kiss the top of her head and we go to the kitchen to pick up where we left off with our project of the day: making salt water taffy. We take some breaths and I do a silly thing with my arms.

"Okay, let's shake it off," I say with a smile.

We cook taffy and later the three of us pull it, cut pieces, and wrap them in parchment paper twists. The burden of the grocery store pushes to the back of my mind for the rest of the day. But, that heaviness stays with me and though I do my best to move on, it never completely leaves. By the time we curl up to watch an episode of a favourite TV show, I'm beyond done, and afterward, I fall into bed feeling empty. It's been a hard day. I expect there are more to come.

SOCIAL MEDIA POST

Tough day yesterday. Maybe it was for you too. I imagine there are more like that on the horizon. We need to shore one another up.

This morning I'm starting the day feeling kind of bruised. Sometimes the encouragers need to be encouraged. Just keeping it real.

Be kind. For the sake of everyone, please be kind. None of us knows what's really going on in the heart and life of another.

Here we go, my friend. Another day in which we will—every single one of us—do our level best to make it through. How 'bout we assume the best about everybody's intentions. We're all just stumbling through this muck one step at a time.

JOURNAL ENTRY – *April 4, 2020*

I stand at the window and look up at the gray sky. Lord, grant us sunshine today. We need it. We feel closed in. The directives to self-isolate feel heavy. Heavier than we imagined a couple of weeks ago when we shared memes about having been preparing for this for our entire lives. By now most of us feel the weight and yet there is nothing but more of the same in the weeks to come. And that's best case.

So, I pray for the sun to shine even as I know that whether it does or doesn't there will still be that grinding noise in the background

SOCIAL MEDIA POST

A news story starts with these words: "We're all so emotionally raw right now." I find myself nodding, not so much at the story it goes on to tell but at the permission to feel raw.

This morning I'm thinking about palm branches and trajectories. I'm listening to messages and music and grateful for the technology that allows me to do so.

I'm still stinging from printed words that hit me in a sensitive place earlier this week and thinking, in turn, about grace.

You know, the artists and creatives who are being so

generous with sharing their gifts, the person across town or across the world who risks vulnerability by posting something about what they're doing or how they're feeling, the person in your house who's probably feeling as raw as you—man, they all need a strong measure of support right now.

We all need a strong measure of support.

Let's just do the best we can today.

SOCIAL MEDIA POST

The delicate dance between staying informed and becoming overwhelmed is a tricky one. A missed step can send us whirling. Dizzy, we sit with our head in our hands waiting for a sense of stability that isn't likely to settle any time soon.

And yet, hope.

Fattening buds on lilac bushes. Seeds dropped into furrows scratched out in the warming earth. A message from a friend asking: "How'r ya doing?"

A Friday we call good that, on the surface, seems nothing but dark. Hope in the grandest scale.

One day we're up, bobbing in the waves and keeping our head above water; the next we're gasping for breath and wrestling to stay afloat. Every one of us wavers between the two. Maybe reach out a virtual hand to help someone sinking today. Or raise one when you're the one struggling.

And grant grace. For the love of all that's beautiful in

this world, give each other a break. Assume the best intentions. Be kind. We're all just walking one another toward home.

On April 8, 2020, all B.C. provincial parks are closed in anticipation of the Easter weekend. [21] International travelers returning to the province (including those coming from the United States) must provide a self-isolation plan. They will not be allowed to return without having a plan in place. [22]

JOURNAL ENTRY – *April 9, 2020*

The things that seemed so important such a short time ago—aren't. I like to think we are learning to step back and take stock; evaluate the choices we've made about what's most important and I believe many of us are.

We choose. Every one of us chooses how we experience these days to a certain extent. For sure those who get sick have much of that choice taken from them, but those of us who remain healthy, decide whether we want to make our own corner of the world brighter or uglier.

Laurinda's employer has put a plan into place that will allow her flexibility, as a working single parent, whose child is no longer attending school in person so Makiya has returned home.

SOCIAL MEDIA POST

We need the gifts our creatives can offer to help us find our way through. Writers, and artists of all kind.

---

[21] https://news.gov.bc.ca/releases/2020ENV0019-000645
[22] https://news.gov.bc.ca/releases/2020PREM0019-000657

Those who give voice to our grief and our joy and those things in between by crafting something tangible from whispers.

Instinctively we lean in to creativity by baking bread, putting paint on canvas, drawing in chalk on sidewalks, putting paper hearts in windows, sewing facemasks and bags and piecing quilts.

Hard times are here. Creativity begets hope.

Sunday, April 12, 2020

This morning we celebrate the resurrection of our Lord. Some gather around screens to watch live-streamed Easter services from home churches or places of worship we now have an opportunity to visit virtually. We are shaken. No longer able to rely on our safe and comfortable traditions, we ask ourselves what we really need to mark this holy day. Quiet, in the stillness of our heart, we breathe a holy hallelujah. This stark peeling back of the things we've trusted in offers an opportunity to find the kind of faith that's real, and sometimes raw; the kind of faith that endures through dark nights like the ones we're stumbling through right now.

God doesn't live in a building. The Divine is right here with us. We imperfect, and currently baffled, ones are the church. Whether we worship from a pew or a forest or our living room sofa isn't the point. The point is that we worship. Alone, together, with the stones and the hills and the trees, we raise our voices.

He is risen!

He is risen, indeed.

Tuesday, April 14, 2020

I see a lot of nonsense and have to remind myself there's always been nonsense. (You understand, I trust, that "nonsense" is a code word for all manner of stuff that paints us as human beings with an unattractive brush.) We try. Most of us do our level best and try to remain kind, but there are those—there have always been those—who chose another path. It shouldn't surprise us. And sometimes—just being honest here—I'm tempted to growl back. To bite. *Sometimes the best you can do is to make someone else feel bad.* I saw those words on a cartoon decades ago and they were funny at the time, in the context. Now they're too close to the surface to carry much humour. It comes from fear, this lashing out at one another. We don't understand what in the world is happening, or who to believe, and we just want this whole thing to go away so we can get back to living our best pre-COVID lives. What kind of person do you want to be? I ask myself. Who are you serving? Which wolf are you feeding? What does your best life look like anyway?

I sit here in the dark and the quiet and think about these things and set an intention about where to put my attention on this day that feels like the gazillionth one since we went into lockdown. I think about the opportunity to come out of this thing different. And those waxy tulips in the middle of my dining table, yeah, I think about them too. And robins hunting for worms on the back lawn. And a brilliant morning sky that invites spontaneous worship. And the feel of warmth from the sun on my arms. The Presence walking alongside me through this. And I breath prayer. Selah.

On April 15, 2020, The B.C. government extends the state of emergency for another two weeks. [23]

Thursday, April 16, 2020

Honestly, we're growing weary. Some days the weight feels heavier than others. It's challenging to see delights which, of course, makes finding them even more important. But some days the effort takes more energy than we can summon. Or maybe that's just me. Lilac buds in the backyard are fat with promise. Or so I'm told. Flower pots dragged out of their winter home stand waiting for me to pull out dried and dead things to prepare for planting flowers. I'll get to it one of these days.

How long? We ask. And we realize it's a question we've posed a thousand times before. It's different now. We're all asking the same question, and kind of scared of how the answer will unfold. We feel the burden of countless others on our shoulders. The words of a woman called Teresa of Ávila who lived five hundred years ago serves as a light.

Let nothing disturb you, Let nothing frighten you,
All things are passing away:
God never changes.

We see that we've all been walking through this thing toward home together, and the ripples we make reach places and people we can't imagine with our fixed and finite mind. It's still heavy. Real heavy. But the weight seems easier to bear with companions such as this. It's not the politicians, the

---

[23] https://news.gov.bc.ca/releases/2020EMBC0020-000697

news reporters, or the armchair critics who meet us in the quiet and help us summon strength to walk through another day. It's the artists and the poets and the ones who invest time to find truth and share it.

Another day of unknowing begins and we resolve to be like those artists and poets and ordinary folk who touch waters of uncertainty and create gentle ripples of wisdom and love both outward and inward. As we are changed, we change. Peace.

SOCIAL MEDIA POST

Confession: I'm feeling overwhelmed. I'm weighted down with anxiety and empathy overload, and burdened by unkind comments from armchair critics. Maybe you too?

Today (every day, really, but Monday seems especially suited) offers opportunity to make a fresh start.

So, let's do that.

Set limits and create boundaries. Go outside and take a walk. Cut back on carbs. Listen to comforting music. Read a good book. Be kind. Be kind. Be kind.

Let's be intentional about the ripples we set in motion.

JOURNAL ENTRY – April 18, 2020

When I wake in the morning, I have to take a few moments to get my bearings. What day is it? Are we still in the midst of a pandemic? Still self-isolating? Saturday. Yes. And, yes.

JOURNAL ENTRY – *April 19, 2020*

The trauma of these past weeks has taken a toll on me—and yes, I dare to call it trauma. The constant grinding in the back of my mind, the isolation, the taking on of burdens, these things weigh heavy and distract me.

We are all in a place of going through. There is no turning back—it's not an option. We will come through eventually; the question is to what? We can lose our bearings in this shadow and lose our way so we must listen with ears attuned to the still, small voice of God that calls us to move toward it. Otherwise we risk coming out of the shadow at a place we never intended and the road back to where we thought we were going may be rockier and more treacherous than the shadow ever was. Contemplating is all the more important these days.

JOURNAL ENTRY – *April 20, 2020*

The question shifts from "what can I do to feel better," because I'm knocked off balance by the pandemic and the overload of empathy and anxiety, to "how can I serve God in this time." I am not sure of the answer.

JOURNAL ENTRY – *April 22, 2020*

A warm day with sunshine. A new project for Gerry. And the morning seems brighter. Having purpose and something to look forward to is like healing balm in these days of the pandemic when we don't know what or who to believe.

JOURNAL ENTRY – April 22, 2020

Sometimes, now, my prayers are as dry and crispy as corn flakes and seem to be of little value. For a time, I wander. Then, the pain I feel magnifies to the point that it is a physical thing and the knot in the pit of my gut becomes unbearable. Frantic, my mind flits from place to place considering possibilities. What can I do to make myself feel better? Then I remember the truth.

I am still beloved. The temporary things I've been considering will never satisfy as much as sweet communion with the Divine and even when the presence seems elusive, I choose to press in and listen. Nothing satisfies like the holy presence. As so, I wait.

Wednesday, April 22, 2020

I've been knocked off balance. I suspect most of us have. I'm comfortable in solitude and, even before the pandemic, am happy to spend most of my time at home but it's different now. There's that constant hum in the back of my mind and a measure of fear over the unknown. There's concern for family members and so many others impacted health wise, financially, and in ways we've not yet began to understand.

I keep busy. I've always got projects on the go and, just for good measure, I add a few more and think about other things I could do. But the funny thing is, my motivation for the things that have fed me in the past is low. Photos on the card still in my camera and seed packets left lonely in the laundry room are puzzling reminders that all isn't as it should be.

The slow burn in the pit of my stomach becomes almost too much at times and my mind flits from place to place trying to conjure a solution to soothe the ache. Busy is what comes to mind most often. And yet, even in that I sense something is off. So many aren't busy with work and things that sustain their livelihood and the economy. They would love to be busy. Others are run ragged serving and helping.

I have this book launching in two months (correction: ONE month, because I decided, just today, to release it ahead of schedule), and there are things I probably should be doing in preparation for that, but I'm struggling there too. The subtitle: *A Story About Busyness*. Who might be interested in something like that right now? it seems almost insulting when so many are hunkered down at home wishing they could be busier.

This morning when I was praying, my iPad dinged beside me indicating someone had sent me a message. When I finished my prayer, I picked it up and found a video message about—you guessed it—being too busy. I watched, nodding my head in agreement, thinking about the things I had scribbled in my journal earlier about the ridiculousness of seeking comfort in being busy, how that's long been my *modus operandi* and how I realized long ago that it wasn't working for me and yet I keep returning to it. After the video clip finished, I turned to a page in *The Presence of Absence* manuscript and allowed my own words to solidify the truth I had just listened to.

> *Busy isn't the balm we need to heal. Busy work isn't work at all, it's just a place to hide from the wild things. The real work comes in stillness when we're brave enough to face the things that startle us in the night, to stand at the opening to a cave of unknowing and take the first step forward.*

And, you know, I think it was no coincidence that my friend sent that link my way this morning. I needed the reminder. Busy is still my drug of choice and it's probably that way for someone else too. But it never satisfies for long. It never goes deep enough. I think of the wisdom a man named Benedict left us with. *Always, we begin again.*

And so again, this day, I do.

Thursday, April 23, 2020

I wake from a dream in which someone is standing in my bedroom doorway, telling me she feels like she's getting the flu, then comes and sits in the edge of my bed to chat. My thoughts upon waking go something like this. *No! I'm not allowing this pandemic to enter my dreams and steal my peace any more than it already has. Not happening.* I am relatively okay during the day but lately, after supper as another quiet day winds down, I feel a familiar burn in the pit of my stomach start to smolder and now it's crept into my dreams. I won't have it.

So, I switch up my morning routine and, instead of taking my first delicious cup of soy milky frothy coffee to the dark solitude of the den, return to our bedroom and sit upright in bed to read, write, and watch the sun rise. In time, Gerry pads downstairs to his office for his weekly Bible study group on Zoom and I reach for my own Bible. The day begins in peace.

SOCIAL MEDIA POST

The slow burn I feel in my gut toward the end of the

day. The woozy sensation of standing at the edge of a cliff. The sharp intake of breath and surge of adrenaline that comes out of nowhere.

They're all physical manifestations of the same emotion. Fear.

The world has shifted and I don't know what tomorrow will look like.

Platitudes don't help. They're irritating, more than anything else.

What was, is no longer. We need to grieve the losses and admit we're carrying a measure of fear. And be kind. And grant grace.

It's traumatic, all this social distancing. Necessary and loving, perhaps. But traumatic nonetheless.

My eyes leak. Out of nowhere, tears well. I'm not crying, my eyes just keep watering. For a time, I believe it.

But when I name these things—fear, grief, trauma—they seem less menacing, their power over me decreases. I replace the space they occupied with peace.

For a time. Until next time.

And begin again, and again, and again.

Friday April 24, 2020

Today is our wedding anniversary. Twenty-one years ago today, Gerry and I stood at the front of a small church and vowed to love one another through good and less-than-good times. One might look at these days as a batch of those not so good ones. But we've got good food in our bellies, a comfortable home to live in, healthy kids and brilliant grandkids. We've got books and jigsaw puzzles and a community garden plot where magic is starting to happen. Our investment portfolio is in a tailspin but we still have enough. Maybe one of the most valuable gifts after twenty-one years is the gift of having enough.

While the plans for an anniversary getaway we talked about earlier this year are long since forgotten, we have planned an intimate little celebration involving a takeout meal of lobster ravioli from a local restaurant. Lord willing, there are still mountaintop experiences ahead of us; sure as anything there are valleys as deep and deeper than the one we're in today. But love in the time of corona virus on the occasion of a twenty-first wedding anniversary feels abundant. Not flashy, but rich and enduring. Sometimes crazy-making, still fun and rich with laughter. And in the dark times, because there will always be dark times, it feels like a safe place. A sweet reminder of the gift of having enough. Happy Anniversary, Gerry. I love you seven.

Tuesday, April 28, 2020

The sun rises and kisses the trees with light so golden it makes me believe in magic. The hills across the valley are spring-green and purple lilac buds grow plump. Yesterday morning I saw too-many-to-count mountain bluebirds flit back and forth from the budding Virginia creeper to the lawn and back again, and later cheerful yellow finches did the same. Surely these momentary visions from my living room window are as glorious as anything can be.

SOCIAL MEDIA POST

I woke this morning thinking about the difference between knowledge and wisdom and how there's abundant access to both in the twenty-first century. In some seasons, when I'm afraid, I turn more to one, thinking it will save me, but return to the better one when it becomes obvious to me that it won't.

Many of us are experiencing loss through this time, and loss causes grief. Grief is uncomfortable. It hurts.

And who wants to hurt? But, you know, sometimes it's the place we need to wander while we make our way through. And we'll make it through.

So maybe today we need to look at the new things, the growing things, the things that are transforming, returning, and regenerating. It's spring. What better time to look at a creation renewing to help us remember that all things will become new?

Buds on trees. Green reaching up from the warming earth. Colour returning in the form of spring flowers. Open windows. Birds singing. Hearts renewing. Wisdom guiding.

MAY 2020

Sunday, May 3, 2020

Over one twenty-four-hour period, between the two of us, five Zoom calls take place in our home. Necessary, some of them; productive, a few of them; but when I realize what has crept into this sanctuary, I want to scream "Stop!" How easily busyness invades our space before we even realize it's happening. It's good, this technology that enables us to stay connected, to do business, and to attend events we might otherwise miss, but, like most things, too much of a good thing can become something else.

I want to listen more than I speak and give more of my attention to growing green things than loud and unimportant things. I want to embrace silence as a presence. I want to remain unplugged even after everything's plugged back in again.

Monday, May 4, 2020

Today I'm going to give myself the gift of doing "want to do" things rather than "have to do" things. An antidote to a funky afternoon and evening when it seemed the weight was too heavy. I'll toss seeds in the ground in my garden, dig in flower pots at home, and make a loose plan. Maybe I'll buy flowers. I'll put music on in my woman cave and play with watercolour paint and create something where there was once nothing. Perhaps, by the time the day is done, I will have returned to myself.

Journal Entry – May 5, 2020

Even before this pandemic began, long before it began, this thought kept flitting about in my mind: I'm having trouble being in this world. It had become too much—the anger and intolerance and fear and mistrust, the relentless push for more. I was weary of it all and sought solace in solitude and silence.

Then the pandemic, and the world went home, and even with the knowing in the back of my mind that I was bearing burdens other than just my own, I held on to a measure of hope for a collective awakening and that out of the chaos would come calm.

I've struggled to return to the garden this year. Pots and flower beds here at home remain untouched. These, symptoms of my inner landscape that's out of alignment. Maybe it started before the pandemic, but I blame it.

I sit in silent contemplation and tears fall from my eyes. I don't know why. I am grieving for the world and for those I love—and for me. I hunger for peace.

Tuesday, May 5, 2020

I climb out of the car, and walk toward my community garden plot with my eyes are trained on the plot next to mine. A young man, hair pulled back in a ponytail, and a little girl—maybe two-years-old—are in it. I get closer and see they're both barefoot, and I'm thrilled by the ordinary extraordinariness of dirty bare feet in a garden.

We greet one another, he's new this year, and introduces me to Allie, his little mud-covered daughter. I affix my watering wand to my hose as we chat. I learn they've just moved to Kamloops and are delighted with this little plot of earth as he, his wife, and sweet little Allie now live in an apartment. He tells me where it is, and smiles as he says it because it's close enough so they can walk to the garden. I picture it. It's a small unassuming building in an older, established part of the city. We talk about planting, and weather, and the local farmer's market that operates online these days. He tells me about the farm he used to work on before his wife's job brought them to our city. I watch Allie up to her knees in mud playing with a tractor and having the time of her life in this plot where nothing much green is growing yet. I think this man is growing the most valuable thing of all now—a daughter—and from what I can tell by their muddy bare feet and smiles, he's doing a fine, job.

When I've finished watering and I'm back in the car ready to go home, I sit for a moment and watch as he hoses off his bare feet and slips them into a pair of sandals. That little scene looks a lot like hope. I think that man and his family have the power to change the world. For starters, they just changed my day.

SOCIAL MEDIA POST

It wearieth me oftentimes to read and listen to many things. ~Thomas à Kempis

If he felt this way five hundred years ago imagine the overwhelm Thomas would experience today. I don't have to imagine, I feel it. Keenly.

It demands a hefty toll, this distraction. Even now—especially now—it slinks seductively around corners, beckoning. Look at me! it cries.

For a time, we entertain it, until we realize the cost is bankrupting us. So we turn our eyes back to the better thing, the transforming thing, the thing that is still and simple and quiet and rich.

This morning I remind myself to be mindful of which coffers I drop coins in, and to push back at the distraction. Lest I grow too weary . . .

Because, man, I am weary.

On May 6, 2020, Adrian Dix, Dr. Henry, and B.C. Premier John Horgan present a four-step phased approach to lifting restrictions and reopening the province. We are currently in Phase 1

We will enter Phase 2 in mid-May.

Small social gatherings (up to 6 people) allowed. Resumption of elective surgeries that had been cancelled and regulated health services such as physiotherapy, dentistry, chiropractors, and in-person counseling. Non-essential business can open with safety plans and protocols in place. Employees who have been working at home will be able to return to the office.

Phase 3 is targeted to take place June – September.

Non-essential travel within the province will be allowed and camping in BC parks will again be available. Large concerts and venues remain off limits but movie theatres and small venues with less than 50 people will be allowed.

Phase 4 – "new normal."

There is no stated time for this phase as it is dependent on case counts and the development of a vaccine. September 2020 is the earliest date given. [24]

Journal Entry – May 8, 2020

That there is a presence of evil in the world is without dispute. That deception and confusion are two of its most powerful weapons is also indisputable. It seems that in this time of corona. the war has been taken to a new level. Deception abounds. Everyone is confused and uncertain which version of the truth to believe and, in fear, is lashing out as means of self-protection.

What is my better work? To love God and my neighbour, for sure, but also to remain aware and open to all that is beautiful and true

---

[24] https://news.gov.bc.ca/releases/2020PREM0026-000826

in this world. I have become distracted and fearful. Confused. These are not the things I want to follow or live in.

This morning, I am drawing a line. Enough. I am going to dig in the dirt and plant some flowers and paint with watercolour and sit in the sunshine and walk with God through this day in awe at the unfolding of spring and hope and promise fulfilled. I am going to remind myself that I am beloved and that everyone else is equally so. I am waging war on confusion by turning my attention to the better things. The eternal things. Things like lilac blossoms in my backyard and the life appearing in my garden. I'm going to plant flowers and pray as I do so in wonder at the life springing forth that is so beautiful. I'm reminding myself that my life is also wonder-filled and I am even more treasured and precious than the plants I'm going to put in the ground today.

Journal Entry – May 11, 2020

It's a new season. The days are long again and warmth hinting at the heat that is to come. There are plans to begin opening up the province. Makiya has been able to go to a friend's house for the first time since all this began and, this morning, Gerry and two friends went fishing, masked, while sitting in the boat.

We have begun to settle into this new normal. Yesterday afternoon, I stood in a queue waiting to go into the grocery store. Grocery shopping has been one of the hardest things for me these past months. It struck me, as I stood in proper socially distanced form, that part of the reason may be that we're forced to treat fellow human beings as toxic. This seems contrary to what we are charged with doing—love our neighbours. Yes, one can spin it and say we are loving our neighbours by remaining apart from them, but the fact remains that in the back of our minds we are seeing them as toxic to us and, therefore, unsafe.

If I, as an introvert who ordinarily shies away from people, feel this dichotomy, then what must it be like for those whose emotional tanks are filled by being around other people? No wonder we are all walking around somewhat dumbstruck and confused.

Monday, May 11, 2020

One morning I stand in line, appropriately distanced from the woman in front of me and hoping the person behind me is extending the same courtesy, waiting to get into the garden center. When I arrived a few minutes past opening time, there was already a lineup. Plants and flowers are means to self-care I tell myself. It will be worth the wait. And so, I stand in line in the wind, wishing I had worn something warmer, waiting for my turn to enter the guarded fortress that the garden center has become.

"You can enter door number two," a young woman tells me when my turn comes.

"Thank you," I say, grateful, in this upside-down world, for the opportunity to go into the store and spend money.

I hunt down a cart and navigate aisles with tape arrows directing the way. Oh no. Not this again. I can never seem to figure out the arrows and get myself where I want to go.

What was once a springtime joy, turns into a chore. I end up grabbing ridiculously expensive pre-selected packets of petunias and a handful of other plants. This year I don't spend a pleasant hour browsing and planning and visualizing what beauty will bloom in my flowerpots in the summer. There's no deliberation, mind-changing, and being filled simply by being among plants. I just want to get something and get out.

A few days later I'm queued again, at the grocery store this time, looking sideways at a couple of family units in the line-up. One person per family is the acceptable norm, for safety, yes, but it's also a courtesy, so more people can enter the store in these days when capacity is restricted. The line moves at a decent speed. I rub sanitizer on my hands before the woman guarding the carts and baskets lets me take one.

"You look very nice today," she tells me as I reach for a sanitized basket. I'm startled, but grateful. She's doing a job she never imagined doing and doing it well.

Later, after I've gathered my things, gone through the checkout, and am making my way through the parking lot toward my car, I'm thinking about the struggle of treating one another as toxic. We keep our distance to stay safe. We sidestep to keep from invading the space of another, dumbfounded at how quickly the world has changed and feeling more than a little fragile.

Thursday, May 14, 2020

I carry baby tomato plants in a small box on my lap while Gerry drives to the community garden. My hands brush across their leaves. The scent of hope wafts from them. They have been growing in my laundry room since I dropped tiny seeds into pots in early April, unmotivated, with barely enough energy in me to stumble out to the garage, plunge garden glove-clad hands into seed starting mixture, and fill pots. The earthy smell was like spring. It sparked something as I wrestled with all that was happening in the world.

Now I drop fish fins and random parts (retrieved from the freezer where I tucked them away after Gerry's salmon fishing trip last August) into just-dug holes and pour crushed eggshells from a quart canning jar on top to prepare a nourishing new home for my plants. Later, when the plants are tucked safely in the ground and we're on our way home, a lingering smell from my yellow Tupperware bowl snakes through the air in the car from the back to the front seat.

"It smells like fish in here," I remark.

But it's not the fishy smell one associates with something slightly "off"; it's the aroma of summer, the ocean, and men laughing together on an old fishing boat in the salt chuck—okay, maybe not the aroma of men on a fishing boat where they've lived and slept for two days and nights, but you get my point.

Later, Gerry and I take our cameras and hike up a hill across the road from a shopping mall where the parking lot is empty because the stores are all closed. We shoot photos of bright yellow arrowleaf Balsamroot, flowers that herald spring's arrival around here. The hills smell like sagebrush, hot summer afternoons, dusty bare feet, and melancholy.

Then we decide to get burgers at the drive-thru (it's been the only option for fast food or fast coffee for months) and take the warm bag smelling of burgers and fries to a park where we sit at a picnic bench and watch a young family play with bubbles on the grass across the field. The warmth of the sun on my body and the smells conjuring memories do a work. They lift a measure of heaviness. I think of the power of simple, ordinary things to change the course of a day and it's good. All will be well if I remember these things and remain anchored to the better things. The timeless things. The good, good things. Aromatherapy helps.

Saturday, May 16, 2020

The first rays of morning sun kiss the trees in the green space behind our home and the lilac bush in the yard and the green takes on a hue that is nothing short of brilliant. The right light makes all the difference. I think of the words of a verse I had tacked to the wall above my workspace for years. *Just for today* . . . it began. I don't remember the wisdom that followed but I know I leaned on it in a long, dark season. And now, in this season where dark looks a little different but is no less threatening, the magic of a dawning day brings me back to centre. This. This is what I need. Just for today I will hang on. I will trust. I will be still and know.

Sunday, May 17, 2020

I wake with a reminder dancing in my mind. Think about the true, honorable, right, pure, lovely, and admirable things. The better things. The best things. And I think the Divine has whispered to me in the liminal space between sleep and waking. Low cloud hovers in the valley. There is no sunrise, just a gradual fading of the dark. I think of the garden drinking, the forests being saturated, and settle in to the quiet comfort of a rainy day.

I am baptized when I step out onto the deck to take a photo of the gray. The patter of steady rain hitting the ground offers praise. This is church, sure as anything, in this still moment when I stand in the rain. We will listen to spoken words this morning, broadcast like magic from a Facebook feed to our big screen TV. Church of another flavour happening right there in our den.

We will, I suspect, escape into books this afternoon. Maybe put a few more pieces in the jigsaw puzzle and play a game of chess. Do the thing I once dreamed of having time for: inhabit our home. In a few minutes I will set this device aside, pick up my holy book and read scripture. I will pray as the morning grows lighter and the rain still falls and peace flows like a river.

Monday, May 18, 2020

I have just come upstairs from where Gerry and I were working on our latest jigsaw puzzle. It's a pretty picture that transports me to another place while I hunt for pieces and set them into place with a satisfying push. I pick up my phone and find the most terrible news on my social media feed. One of the Canadian Snowbird planes has crashed, shortly after takeoff, into a house in our city. I call down to Gerry. Details come in through eyewitnesses, news sources, and messages from a friend who lives just a few blocks from the crash scene. And in an instant—one single instant on a day that, a moment before, seemed ordinary—lives are forever altered and one young one is lost. There are no ordinary moments. They are all extraordinary, each one a gift. May we remain mindful.

On May 19, 2020, B.C. moves into Phase 2 of the restart plan whereby non-essential businesses like restaurants, retail, stores, hair salons, restaurants, libraries, museums and health facilities like dentist's offices and massage therapy practices can reopen with safety protocols in place.[25]

---

[25] https://www.cbc.ca/news/canada/british-columbia/covid-19-bc-update-

Wednesday, May 20, 2020

It's a beautiful afternoon so, after watering the garden and pulling a few weeds, we head to the nearby park to walk. It's okay. We're encouraged to get outside and enjoy our city parks (I feel like I have to explain that because I've was criticized when we did it a few weeks ago). People on blankets in the grass, and towels on the beach, appears to be practicing appropriate social distancing.

Something new, since we sat in our car eating burgers here a number of weeks ago, is the sandbag berm snaking through the park. Those who study these things predict a 1-in-20-year flood this year. It's always something. Nevertheless, we enjoy a peaceful walk along the River's Trail then nip up to the other side of the berm and walk back through the grassy park.

We pass the playground and think of Makiya and summer afternoons we spent here in the past and ponder this year's Camp G and G. We consider looping up and going for ice cream at the store that just reopened with social distancing guidelines in place, but decide it's too close to suppertime.

Then home, and puttering and planning and tending to things that need my attention because I've got a book launching next week, and it's a peaceful summerlike end to the day. The sunshine, warm weather, and ability to go out and enjoy it does wonders for my mental health.

Thursday, May 21, 2020

We harvested the first of the spinach. In honour of the special occasion, Gerry takes an early morning trip to Costco during senior hour (the first Costco run since early March) to buy feta, and a handful of other things we've been missing (And yes, toilet paper. The first package to come into our home since the madness began.)

Now I snip spinach and tuck crisp, fat leaves in a bag while I think about salad. We try to eat seasonally and haven't enjoyed a green salad for many months. I've been eyeing this little patch of spinach since I spied the first green shoots when it was still too cool for anything else except fall-planted garlic to grow in the garden. Now it's time.

At home I pull out my big yellow Fiesta pasta bowl and fill it with washed and torn spinach leaves, add blueberries that I flash froze last summer, and sprinkle feta on top. Then I pull out wooden salad tongs and toss the beautiful mixture together. I make a vinaigrette with Canadian wild raspberry vinegar that's been waiting in the cupboard for just such a day and extra virgin olive oil. As I drizzle it over the spinach, I think about a favourite quinoa salad and think I'll make it sometime soon too.

Later we utter involuntary "mmmmm"s as we enjoy flavour of this simple supper of spinach salad and baked salmon Gerry brought home from his

---

what-you-need-to-know-may-19-1.5574829

fishing trip last summer. Salad days are here again. It is the simple things like this that sustain me and block out the noise.

SOCIAL MEDIA POST

As we hear rumblings about "opening up" and "a new normal" we sense a low grind starting up. We are mindful that what it looks like here may not look the same as it does there but we hope we're taking something with us as we move ahead.

Maybe we've learned to appreciate stillness in a new way. Or perhaps we're just as terrified of the quiet as we ever were and are eager to get moving again to drown out the silence.

Sunday, May 24, 2020

It's dark when I wake and I spend the first moments of the day in silent conversation with the Divine. I have questions. Requests. But mostly I just bask in the holy presence. I'm sipping soy milky frothy coffee from a favourite mug as the eastern sky grows pink. I watch as the hues change and soften and the certainty of another dawn brings peace. The tops of tall cedars bob and sway in the wind. They block part of my view. They have grown without my notice and now they are now too big. We've talked about topping them, or removing them altogether. I'll be glad when they're gone and I have an unobstructed view of the morning sky again. I watch as pink bursts and gives way to yellow, then pale blue. And the trees bob and sway and do their best to distract me from the glory of another day breaking. But not today. Not this morning.

Monday, May 25, 2020

"Are you ready for church?" I call downstairs.

"Yup. Be right there," Gerry calls back.

And like we've done every Sunday for the past ten weeks we gather in the den where I work some magic to get my phone display to broadcast on the big screen TV and we have church.

Afterward, we talk about what we gleaned individually from the message and how it influences our choices, then Gerry heads out to the back yard, where he's laying out markers to indicate where the underground sprinkler runs in preparation for a fence building project, and I head downstairs to the woman cave and put watercolour paint on paper.

Later, we drive to the grasslands, to an area Gerry was at with his hiking friends a few days earlier where the arrowleaf balsamroot flowers are still at their peak. We wander in a field and get down on the ground and shoot photos. It's a beautiful way to spend a Sunday afternoon. Any afternoon. For a time, the low grind in the back of my mind is silent.

Tuesday, May 26, 2020

I arrive home from the garden disheveled, with wind-swept hair and spinach and radishes in hand, to find beautiful, celebratory flowers on my dining table. A gift from Gerry to mark my book's birth day. He insists on a photo, so I change my shirt, attempt something with my hair, and he says goofy things to conjure a natural smile. It works. Kind of. Quiet celebration continues around here today. My new book, *The Presence of Absence: A Story About Busyness, Brokenness, and Being Beloved* is born.

Thursday, May 28, 2020

Good morning, Lord. Thank you for the gift of this day. There's this thing that weighs heavy.
Look at the eastern sky.
I don't understand this thing.
See the shades of pink and red and yellow.
I'm concerned about this person and this situation.
See how it changes colour.
I can't wrap my mind around the reason behind this circumstance.
Listen! The birds are waking up.
There's so much pain in the world. It's so easy to become distracted and overwhelmed by it all.
Remember what I taught you?
I'm afraid. I'm in pain.
Remember the most important thing.
What can I do?
Be still.
But what can I do?
Be still.
How?
Look at the changing colours in the morning sky. Listen to the birdsong greeting the day. Peace. Start there.
Then what?
Do the same thing tomorrow.
But, what if it's cloudy?
It might be.
But how will I see the changing colours?

Maybe you won't, but you'll know they're there behind the clouds because you've seen them day after day.

But there's still this thing. I don't know what to do about it.

Love.

What?

The answer is always love.

But what can I do?

Be still. Be filled. And love.

That's it? That's all?

That's enough.

Amen.

Friday, May 29, 2020

With morning comes the weight again.
The antidote.
Sun sparkle on the leaves of a tender tree.
Deep, variegated greens of the leaves of a mature tree nearby.
Shadows on the hills across the valley.
The stillness of the morning.
The sky—pale blue and dusted with haze.
I wish it was clear blue and sunny. Hot.
But this is what we get today and it's still a miracle I watch unfold.

Saturday, May 30, 2020

Some things hit me like a punch in the gut and the terrible seems far bigger and louder than the beautiful. Other times, I lean in, look closely at something small and quiet and easily missed and there I find wonder that washes me in peace. I don't subscribe to the theory that if I do A, B, and C, it (whatever the troubling "it" is at that particular moment) will get better. I don't believe I'm meant to live on the mountaintop all the time. Well-meaning directives to pray more or pray differently insult me. Sometimes I just have to spend time in the muck.

The Divine doesn't show up like a magic genie and pluck me from the midst of it or tell me to "buck up" and move on, but rather sits with me and invites me to linger and pay attention to the thing that's most troubling and consider the reason it's most troubling.

I wrestle—oh how I wrestle—but when I finally come to stillness, I hear a whisper. *I see you.*

And with my face held in holy hands, as my eyes leak and my head aches, I let go. Being seen was the thing I needed more than anything else all along.

The days get away from me. I don't accomplish the things I set out to do or I find myself stuck in a rut of doing that leads back to the same place I started. So, I make a list.

Paint a picture of a leaf.
Make a quinoa salad.
Be seen.

Those are enough for today.

Sunday, May 31, 2020

It's wet. And gray. But there's something about the formation of the clouds. And the shade of the green grass. Barefoot, I step out on the deck with my phone to capture the moment. This particular gray and green is for this time alone. This morning silence is manna for this moment only. A photo won't harness it. Words won't contain it. But perhaps the practice of marking it will preserve it and one day when I'm lost, I'll recall it, and like a map it will guide me.

JUNE 2020

On June 1, 2020 K – 12 schools in B.C. reopen for optional in-class instruction. Children return on a voluntary basis with safety protocols in place.[26]

Monday, June 1, 2020

Good morning. It's Monday. The first day of June. If there was ever a day for a fresh start, this is it. If there was ever a time when I needed a fresh start—well, I expect many of us do. It's been a tough spring.

Summer arrives this month; there's no stopping it. And that surety, like the sun rising every morning and setting every evening, stands like a beacon in the distance. Hold on.

It's cool where we live. Wet. Not typical. Nothing is "typical" right now and hasn't been for months. We—I—need something to change, and even as I tap out these words, I know that whether we have more of the same, or whether this cool Monday in the first day of June ushers in something new, remains to be seen. And is out of my control.

The longer I carry this weight, the heavier it gets. *Let go. Put it down. Let go.* I know. But I can't seem to release my grip and the season of lamenting lingers. I don't believe in toothy smiles and forced joyfulness and "buck up, sister" admonition that heaps guilt on top of the grief. I believe in lament and rawness and *God, this is hard. Damn hard* prayers. And, *God, why can't we be*

---

[26] https://news.gov.bc.ca/releases/2020PREM0026-000890

kinder? And who's telling the truth? And it's too much. It's too much. It's just too dang much.

And then I stand at the living room window shortly after 4 a.m., and the sky's barely getting light and there's a shade of pink in one spot that looks like promise fulfilled, and maybe that's enough to carry me for this day. A single chive blossom in a white vase on the top of my dresser. A fat, sharp radish plucked from the ground in my garden. Loud, white lilies tucked in next to stately and serene roses in a glass vase on my dining table. And peace like a river.

It is well. It is well. It doesn't feel like it, but it is well.

Tuesday, June 02, 2020

The world groans and I am weary under the weight of it. We are in the liminal: the in-between place of uncertainty where distraction tries to take us from our better work.

I stand in my kitchen and look out the window, over the top of a new top-down bottom-up blind, at a treed hilltop I've paid little attention to until now. I lift my eyes up at the start of a new day and am reminded where my help comes from.

I turn, and the vase of quiet roses and large, loud lilies on my dining table catches my attention. I think of my mom every time I catch a whiff of those lilies. They were too funereal for her taste. I find charm in them—especially paired, as they are, with stoic pink roses.

These things ground me.

Earlier, I lay awake long before daybreak in conversation with the Divine and come to a measure of understanding. Peace.

And the variegated green of the hills and the bright white of the lilies, the succulents on my windowsill, the tiny white petunias in my hydroponic kitchen garden; these, and the Keurig coughing and the soy milk warming and and a tiny ceramic dog who has stood guard on my kitchen windowsill all my adult life and the silence of a household still sleeping. And peace.

I pad to the living room and stand at a window that curtains never cover and there see a sky that for all the world looks like ripples on a calm and quiet lake. And creation greets the day. And if the rocks and the hills can't keep silent, how can I? And I am grounded by the tangible and the imperceptible and in the holy hush of morning, there is only peace.

Wednesday, June 3, 2020

I enjoy coffee and conversation with a friend in a coffee shop, and that little piece of the world seems almost normal. Just as I'm about to make one of my granddaughter's discarded Disney princess barrettes part of my style, I connect with my stylist and schedule a hair appointment. I'm getting my hair cut today. (Hallelujah!) My last appointment was in early March, just as the rumblings were starting.

Salad days are here again. The garden is growing—slower than normal due to unseasonably cool temperatures, but it's growing nonetheless. Bluebirds in the backyard. Light at 4 am. Soft pink in the morning sky. Tea. Shasta daisies. A fat, wet brush full of watercolour.
Light rain. Heavy rain. Sun through the clouds.
Quiet little things, amidst the loud and not-so-little things.
And it is good. It is good. It is exceedingly good.

SOCIAL MEDIA POST

It is still a beautiful world. It is still a beautiful world. It is still a beautiful world. When it seems dark, repeat these words. Look at the small and quiet things. The timeless things. Do the work required of you. Remain soft. Listen. Love all, above all. It's hard. I know. But it is our better work.

Thursday, June 4, 2020

Eyes meet over the tops of facemasks. A locked door.
"Who are you waiting to see?"
Maybe I need a secret pass phrase to enter the building.
The white swan met a stout man wearing a brown fedora.
Nope. That doesn't work.
I wait, until eyes I think I recognize show up at the door and unlock it so I can enter the hallowed hall.
Show me your hands. Spritz. Spray. *Okay, you're good.*
But I'm never quite good and I'm never quite comfortable and afterward there's no good-natured banter with the young woman at the front desk.

Instead, I tap a plastic card on a white square device on the ledge in front of my chair and a follow-up date comes by way of a ding on my phone that is tucked safely away in my crossbody bag to minimize stuff I bring into the building.

I can't wait to get out of there. With my hair cut. Finally.

. . . .

An installer comes to our house to set something up but the company he works for has forbidden him to enter our home. Hmm. How will that work? But it does, somehow, thanks to Gerry running wires and me hooking up devices while the installer stands "safely" in the doorway giving instructions.

· · · · · · · · ·

I make an appointment with my healthcare practitioner.

"She'll call you at 10:30 tomorrow morning," I'm told. "It might show up as "unknown caller" just so you know."

Oh. Okay. Good. I'm glad you told me so I'll know to pick up. I don't, as a rule, answer such calls.

There are more than a few things I'm doing these days that I didn't before.

· · · · · · · · ·

And the days go by. And the low burn simmers.
It's so much easier to stay home.

· · · · · · · · ·

The Swiss chard is finally doing something. There's a flower on the pattypan squash plant. I wish I would have planted those sweet peas closer to the fence. The spinach has bolted. It's raining again.

And the news. Oh, the news.

I'm weary before I get out of bed in the morning.

But I still believe in beauty and stillness and grace and love. Most of all love. Even now. Especially now.

Selah.

SOCIAL MEDIA POST

It gets so ugly so fast once we become willing to look at someone, or a group of someone's, as other.

I've done it, you've done it, we all have.

Lord, save us from the lie of other.

Friday, June 5, 2020

I must have known it at some point but the knowledge that the sun rises due east on only the spring and fall equinoxes and that now, as we approach the summer solstice it's more northeast, faded. Watching the sun rise over the hill on the other side of the ridge this morning confuses me. I think about mornings spent barefoot and pajama-clad in the back yard shooting the sunrise—farther east, over the top of different hills than the one it's making a first appearance over this morning. But I sort it out and watch in awe as another day dawns, and it's as glorious as ever.

Different, but no less awe-inspiring than the alive-with-bees clump of purple-pink chive blossoms I sat in front of yesterday afternoon with my camera.

In a world that seems upside down and where I'm not certain what version of reality to believe anymore, these things point to indisputable truth. They are grounding and worthy of contemplation.

Tuesday, June 9, 2020

The room is cold when I wake. Colder than, in my mind, it should be in June but there it is anyway. The fresh morning air filling the room through the open window is still a gift. I rise and pad to the kitchen for coffee. While it brews, I survey the space I've been given.

The moon, like a cookie with a nibble taken from it atop the hills out the south facing window is bright and brilliant. In awe, I whisper "good morning, moon," less greeting the celestial planet and more the One who set it there.

Then I stand at the north-facing windows of our living room and look out at the clear pre-dawn sky (ah, the weather forecasters got it wrong again) and the calm reflection on the sliver of river I see in the valley.

Day begins in peace.

Then I hear sirens from the valley. And more sirens. And someone's day is dawning with anything but peace. And that's the way it goes.

The beautiful and the terrible.

And I'm weary and I'm hopeful and I'm all those things in between and I stand in the kitchen and lift my eyes to the hills through the window above the kitchen sink.

SOCIAL MEDIA POST

It's okay if we disagree on some things. We don't have to see everything in the same light to be friends—to treat one another as human beings ought to treat one another. This polarizing tribal way we're choosing is breaking us.

Every single one of us hurts, bleeds, and is in need of compassion. Every single one brings something of value to the table. When we choose to stand only with those who (we believe) are like us, we lose a good measure of flavour in life.

It's wearing us out and it's wearing us down.

SOCIAL MEDIA POST

Just for today, may prayer be in my action as much as in my words.

SOCIAL MEDIA POST

Maybe the thing I relied on yesterday or last year isn't wholly what I need in these turbulent days. Perhaps this season of turmoil calls for something more radical. Maybe I need to dig deeper.

Get quieter. Get louder. Stand firm. Remain soft.

See the quandary? No wonder we're confused.

I'm just stumbling along the same as everyone else; sometimes going backwards, sometimes standing still. This is hard stuff we're living.

What's helping you through?

Friday, June 12, 2020

My eyes are drawn to the schoolyard where six teenage boys are shooting hoops. That the sight seems extraordinarily ordinary speaks to the time in which we live. Ahead, the stoplight turns red and the convoy I'm in slows to a stop. I'm grateful because it gives me a few precious extra moments to watch the boys. I wonder about the stories they'll tell their children and grandchildren about 2020, the year when everything changed.

We couldn't know, one morning back in March, that we were waking up on what would be the last day of Before. We don't know, now, that this morning might be the last one before something unexpected or unimaginable happens.

There's a phrase in scripture that talks about "redeeming the time"—basically meaning to make the best use of it. A few miles down the road past the basketball shooting boys I consider the concept.

Back in March, we talked about things we had time to do when life slowed for many of us. We reconnected with those who live in our homes. We played board games together, took up new hobbies or recommitted to those we had set aside in our busyness. We watched too much Netflix, read books, and did jigsaw puzzles. We baked bread. Has all of this, or any of this, redeemed our time? Am I redeeming my time?

I'm not talking about productivity in terms of doing or creating something. I'm talking about the important, deep work of pondering, ruminating, and simply thinking.

Asking thoughtful questions and listening for the answers.

Considering my purpose and place in the world.

Really chewing on what I believe about people and time and faith; what I want to keep and what it's time to let go of.

The better work.

I know, we're all getting antsy and as we start to open things up, we want to get going.

But as I pause and watch boys wrestling over a basketball, I think maybe we shouldn't be in such a hurry.

Maybe the work of redemption isn't finished yet.

I need more time to ponder more things and release other things that no longer serve me.

I need to sit on a rock and watch birds soar and listen to the wind.

I need to *be* more than I need to *do*.

I need to listen more than I speak.

SOCIAL MEDIA POST

Amidst the cacophony there are those sitting on the ground looking, in awe, at the wonder of growing things. And others, gazing upward at a starry sky feeling infinitesimally small beneath it.

Worshiping.

And in the quiet comes wisdom that can't be

> *comprehended where attempts to be right or strong manifests as louder.*
>
> *I do not know the answers. I struggle to understand all the questions. But I know there is truth found in the most unexpected, quiet, and solitary places.*
>
> *And I know poets see things politicians are blind to.*

Monday, June 15, 2020

Gerry and I have been playing chess regularly for over a year. When we first started, I made foolish moves and didn't think ahead. It was a given that he'd capture my king but I was determined to improve so I persevered. Loss after loss. Angst upon angst. Until, one day, I won! I let out a whoop, did a little dance and celebrated loudly—perhaps in a less than sportsmanlike manner. Then I went back to losing.

These days, I win a reasonable number of games. My appreciation for the strategy required to control the board increases every time we play. I enjoy chess as much—possibly more—than when we started playing.

I decided to dabble with watercolour painting a couple of months ago and I'm having a grand time with it. I sit at my table, mix colours, and create images that are not technically good but are satisfying to me nonetheless. I watch YouTube videos and get a good measure of fulfillment from observing the process and picking up tips.

In time my work will improve, for now I'm content with the process and the art I am making. It's not good, but I hesitate to call it bad. Watercolour is doing what I need it to do in this season: it's giving me space to meditate and ponder using a different part of my brain.

Today is Monday. As I think about the week ahead and the things, I hope to accomplish I leave plenty of free space in which to sit in my woman cave, listen to music, think deep thoughts, and wash paint on paper.

Tuesday, June 16, 2020

When I decided to start playing with watercolour I was overwhelmed by choice. Paints, palettes, paper, brushes. I researched and studied and made decisions that were right for me—all the while washing paint on wet paper and being fascinated by the process. I wasn't sure what I wanted to paint. Loose flowers, more true-to-life botanicals, abstract images, landscapes. So I dabbled with a little of each, and came to a decision for what's right for me right now: prairie landscapes. Surprise, surprise.

With a narrowed focus and intention to play while I practice, I can easily spend hours washing paint on paper making "bad" art that's good for my soul. Yesterday, I painted a field that I love more than anything else I've painted to date. A distracting and technically terrible tree lives on it, but I'm able to look past it to the subtle nuances of the field itself. I positioned it on my writing desk for inspiration.

Skies and fields. That's enough for me right now. In time, I'll look back on these early attempts and smile at my rudimentary effort. For now, I'm delighted. In this newfound hobby I see metaphor. Principles are reinforced. Pondering, I find peace. I refer to painting as my therapy. I'm learning, even as I'm creating. I think that's how it's supposed to be.

And I risk vulnerability by sharing some of these early efforts because we learn through the transparency of one another. Your comments yesterday reinforced what I'm coming to believe about watercolour and all art—what I've known to be true about writing for years—there's no wasted effort. We learn through the process and we connect through the craft. We were created to be creative—whatever that looks like.

Thursday, June 18, 2020

I'm so weary. Of all of it. And I feel guilty for my tiredness because there's work left to do. There's truth to be touted (after wading through the weeds to figure out which truth is the true truth). There are causes to support (after investigating to get to the root of said causes to determine if they are what they say they are). There are misunderstandings to clear up (because if I look at someone the wrong way or don't dress myself up to look just like them there's bound to be issues). And I'm sorry, but I'm just so tired.

Gardening doesn't excite me like it did in years past. Oh, it's growing and we're feasting and there are weeds to pull and work to do, but the better work of pondering and imagining and viewing the garden through the eyes of a poet isn't getting done.

There's work on my desk. I make lists and watch self-imposed deadlines pass without checking the boxes. The pile gets higher, the weight heavier, and I've little desire to do anything about it.

I struggle to read and to write. The level of focus and concentration required, for now, is lost. These simple pleasures are no longer fulfilling, but chores I slog through with minimal satisfaction.

Maybe the work in this season is different than it was last year, last decade, last century. Maybe the work now is the most important work of all. Maybe it doesn't look like work.

The shifting sand throws me off balance. Not gonna lie. I'm wobbling. We're all staggering around like drunken sailors wondering what happened, trying to sober up enough to regain our bearings. We knew it would be hard, this changing and breaking down and rebuilding, but we didn't think it would be like this. We know there's even harder stuff to navigate down the road. We're kinda scared.

I think I should be able to weather this storm better than I am. I wrote an entire book about navigating my way through the squall, for goodness' sake. And by "writing" I mean more than just tapping out words because writing is so much harder than that. Deep work precedes words being formed. So, I think I should have this figured out. But I don't and that's part of the beautiful terrible truth of this life. We're not meant to go it alone. We're invited to stand on the deck long before the sun has risen and, while the rest of the neighborhood still sleeps, look up and over and around and whisper a one-word prayer.

"Help."

Friday, June 19, 2020

It's Friday. Even though I've been retired from my corporate life for six years it still feels like the end of the week and an opportunity to look at what I got done and what's left to do. What I got done this week was, in short: nothing. I put two things on my "to do" list on Monday morning and neither are complete. I'm running dangerously close to a deadline on one of them.

But I visited with two friends and I sat on the deck and got lost in a book for the first time in a long, long time. I thought about undulation, what C.S. Lewis referred to as the natural ebbing and flowing (troughs and peaks, he called it) in all areas of our life. Ah yes, that's it. I'm in a trough. And, you know, it's okay. Some of our deepest work is done in troughs. Sometimes troughs are simply a place where we wallow, and it looks like nothing much is being accomplished. But there is, of course, work being done, and oftentimes it's the better work.

So, practically, I must tend to that one thing on my list today and at least make some progress on the other. If I spend a good chunk of time lost in a book, that's work equally as important. Now, in a trough and later when I return to a peak.

SOCIAL MEDIA POST

The world needs your scuffed up self and the things you create whether by intention or accident.

We need you and the quiet moments we spend together listening and holding one another (even virtually, if that's all we can manage right now).

*We need the peace you cultivate in a garden,
through art, or as you stand at the sink washing
dishes at the end of another noisy day.*

*We're feeling a bit manic, on the edge of hysteria.
We see in a mirror dimly. We're afraid.*

*We're mad to control things that are out of control
and we keep forgetting sometimes the better work is
just to be still.*

*We, and the world, are so, so broken. We need that
patch of peace you contribute far more than
anything else.*

Sunday, June 21, 2020

I tune in online to watch the summer solstice at Stonehenge. It's cloudy at Wiltshire, England and there isn't much to see. The only sound is the wind. I watch for a while, remembering what it was like when Gerry and I stood on that ground in the cordoned off area looking at the stones, and take a moment to scroll through comments made by others watching.

They are refreshing. No anger. No fighting and arguing. No name-calling. Just peaceful greetings from people all around the world. It is as if they—we, I suppose—come together in harmony, opting out of the madness happening around us. We set aside our opinions and our right-fighting and our anger and simply sit in silence and watch light change and clouds move above monolithic stones. Many feel a need to connect with others. Some express gratitude to English Heritage for arranging the livestream. Others raise a virtual hand just to say "I'm here."

"Greetings from Scotland."

"Watching from Charlotte, NC."

"Hello from Mexico City."

And people gather together virtually around something as ordinary as a sunset over something as extraordinary as a livestream broadcast at the site of these massive stones and there's just a sense of peace.

"It's so wonderful. The clouds are beautiful."

"Thank you for sharing this peace and calm."

"So soothing and peaceful."

I'm so worn out by the polarization and disregard for basic decency, the half-truths and out-and-out lies, and the sense that we've opened a box and released something horrific. In a world where if I say something's pink someone will argue and say it's really purple and what kind of fool am I for thinking it's pink anyway and we can't remain friends in light of such disagreement, the stones are a haven. I don't think there's anything supernatural about the henge, at the solstice or any other time, but there is certainly something magical about a peaceful gathering of 127,000 people from around the world gathering virtually around them.

On June 24, B.C. begins a gradual transition to Phase 3 of the reopening plan. Hotels, motels, movie theatres, and resorts can reopen with safety measures in place and people are encouraged to take part in safe travel within the province. B.C. parks open to overnight camping. Family members of residents in long-term care homes can visit. [27]

Wednesday, June 24, 2020

"Do you think you're falling into a depression around this COVID thing?" Gerry asks.

"Yes," I respond.

But the weight is about so much more than the pandemic, and depression doesn't fully describe what's happening in and around me.

When things get loud, I tend toward quiet; these days I lean in even more to healing silence. The cacophony feels like an assault, so I sit in my woman cave and wash paint on paper while procrastinating about things I have little desire to tend to.

I walk out of grocery stores, overwhelmed by arrows and the COVID dance we do around one another and the general sense of heaviness. I guess I don't need that thing, whatever it is, after all. I'll try again another day.

I pay a visit to the bookstore—a place I've often gone when I need to return to myself. Forty people at a time allowed. An employee keeps count of the bodies entering and leaving. Chairs have been removed. No lingering allowed. The magazine section is cordoned off. The doors to the adjoining coffee shop are closed. And it's cold. Uncomfortably so. I guess they don't want anyone to get too comfortable in the stacks. So, I leave.

I wrote about a season of depression in *The Presence of Absence* in a chapter called *Dark Night*. This is less a dark night than it is a gray day and please, oh

---

[27] https://news.gov.bc.ca/releases/2020PREM0033-001159

please, let the sun shine bright soon. The gray feels oppressive. Less a blanket of comfort than a thing that suffocates. But the gray times are peppered with coffee and one-on-one conversation in shops and parks, and these things are good. They keep me afloat and give me things to ponder. They keep me connected and restore my faith.

I go to the garden and cut scapes from the garlic and think about a Creator who imagines such whimsy. I pull tiny weeds and tidy things up; pick lettuce, radishes, and the first Picolino cucumber for a supper salad.

At night my little Yorkie, Maya, crawls over us and tries to get as close as she can. She snuggles in. She climbs on top of our heads. The wind through the window, the rattle of the bedroom door, and the sound of curtains flapping unsettle her.

I get it, girl. I feel ya.

All is not as it was. It all feels a little bit shaky.

I read the Psalms. I lament.

I lean in. I lean hard.

Sunday, June 28, 2020

Gerry brings home two flats of plump, sweet raspberries. I wash and crush some; cook and stir and sweeten them; fill jars with jam and set them in the water bath canner to process. It's ridiculously cool outside for late June but in the kitchen where I work, you'd never know it.

While the jam processes, I spread washed berries on trays to flash freeze before putting them in bags. I tidy the kitchen mess.

We munch hot dogs and play chess. Nibble raspberries.

Gerry spends the afternoon nursing a hiking injury on the couch with a book. He makes a difficult call. This summer—this year—is not turning out the way anyone planned back when we turned the calendar to 2020 and looked through smudged lenses to what we thought we'd be doing by now.

I read, wash paint on paper, then curl up under a blanket to watch *Portrait Artist of the Year* on TV and nurse a malady of my own. Thunder booms. Rain falls. Afternoon passes. Day turns to evening. And the Divine is with us and in us, and this ordinary day is holy.

SOCIAL MEDIA POST

It's so easy to get caught up, isn't it? Maybe just for today, we let go and grow still. Listen. Pay attention. Release the need to accomplish something and fall softly into love.

True sabbath.

JULY 2020

SOCIAL MEDIA POST

I'll take the quiet places over the crowd any day. Wisdom lives there. She doesn't shout or force her way in. She waits for poets, contemplatives, and those with an ear tuned to listen, to seek her out. Then, she shares her riches.

Thursday, July 2, 2020

I wake from a disturbing dream, bringing some of the burden with me, and feel the need to orient myself. It's Thursday (though it feels like Monday after yesterday's Canada Day holiday). The person in my dream hasn't been in my life for decades. I have to go for blood work today. I listen to the steady sleep breathing of Gerry and Maya ebbing and flowing like a tide. The morning air is cool on my arms. I hear the low rumble of a train in the distance. I see a crack of light under the door indicating the hydroponic kitchen garden light has come on so it's after 4:00 a.m.—judging by the light, not much after. I have to pee. I want coffee.

And day begins.

I wander the house as the coffee brews, going first to the south facing window in the den and then to the north facing window in the living room—the window of beautiful views. The sky is gray and unremarkable, but no less able to elicit a bubble of worship.

You have brought us in safety to a new day.

I take a tall mug of soy milky frothy coffee with me back to bed where I read a few things, think about things, and write about other things. These first minutes of the day set a tone.

It is well, it is well, with my soul.

Friday, July 3, 2020

I wake to find a dog sitting on my head. Maya must have been scared by the wind in the night but it's calm outside our window now. It's about 4:30 and starting to get light. There's light cloud cover and not the oppressive gray we've been under for days. We haven't had summer yet—or not the summer we're used to around here. Two days ago, we enjoyed the coldest Canada Day in recorded history.

Gerry's bundling up and going fishing this morning. I'm not sure how I'll fill my time. Painting. Writing. Gardening. Photography. Reading. There are plenty of options. There's no reason to be bored.

A couple of writing projects are calling. I pulled out multi-coloured index cards yesterday to do some planning and outlining. We'll see where it takes me. Some shorter work too. And book work, as *The Presence of Absence* makes its way out in the world. One thing's for certain. I won't spend any time on the deck with a book—it's far too cool for that.

I set some intentions a week or so ago, needing to do something about the low-grade depression I felt myself falling into. They're helping. On the outside they don't look like much but, for now, they are part of my better work.

> *Gradually, you will return to yourself,*
>
> *Having learned a new respect for your heart*
>
> *And the joy that dwells far within slow time.*
>
> *John O'Donohue, For One Who Is Exhausted: A Blessing*[28]

Friday, July 10, 2020

It's been a week where every day felt like Friday so I'm relieved this morning that it's finally arrived. It's been a week of slow and steady, weary and wonder, doing things and letting other things go. I wish it was warmer

---

[28] John O'Donohue, *To Bless the Space Between Us: A Book of Blessings*, (New York: Doubleday, 2008), 125.

but I remember smoky summers when forest fires ravaged our province and I am grateful for clear, fresh air. Summer isn't turning out the way we expected but it's unfolding as it should. I must trust that.

I lean in more to intention. I think about stages and phases and how we look for signs but none are forthcoming and, if we're wise, we stop looking and do the better work of learning to love God and our neighbours. What have we learned these past four months? Do we hold things looser? Pay closer attention? Are we listening?

So many things hurt my heart and I learn to protect and preserve it so I can tend to my better work. I focus more on creating than consuming. I read good books, listen to good words, seek solitude and silence, and pray. Maybe the thing we need most of all is to abide. We've been too busy to see it. We thought we'd find answers in accumulation and promotion, we thought we'd quiet the noise by making ourselves louder, but the void only grew vaster. Now we look up at the miracle of dawn and dusk and pluck tiny flowers from the yard and set them in a clear glass vase on the dining table and find peace.

Yeah, I wish it was warmer, that we weren't in the midst of this pandemic, and that we could trust unbiased news reports. But it's not and we are and we for darn sure can't, so we look to timeless and eternal things to ground us. It's what we needed all along. And the Divine embraces us and the poets guide us and it is well.

Wednesday, July 15, 2020

My granddaughter and I dabble with watercolor in my woman cave. It's her first experience with the medium and, as a creative, she enjoys every new step. Mixing paint. Washing it onto wet paper and watching it bleed. Pulling tape off the edges of a finished painting. All deemed, in her words, "satisfying." She hands her painting of a night sky to me when it's finished.

"It's for you," she says.

I'm taken aback. It's her first watercolour.

"Are you sure?" I ask.

She nods, and I prop it up on my writing desk in front of my word-a-day calendar where it will remind me of this simple evening.

"Can I look through your bin?" she asks.

"Of course!"

And she pulls out the small plastic bin from beneath my desk where I store random scraps paper from watercolor play and finished paintings.

She expresses appreciation for one.

"You can have it," I tell her.

And she looks up at me almost shyly.

"But it's your art," she says.

And I gesture to the acrylic painting she did a few months ago that hangs on my wall, and the watercolor she gifted to me a few minutes ago, and laugh.

Point taken.

She smiles and sets the painting aside for herself.

Her mom joins us and by the time we've finished looking through the bin they each have paintings set aside. Simple gifts.

We three have exchanged art in many different forms over the years. Tucked away in my home are some of the first rudimentary stick drawings my daughter did when she first learned to hold a pencil. Elsewhere, construction paper chickens and other pieces of my granddaughter's early creations. An acrylic painting she did recently adorns the wall in our bedroom. We treasure things for their aesthetic but mostly for the heart that created and gifted them.

"Are you sure?" we ask.

But what we're really asking is whether we're worthy to receive a treasure so dear as a piece of someone's heart manifested in art.

Creative expression feeds us and gives us an outlet as we craft something with paint or words or whatever medium we choose.

It teaches us to be open and generous.

It shows us how to give and receive with grace.

It is a picture of creation itself and a reflection of the original Creator.

On July 17, 2020, faith-based organizations in B.C. are informed they can hold in-person services with a maximum of 50 people in attendance, contact tracing, and safety protocols in place.[29]

Saturday, July 18, 2020

What a beautiful week it has turned out to be.

Summer finally arrived bringing with her reasonably warm temperatures and sunshine and we've soaked it up with Daughter and Granddaughter who are visiting.

Our backyard project moved forward with the installation of privacy barriers where the tall cedars once stood. Now we're on to the fun stuff: landscaping.

There's been an abundance of simple happy.

The garden growing and feeding us.

Flowers blooming and making things beautiful.

---

[29] https://crestonunitedchurch.ca/wp-content/uploads/2020/07/Guidance_Faith_Based_JULY_17-1.pdf

Fragrant sweet peas in a small glass vase on the dining table.
Granddaughter reading to us from her latest writing projects.
Board games.
Roll kuchen.
Burgers and hot dogs.
Potato chips and ice cream.
Salads.
Hiking. (Gerry and Daughter loved it. Granddaughter and I will choose a less strenuous visit to the coffee shop next time.)
Hugs. Laughter
Family.
Grace.
Next week we will return to regularly scheduled programming with hearts full.

Tuesday, July 21, 2020

A news source puts out a summary in the morning: *What you need to know.* Below the headline it lists bullet points and links to more detail about each of the "must know" stories. I glance at the headlines with a critical eye. Nope. Don't need to know any of those things.

I need to know it's nearing time to harvest the garlic and there are tender young beans ready for picking. We're almost out of soy milk. We're in for a string of warm summer days. Blueberries have arrived at the green grocer.

But, the news cycle keeps spinning, trying to tell me what I need to know and generously feeding me the flavour it deems most important.

I need to know that the noise distracts me from the better work of loving God and my neighbour. I'm not very good at either of those things and distraction is the last thing I need. The buzz gets in my head; I grow more anxious with each new headline. And if that's not enough to disturb my peace, there's the constant criticism from everybody over everything.

I need to know I'm beloved. I need to understand more of the wisdom gleaned in solitude and silence. I need to see how insidious distraction is at keeping me from the timeless, most important things. I need to practice loving well.

Another day begins, bringing with it the temptation to give up my peace in favour of the "need to know". Choose wisely what you allow space for in your thoughts, I tell myself. Live beloved. Love well.

It's hard, and I stumble more often than not. I stray from the path and get lost in the dark. I feel that lump of something in the pit of my stomach and it aches. All is not as any of us thought it would be by now and smoke clouds our eyes as we try to look farther down the road.

Shortly after four in the morning I pour warm frothy soy milk over fresh brewed coffee, drizzle a bit of caramel on top for a start-to-the-week treat, and take my mug out to the deck where it's still dark but cooler than it is in the house,

There's a comet visible in the eastern sky—NEOWISE, they call it. I've paid just enough attention to the news to know the bright light is the comet. It's cool, I suppose. I should probably be more thrilled but comets aren't my love language. Still, it brings me to prayer.

Oh God you are always with us and you have brought us in safety to this new day. Teach us to love.

Wednesday, July 22, 2020

Sometime during the night Gerry opens the door leading from our bedroom to the deck. Thanks to the cedars he removed a few weeks ago it opens on to an unobstructed view of mountain, valley, and big sky. This morning, a few clouds add interest. Pinks and blues step lightly around one another as the sun rises and it is glorious.

I think about getting my phone to capture a quick image but choose the better thing instead. To sit and watch and worship. I am hungry for the Divine and so very weary of the rest.

> *Be soft. Do not let the world make you hard. Do not let pain make you hate. Do not let the bitterness steal your sweetness. Take pride that even though the rest of the world may disagree, you still believe it to be a beautiful place.*
>
> *Iain Thomas*[30]

I have been pondering the fact—yes, I regret to say it is a fact—that a measure of hardness has settled in me this year.

I need to pay attention to sunrises and hummingbirds and other such magical things; to get lost in the aroma of fresh baked bread and the taste of sweet summer fruit.

I need to push through this propensity to hold my thoughts close out of fear of condemnation. It's hard when it seems even the simplest things are misconstrued and judged.

I don't want to argue.

I don't want to be hard.

When my boundaries are encroached upon my first reaction is to withdraw to a place of safety to regain strength. These days I just want to stay where it's quiet and I don't have to justify or explain.

---

[30] Iain Thomas, *I Wrote This For You*, (Kansas City: Andrews McMeel Publishing, 2018), 3

Before we knew that this year would unfold as it has, I planned to go on personal retreat this summer. I grieve the loss of that opportunity and look for pockets of retreat in unsteady days instead.

Books are my companions—as usual. But some days I struggle to read them. My monkey mind swings from branch to branch clutching my attention in its grip.

I need a project. I have too many projects. I just want to sit on the deck. I need a book I can lose myself in or one I can sink my teeth into. I want to learn. I want out. I don't know.

Another email from the library letting me know I can phone to make arrangements to pick up a book I requested. Books handed out at the library in brown papers bags. Who'da thunk it?

Another trip to the grocery store where we queue to get in, sanitize our hands, and wait for a sanitized basket or cart to be brought to us.

Another conversation where I struggle to hear what the other person is saying behind their facemask or plexiglass safety barrier.

Another news story. Another contradiction. Another disagreement.

It's all just too much.

But in the predawn sky I see the hand of the Creator. Virtuoso. Love.

I don't want to be hard so I pause here.

And tomorrow. And tomorrow.

Monday, July 27, 2020

Another Monday in COVID time and we're all still holding our breath a little—or a lot, depending on the hour or the day. It's the last one in July and how in the world did we get here already?

In other times (BP: before the pandemic), when someone we knew was going through a trial we rallied round. We sent cards, flowers, text messages, delivered meals, ran errands, or just sat with them. It's harder now because we're all going through a trial. We're all staggering around wondering what's happening; tallying up losses and carrying grief; tossed to and fro while trying to remain solid on ground that's continually shaking.

Is the weight you're carrying feeling heavier?

I've been thinking about community and hungering for deep connection, while at the same time finding it easier and more comfortable to remain in solitude. A little off balance. Know what I mean? Self-care. Community care. Creation care. Where does it fit? What does it look like? I pose a question: Where did you see the hand of God today? I challenge myself to pay attention. To the sky, to the earth, to the whispers, to the ordinary.

I think I should do more. Or less. Or something different.

I turn off the news.

I check my heart.

Speaking of hearts, how's yours?

Mine's feeling more than a little constricted.

Here, in the interior of British Columbia we're in for a heat wave this week. A good measure of dry Kamloops summer heat is just what I need. I'll spend a good portion of the day on my deck with books, ice water, a notebook, and my thoughts, trying to make sense of it all but knowing I won't.

I'm hungry. Starving, actually.

In need of a feast in the midst of this famine.

And the week begins, and the month winds down, and we sweep away a little more of the chaff. Breathe deep. Pay attention. Begin again.

But God. And God. Still God.

SOCIAL MEDIA POST

Every day I choose whether to focus my attention on the beauty around me or give in to the terrible that tries to snake its way into my mind. I don't always choose wisely. Some days are harder than others.

I said somewhere that 2020 is kicking my mental health butt. Maybe it's that way for you too? Some days (okay many) I feel as if I'm losing ground.

Today I'm leaning in to prayer, intention, and most of all love. Let's link arms and do this together, okay? We know there's far more good than we're being fed. We know there's far more love, and that it's stronger than anything else. We know this. Let's live it.

SOCIAL MEDIA POST

I know. There's so much to debate and disagree about these days (actually, healthy and respectful debate would be a refreshing change) and some of those things are important.

But look around.

There are people in your sphere who need you to be present. They need eye contact and heart contact. You need it too.

We're all hungry to be seen. To be with someone safe enough we can drop our (virtual) mask with and be real and raw and seen is priceless.

I'm not always good at being that person. I'm working on being better. Some broken person needs me to be present just as I hunger for the same.

Let's set an intention together to try. Okay?

On July 29, 2020, the B.C. government announces a one-time investment of $45.6 million to support school districts and independent school saying "This investment will ensure the increased cleaning of high-contact surfaces, increased number of hand-hygiene stations and the availability of masks upon request, among other safety measures."

"Families will hear from their school district or independent school throughout the summer with updated health and safety guidelines for elementary, middle and secondary schools, as well as learning groups, schedules, enrolment and registration information with the final details being submitted to the ministry and posted online by the districts on

Aug. 26, 2020."[31]

Thursday, July 30, 2020

It's hot. Kamloops summer hot. Oh, how we love it!

I head to the garden early to harvest beautiful tri-colour beans. Back home I wash, snap, blanch, and tuck them in freezer bags.

I sit on the deck and read what was once my favourite book (*The Velvet Room* by Zilpha Keatley Snyder). I lost myself in it countless times when I was a child; I do the same now and it's just as sweet. I'm going to give it to my granddaughter. I hope she enjoys it.

I write. Tapping out words for an article and scribbling more words in my journal to sort some things out.

We drive to a viewpoint, sit on a bench, and look out over the city. I fiddle with my phone to take a photo and miss the whole point. I'm still learning.

I water flowers in pots and tender young plants in my backyard garden. The new growth is a picture of what's happening inside me. I see some things in a fresh way. Shifting sands, yes, but that's not necessarily bad. There's peace in putting some things down and turning toward others.

It's been a tough year for everyone everywhere. I've said here and elsewhere how 2020 is kicking my mental health butt, and it has. And it is. But suddenly it's different.

The summer heat helps, but it goes far deeper than that. I'm working things out. Going deeper. Hearing and seeing clearer. These are the gifts that can come when we go through a dark night.

Gerry's going on an easy hike with friends today, the first in months since he injured himself in a fall. He's kept himself occupied with a backyard project but his heart is in the hills. He'll be happy to return—albeit at a slower pace for now.

I'm leaning into listening. And stillness. Solitude and silence. Intention. Grace.

This day is a gift. I won't squander it.

Friday, July 31, 2020

It's simple.

---

[31] https://news.gov.bc.ca/releases/2020EDUC0040-001415

> Be fair, forgiving, and humble.
> Love God. Love my neighbour.
> Micah 6:8
> Mark 12:30-31

I will spend the rest of my life figuring out how to do these things, doing them, not doing them, and trying again to do them well. Whether I worship with others in a sanctuary, a cathedral, a park, on ZOOM; in solitude; or while walking through a forest, along a beach, or tending a garden—if I'm not intentional about doing these things, I'm missing the point.

Whether I pray according to a liturgy, in silent contemplation, conversationally, or one word at a time ("help," "thanks," or "wow," as Anne Lamott writes about in her book of the same name), if I'm not mindful of walking these things out in everyday life then life then truth has escaped me.

When—not if—I point my finger more often than I look in the mirror, I lose sight of what's most important. When my comfort seems more important than connection . . . When I give more of myself to the cause of the day than to the person standing next to me . . . When knowledge seems more important than wisdom . . . I've forgotten.

I need to change course and return to the better work of figuring out how to love well.

And do it.

SOCIAL MEDIA POST

Listen. To the Divine, to your inner voice, to your gut. To people, the sunrise, and the turn of a crimson rose petal. To the things you missed over here while your attention was over there. To the longing.

AUGUST 2020

Monday, August 10, 2020
There's nothing especially remarkable about the sky right now. I've been watching it gradually grow light, and for a while I thought it might be spectacular. Not so. Not yet.

There are more days like this than there are extraordinary ones—in terms of sunrises and experiences. We must learn to appreciate the ordinary, and see through it to find specs of the extraordinary, or we're doomed to a life of mundane.

It is calm here this morning. Cool air through the open bedroom window, the contrail of an airplane surfacing memories of past travel and gratitude for home, the distant sound of highway traffic: these my early morning companions. It is noticeably darker when I rise these days. The season is changing. We're gently shifting toward something new. The challenge is not to attempt to squeeze as much out of what remains of summer as possible, but to walk softly through days that unfold as ordinary as this one.

Around here, as I said, it's quiet. Laurinda arrived yesterday, loaded up Makiya's things (more now than when she arrived as we stocked her up with art supplies while she was here), and took her home. Gerry accompanied them, on a mission. And now, this morning, as Maya snores gently next to me and I sip soy milky frothy coffee in the fullness of a solitary dawn I sense and embrace the shift. What was, was. Now, we move forward to what is to come.

There's a touch of wonder breaking now as the sun rises. Not enough for me to snap another photo, but a promise. Quiet promises and abiding faith are enough. Today is Monday, the second one in August, in the nineteenth week of Ordinary Time. Day begins

Monday, August 31, 2020

Well, we did it. We made it through spring and now on this the last day of August, for all intents and purposes, we're wrapping up a topsy-turvy summer. It's dark when I rise now, and there's an unmistakable chill in the air. Even in the afternoon when it's warm (or hot—there's still a good measure of summer-like days on the horizon) you can feel it. The tree across the street in my neighbour's yard drops the odd leaf. Elsewhere, shades of green take on different hues as plant life prepares to change.

The marathon days of canning are over. Now I pick blushing tomatoes and put them in a box in my laundry room until there's enough to make a batch of soup. I save seeds, pull out plants, and survey the changing garden landscape. She remains generous with her gifts as she prepares for the restful fallow season ahead.

We've moved from an unimaginable spring through an uncertain summer. I'm ready for autumn like never before. It's always been a season of comfort. We need comfort like never before. Pass the blankets and reading socks, pull out the crockpots and candles. We'll have to be creative in our pursuit of creature comfort this season, but we've already proven our resilience and ability to adapt this year.

In the interest of caring for my mental health, I limit my exposure to some things and open arms wide toward others. These shifting sands present challenges—some hard to weather, others good and necessary. We're all broken in unspoken ways, cracked and chipped and so beautiful in our imperfection. I remind myself over and over: don't let the world make you hard. What is today, wasn't yesterday, and if we don't learn to bend, we will shatter.

And so farewell August. You were one like none other.

SOCIAL MEDIA POST

I'm finding it hard to be in this world. Some days the weight of the anger and the fear feels like more than I can bear. It both grieves and paralyzes me. It makes me quiet. I want to withdraw. I do.

Sometimes a season of stepping back is necessary in order to heal and grow stronger but to remain there doesn't seem right. The world needs me and it needs you and to allow space for only the loudest and angriest voices is to give up.

In the midst of the cacophony the poets and artists and those with soft hearts who struggle to put one foot in front of the other in the midst of the muck may have the wisdom we need but we're too busy protesting and right-fighting to hear it.

Keep showing up. Keep lighting candles.

(Note to self. And those who need it.)

SEPTEMBER 2020

Wednesday, September 2, 2020
I'm going to the community garden to water and pick blushing tomatoes. I pick early, allowing the fruit to ripen in the safety of my laundry room, to foil destructive garden thieves who are apt to pluck growing things from garden plots at this time of year. My laundry room is a party of ripening tomatoes, garlic, and summer squash right now.

I'm melancholy. Were it not for my garden, I'd be just as happy to stay home curled up with books or my journal, but the garden beckons. It's just as well. Maybe tending growing things will lift me out of my funk. There's no specific reason for it; it's just 2020. The pandemic, uncertainty, anger, mistrust, and fear all manifesting in ways that rip at me.

I've been working at paying attention to better things and asking myself at the end of the day where I saw God in the past twenty-four hours. Now I feel empty for no particular reason, with just enough hope that I'll see something at the garden to lift my sagging spirits.

I'm driving down Valleyview Drive, a long street where some section of it has been under construction every summer since we returned to Kamloops six years ago. Sometimes I bypass it and take the highway instead, but, even with the construction, it's a more peaceful route. I choose it today.

Traffic is slow. It's supposed to be slow. We meander past houses and schools and people out for an afternoon stroll. A bus at the front of the line stops now and then to let people on or off, slowing down traffic even more. A young mom and her daughter walk along the sidewalk. The girl, maybe nine or ten-years-old, waves to cars as they go by. The driver of a big gasping garbage truck taps his horn twice in response. She raises her hands in celebration.

And there it is.

Something of joy in the young girl prompting her to wave in greeting to strangers driving by, and simple jubilation at a response. *I see you*, the quick beep-beep tells her, and she celebrates. Care on the part of the garbage truck driver taking a second out of his workday to respond to her wave with two quick taps on his horn lifting both of their spirits for that split second.

I imagine the girl and her mom carrying on toward home, their conversation turning toward something else. Maybe a bird in a tree, or a flower in a yard they pass by. A chipmunk, perhaps. Or cloud formations above. The moment of greeting between the girl and the garbage truck driver lost in memory.

And the driver, weary and heading toward the city yard to drop off the garbage truck and climb into his own vehicle to head home to his family—or maybe to a quiet space that feels far too empty. Something prompted him to do one small thing to make that little girl smile and raise her arms.

And there, in that moment, is the thing I wanted to see: God moving. No thunderbolts, burning bushes, or seas parting—just a spark of kindness in one and joy in another and these spilling over into my melancholy heart. Just a moment. Just a little bit of love. And I smile.

SOCIAL MEDIA POST

So, we keep showing up. Even when it's hard and we feel like the evil and the anger is bigger than anything we can muster, we try our darndest to just show up.

Something or someone reminds us that the things that are seen are only part of the overall story and remember that the small, seemingly insignificant, things have the power to change the world we inhabit.

So we show up. In whatever manner we're able, we are present.

We don't believe the loudest voices are necessarily the truest voices. We muster courage. Sometimes we swim against the current.

We believe love is the most important thing and we spend a good chunk of our time listening and figuring out how to live it.

We punch holes in the darkness one conversation, one gesture, one peaceful act at a time.

Tuesday, September 8, 2020

In the morning, when Gerry takes Maya out for her morning constitutional, he finds evidence of an overnight visitor on the front lawn and in the evening, we watch three hungry black bears amble by on the other side of the fence in the back yard. In between, amid hugs and laughter (and maybe a few tears), we say goodbye to Laurinda and Makiya. We feel restless after they leave—the house is SO quiet after the weekend activity—so we go for a drive on country roads where I sip coffee and speak of my lingering melancholy while Gerry comments on subtle changes in the green on the trees.

Now Labour Day is over and we're on a trajectory toward fall. The forecast still looks like summer but I'm developing a yen for cozy. It's a funny in-between time. The garden is still generous with offerings of squash, tomatoes, cucumbers, and Swiss chard. A second sowing of beans is about to flower, beets grow larger day by day, and the single long loofa I've babied throughout the season gets bigger and fatter every day. It's my prize this year and the first thing I inspect when I go to the garden. I look at other things with an eye toward pulling them out. Spiders and their sticky webs are everywhere.

In the quiet of an early September morning, I watch the eastern sky change and can't help but worship. Then I turn my gaze back into the room where I sit and remind myself that the Presence is just as much here as it is out there. I close my eyes and whisper prayer. Even in the in-between, maybe especially in the in-between, I seek and find and am filled.

Thursday, September 10, 2020

There was something extraordinary about the server who brought a Belgium waffle piled high with whipped cream and strawberries and a plate of bacon, eggs, hash browns, and toast to the table where Gerry and Makiya were enjoying a morning of grandfather/granddaughter time. She was notable enough that Makiya told me about their interaction and the kind way she engaged with them later. The woman made an impression on an eleven-year-old girl.

Later that day, Makiya and I stopped at our favourite coffee shop for a refreshment and the barista impressed my granddaughter with her manner as she took our order. We were all wearing facemasks—they're mandatory there now—and separated by a plexiglass partition that makes it challenging for this grandmother to hear. But somehow a connection was made. When we left, pulling off facemasks with one hand while holding drinks in the other, we were smiling.

And still later, Makiya and I are in an unfamiliar store looking for unfamiliar products and a woman behind us overheard our conversation and stepped in to help us. She, just a customer like us, taking time to be generous with both her knowledge and experience, made our afternoon. It was one of those extraordinary ordinary encounters.

Makiya and I talked, as we headed toward home, about the gift of these three people and how their kindness toward us, in turn, elicited feelings of the same in us toward others. She brought it up later at the dinner table, sharing the experiences with those who hadn't seen it first-hand. I'm convinced moments like these have the power to change our world.

The thought keeps tumbling in my mind: *I'm finding it hard to be in this world.* And I am. The assault of politics and the pandemic has a tendency to stain almost everything. Remember when we could be in relationship with people who didn't necessarily share our viewpoint? Remember healthy, respectful discussion? Remember when we valued people above politics?

I have a vision in my mind of me walking away from the crowd, leaving them to their arguments and right-fighting. Some days I struggle to find a place of peace away from the noise, but I keep looking for it. And when I go out, because sometimes I have to go out, I make it a point to be extra kind in my interactions. To grant grace. Because we're all just doing the best we can to muddle through another day.

Sunday, September 13, 2020

On March 11, 2020, the World Health Organization (WHO) declared the COVID-19 outbreak to be a global pandemic. We're six months into this thing. Half a year has gone by as we have wrestled with trying to understand, explain, and make our way through day by uncertain day.

Are we stronger for having come this far? Kinder to those we come into acceptably distanced contact with?

Have we learned to live, if not comfortably, at least wisely, in the "I don't know?"

Do we feel supported and loved in our community? Or are we plugging into different communities?

Are we doing our best to love well? Failing. Then trying again? Granting grace to those whose opinions and perceptions are not the same as ours? Listening? Learning?

Do we long to return to the status quo? Or have we learned that different, while certainly uncomfortable, can lead to fresh, new things?

Are we encountering truth? Letting go in order to move forward?

Contributing more than consuming?

Holding on to our faith or finding it?

Do we just want things to go back to the way they were before March 11, 2020 or are we willing to consider that a shaking of this magnitude might lead to dust settling in ways that reveal something we need?

I know. It's been terrible, it remains terrible, and a virus is only part of the terrible.

I have far more questions than answers, but I'm learning to lock eyes with the Divine and lean in deep and hard. To let some things go. To be okay with not knowing it all (like I ever did) and measure my progress not in terms of things accomplished or accumulated but in the depth of my faith and the magnitude of grace I extend and in the manner I love.

How'r you doing six months in? Got questions? Maybe a few answers?

Let's lock (virtual or physical) arms and walk forward together.

SOCIAL MEDIA POST

It's been a tough week and it's only Tuesday. It's been a tough year and it's only September.

I've struggled—I am struggling—more with my mental health than I have in decades. Maybe you too?

This morning I was reminded of some truth I worked through and thought I had mastered.

I wrote an entire book about it, but still lose sight of the truth of my own belovedness. I get caught up in thinking I have nothing of value to offer. That my individual brokenness disqualifies me. That I'm invisible.

And sometimes I spiral.

And it gets dark.

I expect you may know some of which I speak.
Maybe you dip a toe into the darkness sometimes
too.

Maybe this year is kicking your mental health butt
too.

Talking (texting, emailing, messaging) with other
broken and beloved ones helps.

Let's do that.

Let's connect.

Let's remind one another—and ourselves—of how
needed we are.

Let's SEE one another.

Sunday, September 20, 2020

It's dark when I rise these days. Still night, really. Certainly, too dark to step out on the deck and greet the morning (I stopped doing that a few weeks ago when I encountered a black, hard-shelled creature the size of a Volkswagen).

I sit in a wing chair near the window where, eventually, I'll be able to see the eastern sky grow lighter, and reach into a basket next to the chair for my Bible, journal, earbuds, and my copy of Robert Benson's *Venite: A Book of Daily Prayer*. Day begins.

There's a now-familiar lump in my stomach again this morning. I'm not sure if I'm depressed or discouraged, if I need to buck up or curl up. All I know is that I'm not the self I wish I was, and I haven't been for months. I read scripture and chew on it for a time. Scribble thoughts in my journal. Pray (that's such a short, simple word for something that can be so deep—yet still simple). Listen to a webcast. Try to figure things out. Sip coffee.

Later I'll stand in the shower, allow the comfort of warm water to rain on me as I lean on the wall, arms raised, tears mixing with the shower water, crying out in prayer. *Help*. There's a snippy little critical voice in the back of my mind telling me dangerous things I dare not pay attention to. It mocks me and the goals I set—especially the one about finding fresh ways to write timeless truth for the benefit of others. I struggle to write anything other than in my journal and when I do it comes out dark, like this post.

But maybe that's okay in this literal and figurative dark night. Maybe someone else needs a companion when the happy-clappy kind of faith just doesn't cut it anymore. Maybe being honest about the struggle, the weight and the heavy pit in the centre of me, and the fact that some (or many) days I come out the other side of my morning prayer none the wiser or better for having spent the time but knowing I'll return the next morning anyway, will offer someone a measure of encouragement.

Maybe that's enough.

I look left, and up, and there, just barely, I see light in the sky. Every morning. Without fail. After dark comes dawn. Day begins. Amen.

Wednesday, September 23, 2020

It's not uncommon to see deer where we live. They meander in the field behind our house, sometimes standing on their two rear legs as they reach for tasty morsels on high branches. They make salad of tulips in my front garden in the spring, to the extent that I've given up trying to grow them. They're not uncommon but a deer sighting always makes us pause and watch.

One day this spring, when Makiya was here, and we were navigating early days of the pandemic, we were doing something together when Maya went mad barking in the den and Makiya went to investigate.

"It's a deer!" she called out.

Before I could join her at the window she cried out: "And another! And another!"

Together we watched six deer on impossibly thin legs, their large ears alert and likely picking up the sound of our barking pup, meander up from between our neighbour's houses, past ours, up the cul-de-sac and out of our vision. It was a special moment we shared.

Now, I'm driving down the hill that leads from our neighbourhood toward the East Trans-Canada Highway and I tap the brake as I spot one coming toward the road from the right, making signs like she's going to step out onto the road.

A man walking up the hill stops when he sees her. He lifts his phone and takes a photo. The deer, maybe disoriented to find a busy road in the midst of her wilderness walk, pauses. She hesitates, then turns around and heads back into the bush. It's only a moment, but one that connects the man, me, and the deer before all three of us carry on with our morning.

I'm heading to my favourite park to walk. I know. It seems somehow counterintuitive to drive somewhere to go for a walk, but there you go. I prayed before I climbed in the car, melancholy, and bearing that weight again: "Let me see you."

My ask wasn't for a burning bush or a booming voice or anything other than a glimpse of the heart of God. I believe in metaphor and poetry, and I've seen the Divine in the ordinary in the past. I could use the encouragement of such an encounter today.

Was it the deer? I wonder as I drive through town toward the park. "Was there something about seeing the deer that I missed?" Because, while it caught me off guard and it was cool, the way seeing a deer always is, it was nothing extraordinary. If there was a message about grace or my belovedness or anything else in the deer encounter, I missed it.

At the park, I start out on the native plant walk—a fancy name for a trail that winds around the back of the island through a familiar area where ghosts of memories linger. It's less busy on this trail. Perfect for prayer walks and contemplation. There's rustling on the side of the path, and through the trees I catch sight of two deer—a mama and a baby. I slow my pace so as not to startle them. Mama deer comes out through the trees, pauses at the path, and turns toward me. She's no more than eight feet in front of me. I stop and, in my mind, respond to her look. *After you.*

Mama and Baby step out onto the path and begin walking down it. I follow at a much-slower pace, watching. There's still rustling in the bushes beside the path and I think another deer must still be in there. The baby turns back, returning to the sanctuary of the bush, while Mama carries on down the path. A man, another walker, catches up to me and we walk together for a while behind the deer.

"Follow the leader!" he jokes as we two keep a slow pace behind the deer.

Then, tired of being slowed up, he increases his pace and moves out in front of me to pass the deer. A woman coming toward us in the opposite direction keeps an eye on the animal but makes no sign of slowing down. And so, the man and the woman pass by and the deer wanders off the path toward the river and I'm still almost tiptoeing and made breathless by the encounter.

Magical. Time stopping. Wonder-full. That's how I experience it.

The deer is out of sight now, and I carry on down the path. I'm thinking about the slow, intentional, graceful movement of deer going about their morning business foraging for food, not overly troubled by walkers sharing their space. Aware of us, but not afraid of us.

Bears are a danger at this time of year as they wander neighbourhoods looking for trees fat with unpicked fruit, gardens still producing, or unsecured trash cans. It doesn't always end well when bears get too comfortable in our neighbourhood. Same with cougars. I heard of one wandering the streets this week in my hometown, and it didn't go well for the cat either.

But we've learned to coexist with deer, and they tolerate us in the spaces they call home. It's unlikely I'd be able to walk up and touch a wild deer but I'm happy to enjoy watching them from a distance, with their strong stick legs, dark and deep eyes, large velvety ears turning like radar at the slightest sound.

Was it the deer? I wonder again, as I round the corner past the bat house toward the opposite side of the trail.

Later, I arrive home refreshed by my walk and prepare lunch for Gerry and I while he sets up the chessboard. I don't know about there being anything supernatural in my deer encounters but I do know that ofttimes the ordinary moments, upon examination, are packed full of extraordinary. Maybe this one was, or maybe it wasn't, but the pause was rich with fodder for contemplation for the rest of my walk.

Monday, September 28, 2020

Gerry and I took a short trip this weekend and some of the gifts were conversation en route, hope resurrected, and releasing the weight of "is this all there is?". I've been wrestling with depression—there, I've written it. I spoke it aloud a few days ago and now I've written it so it's official. I've been in a dark place. Maybe there are more shadows ahead but the respite of a few days away lingers sweet this morning. I am resting here for now.

OCTOBER 2020

Friday, October 2, 2020
I move my morning basket from beside the wing chair in the living room where I have watched the sky in all her splendour declare the glory every morning, to the den. Now, and through the dark months ahead, I'll greet the day there, on the leather sofa under a Sherpa blanket. Cozy. In solitude and silence.

As coffee brews and soy milk warms in the kitchen, I lift from the basket my Bible, journal, earbuds, and a selection of other books that are my companions in this season and make a nest for myself on the sofa. Then, mug of soy milky frothy coffee in hand, I settle in to read wisdom and pray.

It is Friday. Conversations and encounters from the week coming to a close lingers. This week I've been blessed by friends who have asked: "How'r you doing?" and listened to my answer. Good conversation. Rumination. A seasonal shift.

I'm thinking about the effort we put into image and how we learn to wear a façade so well that, eventually, we fool ourselves into believing something not entirely factual, and how in silence and solitude we cut to the chase.

In this season I intend to read more long form work and ponder truth. I will work at contributing more than consuming. I will shut out the noise and choose, more intentionally, what I allow to shape me.

I will practice loving well in the manner I was created to do so—which will probably look different than how you do it. I will be quieter, sometimes speaking louder without saying a word.

The season shifts and fall feels more and more like a much-needed rest. There's something spoken in the whisper of leaves letting go. Can you hear it too?

Monday, October 5, 2020

The yips and yowls of coyotes wake me again. Their cries so loud it seems they're right outside the bedroom window. Likely not, but they're nearby. It's haunting, this chorus of—what? Celebration? Mating? Aggression? Just checking in with other coyotes in the area? Are there two or ten of them? Who knows? I hope all the neighbourhood pets are safe indoors.

My mind lights on a question I posed when I went to bed and lingers for a moment, listening for an answer. No, not yet. Nothing I can discern through the broken quiet of the night, anyway.

These days there are far more questions than answers. Far more unsettledness than peace. More lament than mountaintop joy. Lament. It's an old-fashioned word but it's the thing I feel more than anything else these days. I write about it in my Moleskine notebook sanctuary where I ruminate on all manner of deep things. I walk through it on solitary walks through quiet spaces. I feel it in every part of me; it presses me from both inside and out.

> *My Lord God, I have no idea where I am going. I do not see the road ahead of me. I cannot know for certain where it will end. Nor do I really know myself, and the fact that I think that I am following your will does not mean that I am actually doing so.*
>
> *Thomas Merton*[32]

Maybe, in this season, to lament is the real work. To stop trying to force insincere joy and lean in to that which seems more real. More honest. More like standing naked before the Creator and taking the things that weigh so heavy and simply dropping them. *Here. You take them. I can't carry them any longer.*

I remember a dream I had in different season where I faced head on into a storm, screamed my grief into it, and it was absorbed. And the filling that came after. Maybe that was a picture of lament. I don't know. Like Merton, I have no idea. But howling in the night seems to capture what this season feels like.

In time, the coyotes quiet, sleep returns, and I rest before rising in the dark to pray. There's such peace in the sanctuary of dark in the solitary hours before dawn. And another day begins.

Tuesday, October 6, 2020

A woman, with an awkward gait that makes me think every step she takes

---

[32] Thomas Merton, *Thoughts in Solitude* (The Abbey of Our Lady of Gethsemani: 1956), 79.

is wrought with pain, carries a long rectangular canvas bag across the grass. She stops when she gets to the edge, wrestles a contraption out of the bag, and transforms it into a chair which she turns away from the park and toward the water. Shrugging out of her lightweight jacket, she drapes it across the back of the chair and sits. The place, and the manner she has chosen, speak to her intention. I envy the purpose with which she, without words, has claimed what she needs.

Another woman walks across the parking lot in the direction of where the first woman set up and I wonder if she is coming to meet her. It's what we do now: tote folding camp chairs in the back of our vehicles for socially distanced coffee visits in parks. I wonder how we'll manage in the winter when outdoor gatherings such as these become too uncomfortable.

The second woman unfolds and sets her chair up a short distance away from the first. She chooses a spot under a large tree that has just started letting go of crispy yellow leaves and turns her chair toward the parking lot. Welcoming. Inviting. And before much time passes, she is joined by another and another and soon there must be a dozen or more women gathered in a circle sharing conversation and sipping from thermoses or store-bought disposable cups filled with their favourite afternoon beverage.

The contrast between the circle of camaraderie and the woman alone is striking.

I almost miss seeing her, but another woman totes a canvas camp chair bag across the grass toward the solitary woman. They greet one another, then the first woman stands and together—awkwardly—they carry their chairs away from the crowd, toward a quieter place out of my line of sight.

Later, when I'm walking, I see the same two women—together, alone—with their chairs side by side facing the water and I imagine them enjoying intimate conversation, maybe even dropping their guard with one another.

I think about how we've adapted, found new ways to gather, and how the park that I favour has installed more benches to accommodate the increasing number of people who make use of the space. (Again, I wonder how we'll manage in winter but push that thought aside for the time being.)

There's a word—pivot—that we use to describe the manner in which we've found new ways to do things. Recalculating, is what the navigation system in my car calls it when I go off route and it scrambles to keep me going in the direction I intended. But maybe it's less a pivot we need, and more a pause. It would be a shame to get to the end of this pandemic (yes, eventually it will end) and find ourselves still going and doing and having missed or forgotten the wisdom found in the pause. Nothing wrong with adapting—we must, or we perish—but I can't help but think there's more wisdom in pausing than pivoting, or, at least, pausing then pivoting. I wonder if we'll miss something big if we don't stop and pay attention.

There's something so good and ordinary about a circle of friends gathering in camp chair circles in parks on an autumn afternoon. Community. And there's something equally as precious as two friends sitting in a quieter spot enjoying more intimate conversation. Relationship. We need both. We hunger when we're starved for either one.

This year has presented opportunity to see things more clearly. To identify things that are chaff and things that are gold. To let some things go. To stop doing the same things just because we've always done them that way. To let go of the past and live in the present. And so many other lessons if we're paying attention. We'll come out the other side knowing things we didn't when we entered this season back in March. More's the pity if we don't. I said, back then, that the world won't be the same after this and I believe it still. And I believe we're fools if we expect it to be. We must pause. Pay Attention. *Then* pivot. And in some cases, just let go.

Saturday, October 10, 2020

A smartly dressed young man climbs out of the polished black car, walks around to the passenger side, and opens the door for the young woman. She steps out, and off they go hand-in-hand toward the park.

I'm kind of agog because that kind of respect is not something you see every day anymore. And, call me old fashioned, but I miss it—personally as well as a reflection of our society. We're more laid back (lazy?) these days. Casual. We're busy with important things but, just maybe, neglecting the most important things.

Some other things I miss.

Family at the table at roughly the same time every night for the evening meal.

A bowl of mushy cereal and Saturday morning cartoons.

Watching Walt Disney and the Beachcombers (only Canadians will remember this one) on Sunday evening.

Five a.m. feedings in a dark and quiet house—just mom and babe awake.

After school snacks. Changing out of school clothes into play clothes. The sweet stretch of time from then until supper.

Mr. Rogers.

Mr. Dressup. (Another Canadian icon.)

Crinolines and white gloves. (Okay, I don't really miss crinolines. But white gloves, yes. And *Jergen's* hand lotion in glass bottles.)

But, you know, there are shadows lurking in memories of these old school things. All has never been exactly as it appeared and nostalgia only takes one so far.

The most important things are intangible, not quantifiable, unseen but not hidden. Timeless. It's hard to list them. We hesitate to name them because they're tied up in tentacles of other sticky stuff but we know them when we see them.

The young couple returns to their vehicle, both to the passenger side of the car. The young man opens the door and waits for the young woman to climb in. Then he closes it and, unhurried, walks around to the driver's side.

Man, it's refreshing. It gives me hope.

Tuesday, October 13, 2020

The sprinklers have been blown out. Lawn furniture, outdoor mats, and flower pots all stowed for the winter. The garden is cleaned out and garlic is planted. Now we wait.

One morning, there's a dusting of white on the hills down the east valley. I pull on long pants instead of Capris, socks and shoes rather than flip flops. We go for a drive, one sunny afternoon, up into the grasslands looking for fall colour but we're too late. It's stick season here. We see patches of icy white on the side of the rough road.

I make soup, and we enjoy hot cups of it over games of chess. The furnace hums songs of comfort. We don hoodies rather than short-sleeved t-shirts. I put a tiny shirt on Maya when we go out.

The liminality of these days invites us to pause. To reflect. Winter is coming and one day it will blow in with a fury, but for now we enjoy the opportunity to wait. To abide.

To be present.

To be.

Friday, October 16, 2020

We go early and cast our vote in the advance poll for our provincial election. An election that's not nearly as drama-filled as another one going on right now but one in which we're honoured to be able to have our say in. While we're waiting in line (with everyone dutifully masked), an elderly man and his wife emerge from the polling station and he drops a handful of pocket change on the floor. Another couple, walking out right behind him, sidesteps and the woman waves her hands expressing aversion at the thought of picking up the change from the floor.

The man is flustered. There's no way he can bend and pick up the money.

Then, a young woman steps out of the lineup to help him. The line moves forward and, eventually, we make our X using a tiny pencil that we're told to take with us. I feel inexplicably cranky when we leave.

Monday, October 19, 2020

Gerry rises and takes Maya outside to tend to some early morning business, and sees it. I've been up for a couple of dark hours and couldn't tell that the tops of the hills were white as if dusted with confectioners' sugar, but now I can. I'm delighted as we watch white fall from the sky. It won't last. The first one never does. But this first snowfall of the season makes me dance a silly jig.

Laurinda and I talk (and laugh!) about hygge season being upon us. I think about pulling out my bamboo knitting needles and starting a project. I put a pumpkin scented candle on my writing desk.

Gerry and I get dressed for church. Did you catch that? Get. Dressed. For. Church.

It's like the old days—B.C.: Before COVID—when he sticks his head around the corner and asks about clothing choice. We worship in person, in a building, with a small group of people, and afterward share conversation and laughter and, man, it is so, so good.

We stop at a store on the way home and decide to come back tomorrow. One of the gifts of being retired is shopping at non-peak times. As we drive up the hill toward home, I'm struck with the sweet Sunday afternoon feeling that lingers in the recesses of my memory.

We arrive home and change out of our "church clothes". I pull something out of the fridge for lunch while Gerry sets up the chessboard. It feels like the good old days before the pandemic changed everything.

After lunch I make tea and we attend a beautiful wedding from the comfort of our den. I magically sync my phone with our smart TV and there it is, big as life. A man and a woman reading vows to one another, and there is hope. All the chaos in the world falls away, and there is just love.

The day hums along, the cacophony forgotten, and there is only peace as I bake bread and pull-out flannel from my fabric stash for a special project. We talk about something special we're planning to do soon and there is sweet anticipation. I had almost forgotten what that feels like.

This simple day, fat with worship and laughter and love and ordinary things I've missed so much, is balm. And I'm so, so grateful for the respite and the laughter and the love and the ordinariness in every moment of it.

Thursday, October 22, 2020

I'm meeting someone and arrive early in a part of the city that's familiar in the general sense but less so close up. I park and watch pedestrians, wondering about their stories, until it's precisely ten minutes before our appointed meeting. A short five-minute walk, and I'm there. I wait. And wait. And a general sense that I messed something up starts to burn.

Once, when I was a little girl, I was supposed to meet my mom on the sidewalk outside of the Zellers store. I waited then too, for what felt like hours, while Mom stood on the sidewalk outside of the Simpsons Sears store kitty corner across the street.

She must have noticed me, her lost-looking little girl trying to retain her composure in the midst of quiet panic, and crossed the street. I remember her scolding, certain that it was she who got the name of the store wrong, though I dared not say so out loud.

Everything turned out in the end but I remember with every cell in my body the sense that I had been abandoned, and how it felt to wait for someone I was afraid wasn't going to come.

Now, I check the time on my phone and see it's ten minutes past the hour. My senses are heightened. Something's wrong.

I check my email (for the umpteenth time) and confirm the address. I check lettering on the building in front of which I'm standing. It's roughly the same, though the letter A at the end throws me off. I look up and around and ask Google and feel a lump of something start to grow in my stomach.

Finally, I walk down the street in the opposite direction from which I came and find the spot. There's no mistaking it now that I'm here, and the woman I'm meeting is sitting on the stairs, calm as anything. Her face breaks out into a smile when she sees me.

I feel stupid, and try to explain, but she brushes my explanation aside. Pays it no matter, really. It's not a passive aggressive brushing of something aside, it's a sincere let's-move-forward everything-is-okay kind of thing that implies the more important thing is that we're together now.

We carry on. The rest of the day and that night carries on. The next day does too. And I can't get the image of that woman sitting calmly on the stairs waiting for me out of my mind. That, and the welcoming smile she broke into when she saw me. The Divine is using that woman, that experience, and that moment to remind me of some truth I have a tendency to forget.

The memory will remain strong, like the one from ages ago in which I did my best to remain calm in the midst of certain maternal abandonment, because it counteracts it. It speaks the truth of holy acceptance that's more powerful than the lie of abandonment.

It's moments like this and whispers of love that I miss when I'm not paying attention, when I allow the cacophony of the world and the accusing voices in my mind to be louder than the still, small voice that speaks life and love. Mostly love. Always love.

As I sit here now, I can almost weep from the sense of feeling accepted—no, more: treasured—when I picture that woman sitting on the stairs waiting for me. That, right there, is what grace looks like. It's a moment so holy that I could have dropped to my knees right there on that sidewalk. It's not acceptance from the woman (though her grace was a gift) but welcome into the love from which I came that is my undoing. I keep forgetting. That woman looked a little (maybe a lot) like God's only begotten sitting there on those cold hard steps. There are always these reminders. And, man, if that's not love I don't know what is.

We try to wrap it up in fancy words that have lost much of their intended meaning and, I'm afraid, lose some folks along the way. When it comes right down it it's just ordinary people doing ordinary things, making space for Divine whispers to flow through them and to them and truth wrapped up in

holy encounters that show us how loved we really are.
And so on. And so on. World without end.

On October 26, 2020, Dr. Henry orders that we have no more than six visitors in our homes. "Enforcement will be stepped up to ensure people are following this new order," Dr. Henry says. Playdates for children are discouraged and the wearing masks in public places is expected, though not yet ordered.[33]

Tuesday, October 27, 2020

We have a new family member and are remembering how three pounds of Yorkshire terrier creates a very large ripple. Our new puppy's name is Murphy. He measures six inches to the top of his shoulders and at ten months, he's not going to get much larger. My morning routine looks a bit different for the time being. I rise at the same time and carry the crate where he's slept out of the bedroom with me, leaving Gerry and Maya to slumber on.

"Good morning, buddy!" I whisper as I set the crate on the dryer in the laundry room and reach in to get the tiny squirming boy.

I carry him downstairs, step into the boots I left waiting at the back door, and shrug into my jacket. I turn the light on and take him out to the "potty pen" we set up for him.

"Go potty, Murphy." I bend down and gently set him down in it.

He looks up at me with those big (relatively) pools of Yorkie eyes and obliges. I heap praise, give him a tiny treat, and we go back into the warm house. Soon, we're settled together in the den. He's wrapped in a blanket with his tiny head resting on my chest as he falls back to sleep, and I'm sipping coffee and praying.

It's awkward to manage my Bible and journal with a sleeping pup in my arms, so I reach for my iPad and call up a couple of apps: *Pray As You Go* and *Lectio 365*. Music and scripture reading, prayer and space in which to ponder. When the daily selections are finished, I sit quietly and linger.

This morning I'm pondering possibility. In light of our world turned upside down this year, and no sign of returning to what was anytime soon, if ever, what if I changed my thinking and shifted from lament (though there's good reason to do so and a purpose to it) toward possibility? It's something

---

[33] https://news.gov.bc.ca/releases/2020HLTH0317-001895

I've been ruminating on for months and something in the prayer this morning solidified it. This season is fat with possibility and opportunity to find fresh ways of being. Yes, change chafes, but it's also a time of renewal—if we allow it. For now, the routine of my morning quiet time—and life as it once was in the larger way of being in this world where a pandemic and politics rage—is, of necessity, different. It will, in all likelihood, not look like it once did ever again.

Enter possibility.

It's a season to learn to embrace it. Learn how to bend, lest we break. Find new ways of doing things. Do new things. Let go. Listen. Feel fresh wind on our faces and turn toward it.

This blanket wrapped pup sleeping on my chest has turned my ordered world topsy turvy and helped remind me that sometimes it takes letting go of what was in order to find something new. I've felt the discomfort of transition for a long time, even before early March when stuff got real in terms of change. I look at Murphy's tiny sleeping head and smile. It's good. It's time.

Friday, October 30, 2020

The week has been a blur, reminiscent of forty years ago when I had babies to care for. My world revolves around a tiny three-pound Yorkie this week as we adjust to new routines. Gifts, delights, blessings, call them what you will, there are plenty. Divine whispers, yes even those. Murphy sleeps soundly through the night in his crate on a chair next to my bed. This is an unexpected surprise for which I am most grateful.

One afternoon we drive to the pet store to pick up something (taking Murphy with us and leaving Maya at home for a time of solitude and silence). The pet store is near a favourite coffee shop so I grab a cup of my favourite brew and we take a short drive just because. (Car ride. My dad used to use that term. It makes me happy).

Murphy is learning to trust that when I put him in his crate for a rest after play time it's for his own safety. He's coming to understand that fussing won't get him out and that maybe it's a good time for a nap after all.

Have I mentioned that I'm exhausted? We're all sleeping well through the night but during the day it's constant busyness. I'm 61. Something's gotta give.

A week ago, a crazy amount of snow fell in one day and then it got cold. It was nice, at first. Cozy. Hygge time. It got old when I was standing around waiting for the pup to go potty a bazillion times a day. Thankfully the weather turned and the snow is all but gone now. (It's coming back, I know. Hopefully not too soon.)

Saturday, October 31, 2020

The predawn sky is relatively clear. Rippled with clouds that glow in the moonlight and allow stars to peek through openings, it's the most light I've seen up there for days. We've been under a blanket of oppressive fog and cloud. A week ago, it was cold and white. Then we were graced with a warming trend that melted every bit of the early snow in the yard but brought fog. Now it's fall-like again, and this morning it's balmy.

I'm outside with the pup. Soon I'll be wishing I didn't have to come outside long before light in the ice-cold of the night, but just now it's a gift. The light in the sky catches my attention as I walk to the edge of the patio and look up. I can't help but worship. Reminded again that the light has always been there even when hidden by cloud, and while perception tries to define my reality there's still the mystery of that which I can't see that is no less real.

Murphy makes a sound, too small to call a bark it's more a trill, and lets me know me he's ready to go back inside. I take one more deep drink of the night sky, tuck it away in my mind for later when I'll need it, and turn toward him. Day begins, slow and gentle, held in holy presence.

NOVEMBER 2020

Monday, November 2, 2020
Now it is November and with the turning of the figurative calendar page comes the temptation to project. What will tomorrow hold? The rest of this month? This year? Anxiety rises with each *what if?* that bubbles to the surface. Yes, we are heading toward the shortest and darkest days of the year. Yes, there are traditions, and we wonder which of them we'll keep and which we'll release. Yes, there is that U.S. election and how all of that will play out. And the pandemic. Yes, we're still riding a strange wave there.

This morning I sit in silence in the den with a sleeping Yorkie wrapped in a blanket on my lap, and return to a liturgy of reading and prayer that quiets the storm. I've risen too early thanks to our mucking with time yesterday, but the extra hour is a gift. I ponder and pray, contemplate and cry out, worship—but find what I need most of all in silence and solitude and stillness.

And I am reminded . . . that today matters.

That looking ahead is all well and good, and sometimes there's good reason to do so, but not just now.

That there will be opportunities to give more than I take, and the choices I make will create ripples I won't even see.

That transformation is more important than transaction.

That the Divine doesn't sort us into categories.

That the world needs your gifts as much as it needs mine.

And that the most important thing I can do today is simple, but I will struggle to do it reasonably well. Love.

Thursday, November 5, 2020
It feels a little like I stumbled. I'm in the midst of one of those slow-motion things where almost comical gyrations have taken over my body as I struggle

to regain my balance. Only it's not so comical. Know what I mean?

In the morning I return to the peace of familiar words and raise my hands and heart in prayer for unfamiliar things and for those that whisper, with a twisted sneer, "remember me?". And when I have done what I can do to start the day full, I turn my thoughts to other things.

Like the swirling movement of the clouds yesterday afternoon that captivated my attention as Gerry and I took a break in the middle of the day to soak in the hot tub.

Like the man I watched when I was waiting in the car wander in the Walmart parking lot who had obviously forgotten where he parked his car. I felt a kinship to his searching.

Like the other man I watched walking toward the store entrance whose gait seemed familiar and it wasn't until I saw his now unmasked face returning that I realized I used to work with him a lifetime ago.

Like the sound of the wind and raindrops tapping on the window and the comfort of wrapping up in a cozy, somewhat ratty, sweater.

Like the wilderness, and the richness I find in the midst.

And another day begins with things to do and the opportunity to put one foot in front of the other and try to do something good in the space I've been given. That's all. That's enough. Here we go.

Friday, November 6, 2020

I think there's a skiff of white outside but I'm not sure. It's still dark. When I came into the den with a Yorkie tucked under my left arm and a mug of soy milky frothy coffee in my right hand, before I bent to pick up dog toys scattered on the floor leftover from last evenings play, I stood at the window and looked out at the slumbering cul de sac where we live. There's something sweet about being the only one awake in the house and the neighbourhood. The sidewalks and street seemed to sport a skiff of white, but not the grass—that's what confused me. Maybe it's just a hard frost, not snow.

I settle in on the sofa and wrap the sleepy Yorkie in a blanket and tuck him in the space beside me where he goes back to sleep. I sip coffee and turn my head to look out over the top of the window covering at stars in the clear night sky.

A few nights ago, when Gerry came home from an evening hike, he called me to the window.

"Look!" he said as he pointed toward the east. "You don't often get to see the red planet glow like that."

And sure enough there was Mars, with Venus was next to it. I was tired from caring for a puppy all day, not as interested as I wish I had been, and husband's enthusiasm didn't grab me. I wish it had.

Now, as I remember that missed moment I remember others, like the one I wrote about in *The Presence of Absence* when a tiny green frog showed me I was living distracted. I lean back, rest my head on the back of the sofa, gaze at the stars and speak to God.

And ponder love.

And God smiling.

And how I miss magical moments too often.

And how the longer I look up at the those stars the more of them there seem to be.

And how maybe that twinkle is coming from God's eye as he smiles at this disheveled woman with a tiny sleeping dog on the sofa next to her, sipping coffee and watching stars and thinking, once again, about the wisdom of letting things go.

On November 7, 2020, Dr. Henry issues orders applicable specifically to the Fraser and Vancouver Coastal health regions banning all indoor and outdoor social gatherings except those with immediate household family members and making wearing facemasks mandatory in public spaces.

"In support of this new order, active inspections are being increased and businesses that do not comply will be subject to fines, and/or ordered to close, until a refreshed safety plan and commitment to comply are established.

"Finally, we are strongly recommending travel into and out of these regions be limited to essential travel only and people within the regions stay within their local community, as much as possible. We ask those who live outside of the regions not to visit unless it is essential."[34]

---

[34] https://news.gov.bc.ca/releases/2020HLTH0059-001922

Saturday, November 7, 2020

I grew up in a little house my dad built that was next door to a church. It wasn't our church—we went to the larger Minto United Church across the street. I crossed the street every Thursday evening for choir practice there, and gathered with other members of the children's and adult choir in the basement on Sunday mornings, clad in our gowns, lining up to prepare to enter the sanctuary.

The church next door to us was a smaller building, not much larger than a house. Once a week after school I went there for piano lessons with Mrs. Knight. (I'm sorry, Mrs. Knight. They didn't take.) In the summertime I'd climb the fence and pick hollyhocks from the back yard. But what I remember most about that church next door was the music. My bedroom was on the side of our house next to the church and on Sunday summer nights when my window was wide open, the sound of hymns played on the piano next door wafted into my room along with the evening breeze.

Last evening, I scrolled randomly through my social media for a few minutes before reaching for my book. And I stumbled upon something beautiful—the pastor of the church Gerry and I attend taking time in the middle of the day in an empty sanctuary to worship in song at a piano. I listened and let the music she made wash over me. It was the perfect way to wind up another tumultuous day.

And now, this morning, as I sit in the sanctuary of my den where I meet with God every morning, I remember that gift our pastor offered and return to it. With eyes closed and hands lifted I listen and worship as her simple, pure, and oh-so-beautiful offering fills the room. Such peace. Such love.

I marvel at how sweet it is that those with gifts such as this share them with the rest of us. And while I might have, one day long ago, wished for the ability to conjure music from the keys of the old piano in our basement, the truth was I crept up the stairs and adjusted the timer to shave minutes off my mandated half hour practice time. And yet piano music, and a voice such as the one I'm listening to now, feeds me deep and well. It's a beautiful reminder of how we need one another.

Now, the medley coming from my iPad switches to a familiar song. *Holy, Holy, Holy*. It's the song the adult choir sang every Sunday as they walked into the sanctuary in formation after we in the children's choir were settled in our places at the front. I didn't understand all that the words meant, but they reached something deep in me nonetheless. Neither did I fully appreciate the piano played hymns that serenaded me to sleep on Sunday nights, but God was in that music as sure as is happening here this morning. Lately, I've been pondering the question of where God was when I was a child and now, I see a piece of the answer. Or, I hear it, even as I sense the timelessness of it.

I tap my screen and listen again.

Don't be afraid. My love is stronger than your fear.

And...
Holy, holy, holy.

Monday, November 9, 2020

"Thank goodness this didn't happen in the winter," we said back in March and April when this thing began. "At least we can go outside." Even when we were in lockdown, we could go outside and turn our faces to the sun and feel the warming and the promise of more. Our provincial health minister encouraged us, for the sake of our mental health, to spend time safely outside.

Around here, at the very beginning, before playgrounds were closed and cordoned off, we played four square and tossed a basketball around with our granddaughter. Later, we gathered in parks with camp chairs and coffee to visit friends. We walked in parks that city workers had retooled to allow us to keep safe distances from one another. Spring turned to summer, and some days we almost forgot the world was in chaos. Sure, it was different, and we made adjustments and let go of some things, but overall, it was still a beautiful season of abundance. We never imagined we'd be here, barreling toward winter with news of lockdowns looming. We look back and smile at our springtime naiveté. Who'da thunk we'd still be dealing with this thing after all these months?

Soon, only the hearty among us will venture outside for any length of time (read: not me) and we'll turn back toward jigsaw puzzles, make sourdough bread, and find other creative things to do indoors. We'll sit by fireplaces wrapped in soft blankets, burn candles, and listen to good music. We'll adjust—we've done it before—and find treasures in the dark.

Back in March, I remarked that the world won't be the same after this thing passes and my granddaughter asked what I meant. I didn't have an answer. I couldn't explain the strong sense I had that we were about to experience a global shift and that what *was* would be no more. Neither have I been able to adequately articulate my belief that in the midst of this thing there lies opportunity—and that we'll miss it if we won't release one trembling hand from the rope we are clinging to, reach for one in front of us, then let go with the other and take hold of something new.

I lean in hard to that which is universal and eternal—the solid things—and find courage to let go and reach forward. In the dark, we find light. There's still that uncomfortable place in the pit of my stomach that churns like stormy seas and burns like glowing embers. I used to think it was one thing, but now I think it might be something else.

I return to the sofa in my den morning after morning and say *come*. I scratch out a few words in my journal, read a few holy ones, and sit in silence and listen. And look for light in the dark.

Friday, November 13, 2020

It's Friday again—or is it already? It's been a week. One of *those* weeks. A week that included a meltdown precipitated by lack of sleep, lack of routine, and no lack of overthinking. Throw in a dash of the news cycle, a virus breathing putrid breath through sneering, curled lips revealing chipped and yellowing teeth, and concern about new restrictions and how that will all play out, and it's a recipe for something not too palatable.

I stand at the kitchen window and watch snow dance like feathers and listen to the scrape of my neighbour's snow shovel on the sidewalk. Then I walk to the living room window that overlooks our back yard (and a ridge hidden in low cloud this morning) and smile at the shoveled pathways in the snow on our neighbour's back lawn for their dogs (such shoveling happens on a much smaller scale on our back lawn for Maya and Murphy).

I sit down on the sofa, curl up under a Sherpa blanket, and listen to the soft snore of tiny Murphy, who is curled up under his own little blanket next to me, while I read a few words, pray a few prayers, and sip soy milky frothy coffee. The pup shifts position, puts his chin on my arm, and looks up at me with dark pools of Yorkie eyes for a moment before closing them and returning to rest. I close my own eyes, wrap my hands around a warm mug, and breathe prayer. It's been another discombobulated and difficult week. Having stepped lightly through my morning liturgy, I linger in the *now*, and rest in the peace of the moment.

Tuesday, November 17, 2020

My favourite coffee shop is closed. It's a small shop attached to a bookstore—both, part of large chains. I've spent hours over the years there visiting with friends or buying coffee and browsing in the adjoining bookstore. A lifetime ago, I used to stop and get coffee early in the morning on my way to work for a Friday treat.

It closed temporarily, earlier this year along with everything else, and when it opened, I gladly donned my facemask and went inside to buy coffee. Once, I even took my coffee into the bookstore to browse for an few unsatisfactory minutes, but the experience was no longer the same as before. (And certainly, wouldn't be now that facemasks are mandatory in the bookstore. Kind of hard to sip a latte while wearing a facemask.) Nonetheless, I patronized the shop and bought coffee to take to the park to visit in the summer months when that was how we socialized, and stopped for a cup when I was having a rough day and needed a treat.

Now it's closed—for good, the report I read yesterday said. I wonder anew what this post-COVID world will look like when, eventually, all of this shakes out. None of us know. We imagine. But it's usually best not to get too far ahead of ourselves. In the grand scheme, the closing of my favourite coffee shop is inconsequential. The fact that I haven't spent a pleasant hour browsing in my favourite bookstore this year doesn't mean much. Life tumbled along just fine before these treats were available to me and it will now that they're not. Well, maybe not fine. Not just yet.

This morning in my prayer time for some odd reason I thought of the title of a YA book from years ago. *Are You There God? It's Me, Margaret* by Judy Blume. I'm not sure that I ever read the book (I was more interested in Blume's *Deenie* because the main character had scoliosis like me.), but I have, for sure, appropriated the title in my own desperate prayers.

Are you there, God? It's me, Linda. I'm a little (a lot) overwhelmed right now. Help.

But prayer these days is different: less "are you there" and more "you are here." I'm still overwhelmed—most days, in fact—but with the sense that I'm not alone in my overwhelm. That on the other side of whatever it is that keeps me from seeing clearly, there's such deep, deep love.

What does any of that have to do with the fact that my favourite coffee shop closed? I don't know. Maybe just a reassurance that though we're living on unsteady ground where things are being chipped away there's still the unseen things that haven't changed. The demise of a coffee shop isn't the worst thing but it's still a sad thing (especially for the ones who worked there for years), but from it will come a new thing. Many other stores are closed and, unfortunately, many more will follow. It feels like we're living in a snow globe and someone keeps shaking it. The news is almost too much to follow.

Prayer looks different these days. Maybe we needed for it to look different.

Wednesday, November 18, 2020

A lifetime has passed since Gerry, Makiya, and I sat in our car in the park eating burgers and fries and looking at a sculpture that spelled HOPE. It was the first of April and we three had been hunkered down at home for weeks, finding lots to keep us occupied, but needing to get out of the house for a break. The park was all but empty, as most places were at the time. Shops and schools were shut down. Those who could work from home, were. There was a shortage of toilet paper and hand sanitizer and flour and yeast. Jigsaw puzzles were out of stock online. It had only been a few weeks but we were already feeling a little punch drunk. Surely this couldn't go on much longer. We three were grateful for the respite of time in the car in the park. Despite it all, it was spring, the season of hope. We felt it in the warming sun. Now we're barreling toward the cold and dark months. The news does nothing to ease the tension so we vacillate between turning it off and being obsessed by it. We stock up on (without hoarding) dry goods, laying in supplies for a winter of unknown.

Yesterday I took Murphy for a walk in that same park and looked at that same *Hope*-ful sculpture. An older couple sat in their car right in front of it, in the place where we parked to eat out lunch back in April, so my view of it was slightly skewed from what it had been before. My own hope is slightly skewed by now too.

I could get all theological and Pollyanna-ish and paste a fake mask back on my face but the truth is that I don't have the stomach for any of that. This is hard. Damn hard. It's wearing. And it's not likely to get better anytime soon. So, I wake with that now-familiar burn in the pit of my stomach, another day begins, and I wonder what to do about this heaviness. I no longer try to muster hope but trust that it will find me. Sometimes we need to let go in order to be caught.

On November 19, 2020 Adrian Dix and Dr. Henry issue a joint statement introducing new province-wide orders. "On Nov. 7, we issued regional orders to slow the rapid transmission we are seeing in social interactions, in certain workplaces and in higher-risk indoor settings, like group fitness activities. We are now expanding and amending these provincial health officer orders across the province."

Social Gatherings

All indoor or outdoor events are prohibited. This includes religious, cultural or community events, with the exception of baptisms, funerals and weddings. These may proceed with up to 10 people including an officiant if a COVID-19 safety plan is in place. There are to be no associated receptions of any kind in any venue. There are to be no social gatherings at residences with anyone other than those who reside there. People who live alone must host no gatherings, but can continue to see one or two of the same members of their core pandemic bubble at home.

Group physical activities

> Businesses, recreation centres or other venues that organize or operate indoor group spin classes, hot yoga and high-intensity interval training will stop for the fall and winter. Sports activities can continue, but there is to be no travel outside of communities for games or competitions, and no spectators are allowed. League organizers should continue planning for 2021 with today's modifications in mind.
>
> **Workplace safety**
>
> All businesses and worksites must conduct active daily screening of all on-site workers using their COVID-19 safety plans. Workers and customers must wear masks in indoor public and retail spaces (except when eating or drinking), and in workplace common areas, including elevators, hallways, group or break rooms, kitchens and customer counters. Office-based employers should temporarily suspend their efforts to safely get employees back to their workplace and support work-from-home options wherever possible.
>
> **Travel**
>
> All non-essential travel outside of one's community is strongly discouraged. People travelling to stay with immediate family members should ensure they do not host or participate in any social gatherings. [35]

Sunday, November 22, 2020

I am tired of thinking about the pandemic. I'm tired of writing about it. I'm weary of its curled tentacles reaching into every aspect of life and leaving

---

[35] https://news.gov.bc.ca/releases/2020HLTH0061-001949

a sticky residue. I've had enough of the polarization—over the pandemic, but also politics and things as simple as the best breakfast cereal with which to start the day. I'm done. I am beyond done. Most of us are.

We are nearing Advent and I hunger for the season of waiting as never before. This year I will listen to Handel's *Messiah* with fresh ears and a heart attuned to what it means to wait. I will light candles and ponder light. I will linger long and lament. And perhaps this is a gift.

In the midst of confusion, and in light of new restrictions, I ache. My body manifests telltale signs of stress. Empty is what I feel more than anything else. I wait. For the end of the pandemic, for the news to report the news, for new life to spring forth from these crumbling vestiges of what we once believed was important. For the desire to write about something other than what I write about here again this morning, For my doneness to transform to hope.

Enter Advent.

A time of expectation. By definition, a season of waiting. Preparation, not in the form of shopping or decorating or attending too many gatherings (ha!), but in growing intentionally still and resting our tired heads on the shoulder of the One for whom we wait, who has already come, and who will come again. A time to just be still. As if we haven't been stiller than ever this year. But it's stillness of another kind we feel in the call of Advent that invites us to enter into mystery and be held within it. And to be held is what we need more than anything else right now. Like my squirming puppy who wants to go, go, go, we need to quiet ourselves and become still in order to be held.

And so, Advent.

Monday, November 23, 2020

It's Monday. The last one before we enter the season of Advent and I wake with a fresh intention to walk through this week different than I have in recent weeks. Some words spoken yesterday, by our pastor in the online church service and by our daughter in good conversation later, nudge me toward a different direction.

I wake early—far too early, even for me—but Murphy deems it the appointed hour and so together we begin the day. We tend to some things, then settle in on the sofa in the den where he goes back to sleep and I enter into the time I hold precious. Now, hours have passed. Maya has joined us in the den and Gerry is downstairs having his morning reading time. It's light outside. It's lighter inside too. Something has broken. I can't explain it. The day and week begin and ordinary time winds down. It seems like a good time to begin again.

This is the way of the kingdom . . .

Tuesday, November 24, 2020

I hear a whisper in a variety of voices over the course of many days—all with a similar message. While there is a season for "big picture" thinking, so too is there a time to dial it in and focus on what's right there in front of me. I think of times when I've been in a plane and flown over prairie and been delighted by the patchwork squares of farmland I see below. For me it's a visual (aside from the pure satisfaction of being near prairie) of the wisdom of tending the figurative plot I've been allotted and making a difference in the world in the manner and place I was created for.

A brief, and socially distanced, conversation with a friend who has come to our door with a gift, tears falling from my eyes as I read words she has written on a handmade card and hold her offering in grateful hands, and I am so blessed by her thoughtfulness.

This is the way of the kingdom . . .

A short conversation. A handmade gift. The willingness to bless someone who needs it more than the giver can know. This. This is the way of the kingdom.

As is tending my metaphorical hectare, and caring for those who abide there and those who are just passing through. Less concern over the things I have little or no influence over, and more for the things—and people—I do. Less outrage. More love. Less self-righteous indignation. More love.

This is the way of the kingdom.

That whisper reminds me of truth I so easily, and often, forget. *El Roi.* The God who sees me. In my anxiety and depression and feeling so—I don't even know what—for so much of this year I am seen and loved and granted such rich grace. Someone, in caring for her own hectare, listens to a whisper and enriched a piece of mine. I will, in turn, cultivate a section of another. And so on. And so on.

This is the way of the kingdom . . .

Thursday, November 26, 2020

Often, I take photographs looking out over the ridge where we live to the hills and clay cliffs across the valley. Less frequently, I lift my lens toward the south because it's just not as spectacular, yet the view from there captivates me in a different way.

Early in the morning at certain times of year, while I wait for the Keurig to cough out my coffee, I stand at my kitchen window and look up at trees and sky and atmosphere and feel myself touched by the elusiveness of it all, but, these days, it's far too dark. Instead, I look from the south-facing window in our den, or pause on the front step when I take Maya outside, and look up. Some days—many right now—low cloud wraps around the trees creating something mysterious, evoking a longing.

Yesterday, I grabbed my big girl camera and my wide angle 10-18mm lens and took a few shots. The images didn't capture the feeling, so I switched to my 50mm prime lens and tried again. Closer this time. Sometimes, though something's right in front of me, I need to look through a different lens in order to see it. I'm switching lenses often these days. Trying different angles. Adjusting my focus. And examining it all with a creative eye in post processing. More often than not I see something fresh.

Friday, November 27, 2020

It's been one of those weeks where the days all run together. New restrictions mean Gerry is at home unable to hike with his buddies and that's hard for him. Me, I'm used to staying at home—it's kind of my super power. We've been intentional about going out for a short while every day to give me a break from 24 x 7 Murphy care, and also to increase Murphy's comfort with being left at home. Sometimes I wonder how we raised two other Yorkies to adulthood while we were both working full time. A drive. A quick errand. Just enough to warrant putting on socks and a jacket.

Sometimes, on Friday, I try to put together a list of five simple things from the previous week I'm grateful for. Here's this week's list..

Friends. Over the course of a single twenty-four-hour period this week six women reached out to me, in various unrelated ways, reminding me of the ripples every life creates and how small things can make a big difference.

Music. I've been listening Handel's *Messiah* performed by the Choir of King's College, Cambridge on Spotify. It's beautiful food for the soul that will nourish me through the remainder of this year.

Jigsaw puzzles. We pulled out the first jigsaw puzzle of the season, and Gerry's made a good start by getting the edges done and I look forward to spending time with it in the coming weeks. We bought a new one yesterday too, fearing another shortage as winter wears on.

Danish butter cookies. The tins they come in may look different but Danish butter cookies always taste the same. Apparently, it's possible to make these at home. I'm tempted to try. Or, more likely, buy another tin.

The weather. There's no snow in our neighbourhood and the forecast looks like we're heading into December still green. Here's to much more of the same!

And so, the week winds down and we inch ever closer to Advent. Can we embrace quiet hope, joy, peace, and love in this season? Ah, there's a challenge we can all step up to.

Sunday, November 29, 2020

Hope. It's been a year of hope deferred. The world, caught up in uncertainty and a host of other things there's no need to name, is weary. We all feel it to some degree and it's getting heavy. Very heavy.

You tell us that hope deferred makes our heart sick. An extended season of hoping, not seeing what it is we hope for come to fruition, and falling into despair as a result wears us down and wears us out. We're all tired and heartsick right about now.

As Advent dawns and the season of longing begins for a world feeling crushed, come. Come and restore a childlike hope, a quiet contemplative hope, and the last-ditch kind of hope that cries out "I'm done! I just can't do this any longer." And as we ponder the mystery of One who came and who will come, prepare our hearts. Restore our hope.

We need it more than ever. I need it more than ever.

Amen

Monday, November 30, 2020

In the sweet stillness of early morning, I light a candle.

There's nothing special about a bit of white wax and a wick in a small glass container but as the flame flickers it casts a glow where I need one.

Come . . .

There's nothing magical about it; it is the hope candle because it's the first one I reached for this morning.

Come . . .

I pray: replace the heaviness in my heart with hope.

Come . . .

And this room—where white lights on the non-traditional tree flicker and coloured lights from my neighbour's house reflect on the window, where the Keurig spits coffee and my bare foot brushes on a crumb on the floor—is made holy.

SOCIAL MEDIA POST.

It's been a hard slog walking through this year. We're all carrying a load that's heavier than expected. Sometimes we shift the weight and get some relief. Other times it threatens to bury us.

I'm praying for hope in this season. Mystical, magical, extraordinary hope. Hope that surprises us. Hope that transforms us.

Let's keep our eyes open. And our ears. And trust that hope will show up in little and large ways. Let's walk into this season expecting.

Let's give hope, share hope, roll around in it and get

covered in it. Let's invite it, make it welcome, and sit with it.

DECEMBER 2020

Tuesday, December 1, 2020
Now it is December. I think I should write something encouraging in these darkening days, but come up empty. I don't want to wear a figurative mask here, so I'll write of the barrenness I feel, and trust I'm not alone in the wilderness. I don't have *Three Steps to Find Happiness, Five Ideas to Streamline This Season, Seven Steps to Celebrate the Perfect Holiday During a Pandemic.* I have none of that; I want none of that. I'm not offering a course, a community, pretty printables, or anything else. I'm just here. Showing up. Finding fresh ways to write timeless truth even when the truth is that slogging through another day seems to take more effort than I can muster. The faith I have is a mustard seed sized. No, I've seen mustard seeds, mine is more carrot seed sized right now. Just big enough to entice me to whisper one-word prayers.
Help.
Faith that's barely big enough to believe that what I don't see is bigger than the giants surrounding me, to trust in silence more than noise, and believe that carrot seed sized faith is enough. To believe in mine and your belovedness.
Another day begins. Another month. Another season and I come here with little to offer but my carrot seed sized faith trusting it's enough.

Thursday, December 3, 2020
Does anybody really know what time it is? I think there's a song with this name. I couldn't tell you for sure, and I certainly couldn't hum few bars. But this phrase has crept into my mind often this year. When I wake in the morning, my first thoughts are anchoring. I establish what day it is and what, if any, commitments I have. I often stumble, as days seem to run together. *What day is it, anyway?* Sometimes I get it wrong and it takes a while for me to figure it out.

With fewer commitments and opportunities to take me out of the house, one would think I'd be on top of things. Instead, I often feel overwhelmed. I hunger for routine; without it I flounder. Day after day of uncertainty does not contribute positively to my mental health. Ironically, I've given more thought to my mental health (or lack thereof) this year than I have for decades and yet the health part of it remains elusive. I know I am not alone in this fog and I find a measure of comfort knowing I have companions in this darkness. I recoil from pat answers that clang like noisy cymbals and avoid those who seem to have all the right answers. Instead, I find comfort with kindreds who, like me, have far more questions. Companions in walking through the darkness that descended this year. Another day begins and I wish I could stop writing about the pandemic and the fog and the floundering, but I can't seem to. So, I drop anchor.

Today is Thursday, the third of December in the first week of Advent in the thirty-eighth week since the pandemic was declared. Does anybody really know what time it is?

On December 2, 2020, Adrian Dix and Dr. Henry issue a joint statement introducing new orders. "The order requires that right now, all indoor group high intensity fitness activity is prohibited. This includes: hot yoga, spin, aerobics, bootcamp, dance classes, dance fitness, circuit training, and high-intensity interval training. Low intensity fitness activity like yoga, Pilates, tai chi, stretching and individual fitness activity is also suspended until new guidelines are available to resume these activities safely. All indoor adult team sport is also prohibited. This includes basketball, cheerleading, combat sports, martial arts, floor hockey, floor ringette, ice hockey, ringette, netball, skating, soccer, squash and volleyball." [36]

---

[36] https://news.gov.bc.ca/releases/2020HLTH0063-001998

Friday, December 4, 2020

I'm hunting hard to find small and simple things to be thankful for in this difficult week when the days all ran together.

A week ago, on her day off work, my daughter and I chatted on the phone for a couple of hours, took a break, and then chatted for a couple more hours. It was deep and good conversation—the kind I only have with her.

We can't meet in our favourite coffee shop anymore, but coffee and conversation in a friend's living room can be equally sweet (And yes, I know we are under restrictions, but our Provincial Health Officer says it's okay to visit someone in your bubble in their home if they live alone. And I hate that I feel the need to justify this.).

Last night I stood at the window, looking out at the moon that seemed brighter somehow. Maybe there's some astrological thing happening right now, or maybe not—I pay little attention to such things. But the moon seemed brighter and it caught my attention and for a moment I paused and prayed.

A scant list for this thirty-eighth week of COVID time. That's almost enough time to carry a baby to term. No wonder we're all feeling weary.

On December 4, 2020, Dr. Henry issues an order banning social gatherings of any size and restricting people from visiting others in their homes, backyards, parks, or anywhere else until January 8, 2021.[37]

Sunday, December 6, 2020

The little electric stove in the corner of the room hums (and makes a disconcerting noise that has me wondering if it's nearing the end of its lifespan) and Murphy, my constant companion, is tucked in his crate watching every move I make. A fading bunch of grocery store flowers is on the table next to the north window. My camera is on a tripod on the table facing the flowers, my favourite 60mm f2.8 macro lens firmly affixed. I've pulled out pieces of black canvas and white foam core from behind the antique stove where they've languished for so many months and arranged them just so.

I look through the viewfinder on my camera, adjust settings, and use a

---

[37] https://www.cbc.ca/news/canada/british-columbia/covid-19-bc-update-december-7-2020-1.5831343

remote shutter to capture images with the least amount of camera shake. I rearrange the flowers, pluck single blooms and use a little flower frog to stand them upright. I move the camera and use the foam core to reflect light as I click the shutter. And click. And click. And I see the hand of God. All the stuff out there falls away and a holy Presence whispers truth as I work in the sanctuary of my woman cave. I see the Divine in these flowers clear as anything.

This is prayer.

SOCIAL MEDIA QUOTE.

We're watching a Josh Groban special on PBS and the singer pauses to talk about how he had to pivot (I've come to despise that word) in introducing his latest album to the world. No tours, but a PBS special instead (to our benefit).

"The world we're used to is not the world we're living in right now," he says, and the words strike a chord with me.

We're not living the way we're used to, and I wonder if we will ever return to what once was again. It's a sobering thought I imagine many, if not most, of us have entertained this year.

It's uncomfortable, this shaking up we've been experiencing for the past nine months. Just when we think we've got our bearings—boom!—the shaking starts again. It's like living in a snow globe.

The only thing that's certain is that we're all feeling it. We respond in different ways but we're all weary and off balance. Every. Single. One. Of. Us.

I often write here about remembering to be kind to one another. To grant grace; to cut one another some slack.

On the heels of learning that current restrictions here will be in place at least until early January, I remind myself of these things.

Be kind. Grant grace. To others, and to that person looking back at you in the mirror in the morning. She (or he) is doing the best they can in a world that is not the one they're used to living in.

Hang on, my friends. Hang on.

On December 9, Adrian Dix, Dr. Henry, and Premier John Horgan unveil details about the approval of the first COVID-19 vaccine from Pfizer BioNTech use in Canada and the plan for rolling it out to British Columbians.

"Next week, British Columbians will begin to receive the Pfizer vaccine, launching our provincewide immunization program. The first limited round of approximately 4,000 vaccines will be administered to Lower Mainland health-care workers who work in long-term care homes and front-line health-care workers essential to the COVID-19 response. Following the initial 4,000 Pfizer doses, vaccines will arrive each week in B.C. in increasing quantities. As these vaccines become more available, they will be expanded to other priority populations throughout

British Columbia."[38]

Thursday, December 10, 2020

My vision is blurred. I squint and tilt my head just so, but still struggle to see what I most want to focus on. What comes to mind most often are two words lifted from one of my favourite songs of the season. Words that have nothing to do with holly jolly or jingling bells and seem to miss the point altogether. *Weary world.* Sometimes I linger in the weariness. I grab a blank and curl up to rest because I'm so dang tired, not from work or busyness or anything other than carrying the weight of this year. Just give me a moment. Or two. Or ten. I just need to catch my breath. And, like old time movies where torn calendar pages illustrate the passage of time, the days pass and we make our way through Advent toward the solstice and twelve days and, eventually, a beginning.

Meanwhile, my head hurts from all the squinting, but I can make out a light through the fog. After a time of rest, I fold up my blanket and take another step closer to the next word in that song.

This year is not the worst I've endured. It's not the first, and likely not the last, holiday season that will be tough to get through. (Actually, it's not that it's especially difficult this year. More that it's . . . I don't know . . . just not.)

Hang on. We're inching toward light.
It's darkest before dawn.
Yada yada.

Let's just get reasonably comfortable in the I-don't-know of this year and keep keening for light. Hold candles for those who stumble. Wait. And, in due time: rejoice.

Saturday, December 12, 2020

> *We are often most in the dark when we are the most certain, and the most enlightened when we are the most confused.*
>
> *M. Scott Peck*[39]

Scott Peck was not a man without fault, nor a stranger to trials. But nothing disqualified him from being a man who, through his book *The Road Less*

---

[38] https://news.gov.bc.ca/releases/2020PREM0065-002035
[39] M. Scott Peck, *The Road Less Traveled: A New Psychology of Love, Traditional Values, and Spiritual Growth* (New York: Simon and Schuster, 1978)

Traveled, altered the trajectory of my, and many other lives. (I use the word "disqualified" intentionally, because there was a time when I thought it applied to me as a result of various circumstances and choices. Now I know better. None of us are disqualified.)

I woke this morning with Peck's words on my mind. "Life is difficult," he told me decades ago in the first words of his bestselling book, giving me permission to accept the universality of what I knew to be true personally. He taught me the wisdom of discipline and grace, love and faith and, while I had many miles to travel before I more clearly understood (I'm still working on getting it), he planted seeds in the mind of a twenty-something young woman that grew deep roots. I wonder what Peck would say about the world we are living in now. I expect he'd just remind us of timeless principles he explored and shared with us in his work all those decades ago (*The Road Less Traveled* was published in 1978), principles that, if we heed them, have the power to help guide us through.

This morning, I'm looking forward to a contemplative virtual retreat thanks to the wonders of modern technology. This afternoon, I think I'll pull out my worn and loved copy of Peck's book, curl up, and reacquaint myself with his wisdom. Goodness knows, I could use a refresher.

SOCIAL MEDIA POST.

There are a lot of "experts." We can put pictures of them on a wall, toss a dart in that direction, and stake our lives and reputations on the one where the point lands.

Or we can research, scramble down rabbit trails and get lost in the dark before surfacing with an opinion and claim that truth as the only one.

Or we can listen to those who see things through a different coloured lens than our own and consider that maybe we don't know as much as we think we do.

Or, maybe and, we can look at the night sky and the glory of a sunrise and realize this is all so much more than we can fully grasp. So we sit on the floor and

> *play Lego with a child, or have an heart-to-heart conversation, or offer a smile.*
>
> *(I know, there's that facemask. But smiles show even when they don't. That's why customer service phone reps are taught to smile when they speak.)*
>
> *Maybe we don't know it all. Maybe that's not the point after all.*

Sunday, December 13, 2020

Once upon a time, around this time of year, we sat in the SeaTac airport sipping coffee and listening to Christmas carols played on a grand piano while we waited for our flight to take us to the happiest place on earth—grand baby land. Then we retired and returned to Canada and, around this time of year, journeyed north to visit family and brought our granddaughter back with us for some festive fun. Now we hunker down at home along with the rest of the weary world. Joy looks a little different, and sometimes we look harder to find it, but it's there in both unexpected and familiar places. Light is coming.

Monday, December 14, 2020

A question is posed in a Zoom room: what's bringing you joy right now? I rack my brain to come up with something—anything—and, when called upon, manage a barely coherent (and, frankly, insincere) reply. The truth is that nothing is bringing me joy right now. I've said here before that I'm wrestling with depression. I'm ready to stop wrestling. To tap out. To just sit with the darkness and see what it has to say. Because surely there's something I need to pay heed to.

Some time ago, I set an intention for what I write. "Find fresh ways to write timeless truth for the benefit of others." I've tried to do that in this space, but I'm struggling with the "for the benefit of others" part. I tap out words, play with cadence and structure, and maybe it's more for me right now than anyone else. Maybe I should take my rambling elsewhere for a while because, really, I've got nothin' for you.

But, you know, I still believe there's something right in the raw and real that reaches us where we are and is more genuine than a happy clappy smile-pasted-in place way of being. Personally, I'm prone to bypass the plastic in favour of the prickly. Maybe you too? Maybe you're a kindred who gets that sometimes swinging your legs out of bed and touching a tentative toe to the floor takes almost all the energy you can muster in a day. Maybe you feel the darkness as a physical manifestation and you know you need to probe it but, man, you're afraid to disturb it too much for fear of what might come out. Maybe sometimes your eyes leak before the day gets going too.

Maybe nothing is bringing you joy right now either.

Maybe you need to know you're not alone in that.

Maybe I need to know I'm not alone in that.

Maybe the "timeless truth" is that sometimes it's hard to muster the energy to face one more heavy day. And maybe the "for the benefit of others" is keeping it real so we know we're not the only one feeling that way. I don't know. Anyway, I'll keep tapping away here, and elsewhere, and in time a measure of light will return. If you're looking for upbeat and positive you might want to step away for a while. Check back in later. There's some soil tilling needed here now. It's bound to get messy.

On December 22, 2020 the first COVID-19 vaccinations are administered in Kamloops, B.C.

Tuesday, December 22, 2020

Today is Tuesday, December 22. We are days away from Christmas and a piece of me feels like I failed Advent. Hope. Peace. Joy. Love. Can I honestly say I leaned in to these things as I intended? Have I lingered in the longing; or has it been more of a stumbling tumbling season of grasping for things and feeling them slip through my fingers over and over again? And is that okay?

Yesterday was the winter solstice. The day started green, pointing with misplaced certainty to a snowless Christmas, but turned white in a hurry. City streets and highways turned treacherous. Somewhere above the cloud at the end of that short stormy day, planets aligned and a "Christmas star"[40] shone bright. We couldn't see it, but we trust it was there. The solstice turned out to be a microcosm of the 2020 experience with its unexpected storm, dangerous conditions, and something capturing our imagination that was going to happen no matter what. It was that "something"—that planetary alignment, that "Christmas star"—that opened my eyes to the inevitability of Advent.

No, I haven't felt it and I haven't seen it—though I've hungered for it—but maybe the pieces I held close for a moment before feeling them fall like

---

[40] https://astronomy.com/news/2020/12/the-christmas-star-appears-again-jupiter-and-saturn-align-in-the-great-conjunction-on-dec-21-2020

grains of sand through my fingers were enough to soften my heart and usher in the mystery. I think about a phenomenon occurring high above the clouds, there being nothing that could have stopped it, and that certainty gives me comfort. As I contemplate things above, and others unfolding here among us; as I return to familiar words and pray familiar and not-so-familiar prayers; I find rest. I don't know what the day will bring but the wisdom of things unchanging gives me peace.

Wednesday, December 23, 2020

It's no secret: I've struggled this year. In recent months the battle has almost overwhelmed. I wrote on my blog yesterday how I felt like I have failed Advent and someone who played a pivotal role in my messed-up life decades ago, and who remains a dear friend of my heart, sent me an email in response to my feelings of failure. He gets it. In a very real sense, he's right there with me just like so many of you are. This has been a hard and harsh year. My friend shared a song, and the backstory behind it, and it helped. It reminded me of things I forget when I feel like my brokenness disqualifies me from—well, pretty much everything.

"Jesus wasn't born for people who have it all together. He was born for those who have nothing," the story says.[41] These days, I'm one of those who feels like she has nothing so I guess that means me.

Maybe, in terms of my intention for quiet contemplation and deepening my faith, I missed the mark on Advent this year. Hope, peace, joy, love. They've been elusive on all fronts. Unfaithful. Weak. Unstable. Yup, that's me.

In a couple of days, it will be Christmas. One like none other in our lifetime. We are feeling worn out, wrung out, and the effort to summon joy is just more than we can muster. The good news is that we don't have to. Manufactured joy isn't what Christmas is all about. We're pausing to remember a birth. A time when love was manifest in a time of unrest, weariness, and political turmoil. A time, in a sense, not so different from today. I know—there's this, and there's that, and we've never come this way before and all that's true.

But God.

And me—broken, weary (so, so weary), feeling a lot like I've failed these days—messed up and feeling like giving up.

And Immanuel. God with us. God with me. God with you.

Maybe we all need Christmas more than ever this year.

Saturday, December 26, 2020

---

[41] https://worshipmatters.com/2020/12/18/the-story-behind-o-come-all-you-unfaithful/

I've always enjoyed Boxing Day. It's quiet and low key—a day of books, jigsaw puzzles, and leftovers. This year Boxing and Christmas Days look much the same, but still there is a sense of exhaling this morning. A hint of reflection and intention with a measure of rumination. There are things to do, but not yet. Not just yet.

As a word person, I begin this day in the company of them. Some come through conversation, others through emails and text messages, still others are whispered directly into my bruised and tender heart. Boxing Day comes like a gift offering both time and opportunity to ruminate on them. Don't rush back into the world if you're able to linger. There are intangible and valuable presents to discover and unwrap.

The other day I took a photo on a cold mid-morning. The sunlight filtering through low clouds cast long and deep shadows on the snow, and there was a sparkle no camera can capture. But it was the interest of the shadows that caught my attention. There is a time for shadows and the thoughtful beauty that's absent in the glare of full-on sun. So maybe this Boxing Day is a good time to be still and look closer at the shadows and see what wisdom might be hidden in them. Or maybe it's a good time to get lost in a book, or the meditative practice of putting together a jigsaw puzzle, or to make art. Maybe it's a good day to just let it unfold as it will.

Thursday, December 31, 2020

It's my habit, during the last week of the year, to reflect and set intentions. To make a list of my top ten reads. To choose a word for the coming year. To tidy up files and create new ones. I've done some of these things. But mostly I've wandered and wondered and tried to put down the weight that's wearing a hole in my psyche.

We walk gingerly toward the dawn of a new year and wonder how history will remember us. We set intentions and make plans knowing full well, as never before, that life can knock our house of cards down in an instant. Last night I lay awake and looked into the dark. I prayed, listened, and wondered about things. I thought not so much of the year that's ending as I did other years in which horrible things happened. Not so much about newsmakers as ordinary folk who stumbled through unfathomable things and remained standing and the character it took for them to do so.

This morning I can't help but reflect on the year we're saying goodbye to. I look at photos and create a grid of memories. Then, because it doesn't capture enough, I create a second.

This was 2020.
Empty, yet full. Quiet, but oh-so-loud.
I have neither energy nor desire to philosophize or do anything other than

consider the gems in the past twelve months. And there were some.
- I published a book. That's a Big Thing in my world but it's lost in the chaos. (Note to authors: don't release a book in a pandemic year.)
- I enjoyed good conversation in parks and coffee shops and on the phone.
- I enjoyed spending time with our granddaughter and daughter.
- I made facemasks out of quilting fabric.
- I sang the doxology while I washed my hands.
- I grew tomatoes. And canned tomatoes. And roasted tomatoes. And made tomato soup.
- I grew a loofah.
- I filled my canning shelves and freezer with an obsession I eventually realized wasn't healthy.
- My chess game improved.
- I read good books.
- I wrestled with my faith.
- I was surprised by grace.
- I let go of some things.
- I played with watercolour paint.
- I got another dog.
- I stayed home. I took walks. I stayed home. I stayed home. I stayed home.
- I listened to the news. I took a break from the news. I set boundaries around how much news I could stomach.

I didn't do nearly all the things I could have done but I did what I could, and now, as the year winds down, like many of you, I'm just tired. I'm going into the new year with few expectations, and a measure of hope and faith— not necessarily a large measure, but a measure nonetheless. I trust it's sufficient for one day and that enough will be provided for the days that follow. We made it through, friends. To say Happy New Year seems trite so I won't. Thank you for reading my ofttimes rambling posts this year. Let's link virtual arms and walk forward into whatever lies ahead together. It's still a beautiful world.

YEAR TWO

JANUARY 2021

On January 7, 2021, the provincial ban on social gatherings is extended until February 5, 2021. [42]

On January 22, 2021, B.C. Premier John Horgan unveils the COVID-19 immunization plan (which was later accelerated).

Phase 1 – December 2020 – February 2021 (already in progress)

Residents, staff, and essential visitors to long-term and assisted living homes. Individuals waiting for long-term care. Hospital healthcare workers. Remote

---

[42] https://bc.ctvnews.ca/b-c-extending-covid-19-restrictions-until-feb-5-1.5257383

and isolated Indigenous communities.

Phase 2 – February – March 2021

Seniors 80+; Indigenous seniors 65+; hospital staff, community general practitioners and medical specialists; staff in community home support settings.

Phase 3 – April – June 2021

Working backward in 5-year increments starting with people aged 79 – 60; 79 – 75; 74 – 70; 69 – 65; 64 – 60; people aged 69 – 16 who are clinically vulnerable

Phase 4 – July – September 2021

Working backward in 5-year increments starting with people aged 59 – 55; 54 – 50; 49 – 45; 44 – 40; 39 – 35; 34 – 30; 29 – 25; 24 – 18 [43]

Monday, January 25, 2021

I entered the new year wrung out and empty with little desire to tend to beginning-of-the-year things that ordered my days in previous Januarys. So, I didn't. In the morning I got dressed in my "daytime pajamas" and leaned in to the meditation of holding my pup in my arms while piecing a jigsaw puzzle. Hour after hour I focused on little more than shapes and subtle and not-so-subtle changes in colour and pattern. I eschewed the news and avoided social media and pondered kingdom things. In the evening I changed into my "nighttime pajamas" and climbed into bed with a book. Day after day of not much more than this.

Some of you sent messages: texts, emails, even a phone call or two, just to check in. Others, knowing of my struggle, prayed. In time, from the depth of

---

[43] https://news.gov.bc.ca/releases/2021PREM0005-000119

darkness with which I entered this new year, I sensed a softening of sharp corners and found energy to begin tending to other things. Gerry encouraged me to get outside, so we took the dogs for walks and went for drives.

I pulled out recipes, planned meals, organized paperwork, and tended to Story Circle Network[44] (an organization that promotes and creates opportunities for women to tell their stories. I'm a long-time member and serve on the board of) business. I played with the dogs. Gerry and I played chess. I played with watercolour and created art just for the sake of creating art. Eventually, I began to hear a whisper. *Be loved.*

One day, Gerry and I sat in the hot tub on our back patio looking out over the ridge, and there, clear as anything, in the branches of a leafless tree I saw the shape of two people sitting side by side—one figure leaning in to the embrace of the other. I was mesmerized by the image and wondered how it was that I had never noticed it before. I knew there was a message for me.

There is this independent part of me that wants to be in control and tries to convince myself that I can do it—whatever *it* is—by myself. Sometimes it takes a season like the one I have just come through to recognize the folly of this kind of thinking. The indisputable truth is that I am loved by family, friends, and most of all with a Divine love the immensity of which I cannot fully fathom. (You too, by the way.) That whisper—*be loved*—reminds me that I was never meant to carry burdens all by myself, and when I try to do so I'm prone to break—and I did. I broke, and the first gift of 2021 to me was that brokenness.

I am not abandoned or ineligible; rather I am, and always have been, loved. Maybe, like me, you're prone, in times of stress, to deflect that love. It doesn't leave, it's still there, waiting for us to put down our shield and lean in to Love's embrace like that image in the trees reminded me. It's not conditional on anything we do or don't do, it just *is*; and it's only from the place of being loved that we, in turn, are able to love.

Tuesday, January 26, 2021

For a time, I watched the moon. Rising, as is my practice, in the wee hours, I stood at the window on a succession of days when the night sky was clear, and grounded myself in its movement and crescent shape that was thinner every day. The cacophony of the world at large, silent. The rhythm of the changing night sky, a certainty. Now I watch new green shoots of lavender in the hydroponic kitchen garden. I brush my fingers across the leaves and pause for a moment of aromatherapy. The little corner on my kitchen counter where a fresh crop is just getting started looks an awful lot like hope.

As is my practice in January, I purchase a small bunch of pink tulips at the grocery store and put them in a vase in the middle of the dining table. Their

---

[44] https://www.storycircle.org/

waxy petals are a promise in this first month of the year when it is cold and white outside. I sit in the den, with my tiny Yorkie curled up asleep on my lap, and read scripture. Then, I lean back, close my eyes, and whisper prayer. The liturgy of ordinary days does its work and little by little the cloud lifts and the voice of truth speaks clearer than that of despair.

Thursday, January 28, 2021

Yesterday was my birthday, but we don't make a big fuss about birthdays around here. "It's just another day." I say the same thing every year. When I was very young, I felt a certain glow on my birthday but I've had enough of them by now that the sheen of celebrating the day has worn off. There are still sparks of joy in the form of phone calls, messages, cards, flowers, and something sweet like cheesecake to mark the occasion, but I'm always relieved when the day has passed.

Yesterday, I thought about Mary, my birth mom, and the way she must have experienced January 27, 1959. To say it was difficult for her would be a gross understatement. The pain of giving birth to a daughter in a delivery aided by forceps, alone and with no support from loved ones, then having her baby taken from her, never to have the opportunity to count fingers and toes or inhale the sweet baby scent, is unfathomable. It's taken a long time to get here, but I have nothing but compassion for her and the grief she most certainly carried for the rest of her life.

For my part, coming into the world under a cloak of grief, shame, and secrecy has made it difficult to have a sense of my own intrinsic value. For the most part, I stay in the background, not wanting to take up too much room, not confident in my contribution and content to remain invisible. But God who loves me is showing me something different now. Everywhere I look I see messages. I hear whispers reminding me I am loved, prompting me to allow myself to be loved. A tender shift is happening.

The older I get the more I realize how little I know and how much more willing I am to lean in to Divine mystery. Maybe that's wisdom, truth finally getting through, or perhaps it's a new season dawning with perfect holy timing. I don't know, and I don't need to know.

On January 29, 2021, B.C. residents are advised not to travel outside their communities for non-essential reasons.

Friday, January 29, 2021

That I am optimistic enough to attempt to pull together a list of favourite things from the past week is a statement in and of itself about the lifting of the metaphoric fog I've stumbled around in for months.

A pedicure. For years, going for a pedicure has been a regular indulgence I slotted into my calendar. I don't see that stopping anytime soon—or ever. I still miss the place (and the price!) I went to when we lived in WA but after seven years living back in Canada, I've adjusted.

Coffee and conversation. We've learned to be creative and intentional in the ways we connect with one another and developed an increased appreciation for face-to-face conversation. Enjoying a cup of coffee this week with a friend was a special gift.

Float therapy. For years, ever since I first heard of floating in a sensory deprivation tank, I wanted to try it. Ninety minutes of pure solitude and silence? Sign me up! It became one of those things I wanted to do but would probably not have taken the first step toward doing. Enter my husband who gave me a gift card to the local float therapy place for Christmas. I put off going for the first time, wanting to be in the right headspace for the experience, but when I finally went, I was hooked. I went this week for the second time and purchased a membership. I'm not going to describe my experience because it's personal, and likely different for everyone. Suffice to say that it's my new favourite thing.

Watercolour. I'm taking an online beginner watercolour painting class and am having fun. That's really the point.

Getting organized. After spending the first three weeks of this year mostly doing nothing (and making no apologies for it), this week I tended to things needing my attention. It feels good to have crossed some things off my ever-evolving to do list and feel like I have a measure of organization in place for some projects and life.

This week, in some ways, feels like the first one of the year. It was a good one. There's still so much uncertainty in the world but there's peace in the midst. Unplugging for a time was the right thing for me. Maybe I'll do it more often.

Saturday, January 30, 2021

Murphy and I are in the den. He is curled up and snoozing on my lap while I read and lean in to early morning solitude. In the distance I hear the hum of a phone vibrating, and a ringtone that goes from barely audible to loud. *Sigh.* I pick up my sleeping pup and we pad to the kitchen where Gerry's phone is breaking the morning silence with an alarm. It's Saturday. Men's Bible study. Usually, my husband leaves his phone on his bedside table on Friday nights but he must have forgotten. I swipe to dismiss the noise, head to the bedroom to make sure he's awake, and then Murphy and I return to the den.

My little Yorkie is wide awake and it takes a while for him to settle down again. Back and forth from my lap to the space beside me, then round and round to find a perfect spot. He gazes up at me with those big beautiful dark Yorkie eyes and finally settles. I return to reading.

Then, I hear Maya barking. Gerry must have gone downstairs to shower or prep for his study and left her on the bed. She's older, and no longer confident in her ability to use the stairs we had made for the bed years ago when she was a puppy. *Sigh*. I shift sleeping Murphy again, pick him up and go to the dark bedroom where Maya waits to be rescued from the bed. I pick her up and, with a dog under each arm, go downstairs where I find Gerry already at his desk.

"You left Maya behind," I tell him. "She was barking."

We transfer Maya-with-the-full-bladder from my arms to Gerry's, and Murphy and I head back upstairs to the den while my husband pulls on a coat and takes Maya out to the back yard. Murphy and I go upstairs and take our places on the sofa in the den. He performs the same routine to find a perfect spot in which to snooze while I wait for him to find it. He has just closed his eyes when I hear a familiar quiet "harumph" at the closed den door. Maya wants in.

Again, I shuffle one snoozing Yorkie and pad to the door to let in another. I pick Maya up and deposit her on a blanket on one sofa then settle back into my place on the other. Murphy performs the same find-a-perfect-spot dance and curls up on my lap.

Now, both dogs are sleeping and I hear Gerry on Zoom greeting his study group. All is well, and finally still. in our little world. I could really use a second cup of coffee to replace the cold one on the table next to me. I'm weighing my options.

FEBRUARY 2021

Monday, February 2, 2021
Once upon a time, not so very long ago (though it seems like a lifetime has passed), it was a simple thing to drive down the hill from the neighbourhood where we live, turn into the strip mall, pick up a few sundries from the pharmacy, and stop in at the grocery store for a couple of things. Now I add items to growing lists, turn bottles upside down, and eke out the smallest bit of whatever is in them and make due. I did all of these things to a certain extent before; I do them with more intention now and put off going out to the store for as long as I can.

When my eyes meet those of another shopper and there's a moment of connection, I smile bigger underneath my facemask than I would have in the time Before. I have to, in order for the smile to reach my eyes and be apparent to the other person. Smiling big, though no one sees it, is good for both of us. I'm sure there's some science there.

There's no more "running to the store". There's keeping my distance, waiting for someone to move away from the pasta so I can step in and quickly grab what I need so as to not hold up someone else. There's straining to hear the checkout person who works behind plexiglass and also wears a facemask. There's taking my time.

For almost everything except groceries I prefer to shop online if I can, weighing convenience against guilt for not supporting local businesses. Delivery trucks pull up in front of our house on a regular basis. Sometimes they ring the doorbell, setting off a chorus of Yorkie barking, other times they leave packages by the front door only to be discovered later when one of us takes the dog out to do some business. There are fewer opportunities to catch glimpses of mystery in day-to-day interaction with other people and the world in general because I stay home most of the time. Maybe I just have to pay closer attention.

Day dawns on the first day of the second month of this year. We're inching toward spring when there will be no earthly way not to see the hand of the Divine all around us. For now, we pray for eyes to see and a heart to know. We go slow. We pay attention. In these there is wisdom.

Tuesday, February 2, 2021

I dream I'm in an airport I've been in countless times, between flights on my way home. The situation seems odd for a number of reasons. I don't have a ticket, for one thing. I know there are hours before the flight so I'm sitting and reading in one of the lounges. The thought occurs that I'd be able to relax into my book more fully if I had a ticket in my bag so I set out to buy one and am confused when I don't find the ticket counters aren't where I expect them to be. Gerry appears out of nowhere and points to the stairs. I'm just on the wrong floor. Oh, okay. Good.

Together we morph to the lower level where there are rows and rows of computers at stand-up and sit-down desks. Something for everyone. Purchasing a ticket and printing a boarding pass is strictly a DIY thing. I've got this, I think to myself. But I don't.

I can't figure the first thing out about how to enter my information into the computer, so I move to another. Then another. All around me young people are buying tickets and printing boarding passes, and I lean over and ask for help. A young man tells me what I need to do, but his instructions don't help, so I ask someone else. The scenario repeats again and again and I grow more frustrated with every passing minute.

Finally, a different young man takes us under his wing (Gerry is there now. He's been running around looking for a plastic bucket I left behind at one of the computer terminals.). The young man guides us to a cozy corner where the computer looks different than the others and offers instructions on how to enter my information. I get hysterically giddy and tell him that once upon a time I was a computer programmer and the fact that I'm having so much trouble is a hoot.

I'm rescued from the situation when I'm wakened by the sound of Murphy making noise in his crate next to our bed letting me know he needs to pay a visit to the facilities.

One wonders what the mind is trying to work out when we sleep. I can pinpoint thoughts of the airport to scenes we saw on the news last evening. I once spent a good chunk of time in airports, so I get the connection. There's a hint of feelings about this stage of life too. Piece by piece I can see connections; the dream as a whole is just chaos. A little like life, yes?

It's hard to make sense of the big picture sometimes—like now—but in ordinary moments, when we pay attention, we find anchors. And delights. And, yes, moments of mystery. I believe there's great wisdom to be found in the simple, ordinary things. Always, but especially when the big picture seems hard to grasp.

Wednesday, February 3, 2021

I'm thinking about a weeping willow tree this morning. It lives in a park on the other side of the city—my favourite park in the area, one fat with memories and history. Over the course of forty years, I've walked in it and wept in it, ridden a bike along its paths, cheered at my son's baseball games, played golf, taken photographs, and done countless other things within its boundaries. I wonder how long trees like this grand old one can live so I look it up. The average lifespan is fifty years so the tree I'm thinking of is in the winter of her life. The thought makes me want to stop by and visit more often.

On February 4, 2021, Dr. Henry issues an order making the wearing of non-medical masks mandatory for middle and high-school students in the province.[45]

On February 5, 2021, she announces that the ban on social gatherings is extended indefinitely.[46]

Saturday, February 6, 2021

These days I go slow and give myself permission to put balls down. Juggling was never my forte anyway. I'm still jigsaw puzzling, leaning in to the therapy of hours spent putting pieces in place and making something from the chaos of random shapes and colours.

I do my best to listen, even when I struggle to hear.

I eat oatmeal and wear cozy socks because these things give comfort.

I curl up on the sofa with the dogs beside me and a book in my hand.

I grant grace—to myself and others. It's not always the first thing, but it is the better thing. I get there eventually.

I do a hurried inventory and buy seeds. Unenthusiastic, but believing things I want will disappear from the shelves soon. Garden fever will kick in

---

[45] https://www.cbc.ca/news/canada/british-columbia/covid-19-bc-school-guidelines-enhanced-health-and-safety-measures-announced-1.5899483

[46] https://www.cbc.ca/news/canada/british-columbia/covid-19-restrictions-bc-february-5-2020-1.5902427

eventually. Or maybe not. Still, I'll plant and tend and learn and harvest, all in good time.

For now, I wear daytime pajama bottoms and don a suitable top for Zoom calls. Zoom. Where would we be without it?

We go for car rides when the sun shines. (Car rides. Isn't that a sweet term? My dad used to load us in the car on the weekend to go for car rides. I'd beg him to take one more turn in the single roundabout in the city.)

We take the dogs for walks. Sometimes we leave the dogs at home and go on a day date, eating burgers in the park and following up with a walk.

I go out to pick up a couple of things from the store. More often, I send Gerry with a list when he's going out anyway.

I check tracking and wait for deliveries.

I wash watercolour paint on paper.

I talk on the phone with my daughter and granddaughter.

A groundhog says it's spring. Our provincial health officer says we'll remain under restrictions for an as-yet-undetermined time.

Every day look a lot like the one before.

Tuesday, February 9, 2021

It has been a very mild winter so far here in the interior of British Columbia. Occasional bouts of snow that melts almost as quickly as it arrives, mild temperatures, and a good measure of sunshine. No complaints here. But this week we're experiencing a polar vortex and for those, like me, who have become accustomed to not having to don our heavy winter coats and pull on a pair of gloves, it's cold.

Yesterday, I had an early appointment I had to go out for and I posted something on my social media about not looking forward to heading out on a morning where the "feels like" temperature was -20C (that's-4F). I was quickly called out by my family in Saskatchewan where it's *really* cold right now. I think the most extreme report was from someone who said it was -39C / -53C with the wind chill (that's -38F / -63F with the wind chill) when he went out to start the car in the morning. That's cold. Really cold. Having grown up in Saskatchewan I know what cold feels like. British Columbia cold doesn't compare to Saskatchewan cold and it's been many years since I stood on the frigid prairie in the middle of winter. I've grown accustomed to a gentler climate so -20C is very cold to me. Friends who live in Texas understood my lament about the cold. To them, my claim about it being really cold at -20C / -4F was legit.

It's all relative, isn't it? Isn't it also an illustration of the way our perception influences our reality? And how there's always someone experiencing something harsher or easier than our current state? It doesn't take away from our own experience, but something to consider.

This morning, my weather app says it feels like -25C out there. It feels like

-44C in Moose Jaw, Saskatchewan where I grew up, and -28C in Prince George, British Columbia where my kiddos live. It's cold, but there are 39 days until the first day of spring. Better days are coming.

Thursday, February 11, 2021

I'm feeling a little overextended. Sounds odd, because I'm home more often than not, but the connected world we live in means it's possible to have a full-ish plate without even venturing out. I say "full-ish" because what feels heavy to me might be nothing to someone else. And that's okay. We're allowed to be different, and it's okay to make personal choices about how much we carry. The sweetness of a slow January, in which I did little visible work and, instead, focused on healthy and much-needed inner work, left me with even less taste for busy for the sake of being busy. I think about going off-grid again. For now, I set boundaries.

In 2021, as we hold on to hope and inch toward spring, the world "out there" still groans as does the one I inhabit every day. My personal groaning has taken on a different cadence. Now there is change and renewed intention. Letting go and picking up. Thirst.

Somewhere along the way I picked up the idea that after a time of drought, when it feels like my prayers fall to the floor with a discouraging thud, if I turn my face, I'll see that the Divine has been there waiting for me to shift my attention back all along. I see it in a different way now. Even in the drought, when I'm parched and starving, maybe especially when I'm most famished, the Mystery still surrounds me. God isn't waiting for me to get my spiritual act together. God sits with me in the muck of every day and, when the mud cakes on my feet and makes it hard to pick my foot up and take one more step forward, reminds me I'm loved and seen and held. Sometimes I have to let go in order to see this.

What is the difference between hope and expectation? The question is posed in a book I'm reading, and I sit with it for a while. I'm still pondering it. Maybe part of the answer has to do with where we put it. I don't let go and *hope* I'll be held, I let go and *expect* that because I'm beloved I won't be left to climb out of the abyss by myself. The rearranging and reframing of my thoughts continues. It's not always comfortable, but that's okay. No one said any of this was going to be easy.

Two things. That's all I have to do. Love God and love people. Neither of these is particularly easy all the time, but they are my better work. I don't do them in order to earn anything. I try and fail and try again and keep trying because I am abundantly loved and it's my natural response to knowing such love. And when I stumble, and the dull thud of my prayers hitting the floor again echoes in the darkness, *El Roi*, the God who sees me, fills the empty spaces and holds me until I'm strong enough to try again. No condemnation. No turning away or waiting for me to get it together. Just love and a Mystery

I can't turn away from.

Friday, February 12, 2021

Toss a polar vortex in the middle of pandemic restrictions and you've got a string of pretty slow stay-at-home days. Yet I'm juggling a full-ish plate. The paradox is dizzying. Here are a few favourite things from the past week.

New art supplies. I'm taking a watercolour painting class and ordered a few supplies last week. A Daniel Smith half pan set, a block of Arches 100% cotton paper, and an Escoda Versatil #10 rigger brush. It was like Christmas all over again when they showed up at the door.

Floating. Sigh. I enjoyed another 90 minutes in a sensory deprivation float tank this week. Ninety minutes of nothing but silence, dark (not all dark is bad dark), and uninterrupted solitude in which I prayed, listened, and just allowed myself to be. Pure bliss.

Brilliant sunshine. Clear blue skies and blinding sunshine. It's what I hungered for in the wet, gray winter months when we lived in WA. Sure, it's cold, but the sunshine is so good for one's mental health.

Jigsaw puzzles. Yes, we're still puzzling. We've done more puzzles this winter than we have in a decade. It's a meditative pastime and a welcome one this year.

We're another week closer to spring. The gardening pages are active with conversation and planning but I've yet to catch garden fever. Living in the moment right now seems to be the better thing for me. Happy Friday and happy weekend. Rumour has it that it's a long one here in British Columbia which means very little to me at this stage of life.

Saturday, February 13, 2021

There's a lot of loud distracting and drowning out.

But I'm convinced by wisdom clothed in stillness.

The kind of truth found hiding in plain sight in ordinary things and extraordinary moments.

A word in season.

Eye contact.

The scrape of a paring knife on a potato. A pile of peels.

A man standing at a kitchen sink washing supper dishes.

Fresh bread.

Homemade soup.

Weekly rhythm.

Even now.

Especially now.

Tuesday, February 16, 2021

It's dark when I stand in the kitchen, wait for coffee to pour from the Keurig and stretch. My eyes wander and light on a little plaque above the window. *God bless our home*, it says.

God bless our home where we are sequestered, safe from a virus named COVID.

God bless our home where two people live with two Yorkshire terriers. The smallest and youngest at three feisty pounds, who alters the cadence of our days.

God bless our home where we do jigsaw puzzles and read books and surf Netflix, mostly in vain. Where we eat fresh still-warm bread and wear pajamas and lose track of the days. Where we Zoom into community and look at the faces of people in living rooms and home offices and do our best to connect, thankful for the technology but hungry for more.

God bless our home where our grandchildren haven't been for months. Where we peer at pictures on screens seeing both change and growth and grow melancholy at the thought of what we're missing. Where we remain thankful for technology that allows us to connect but hungry for hugs.

God bless our home where we pray and lament. Where we're thankful but mourning. Where our faith ebbs and flows.

God bless our home.

Thursday, February 18, 2021

The cold snap eases its grip slightly, begrudgingly, giving in to the inevitability of change. If we hadn't rocked over our front flower bed last year, I imagine I would have seen the green of brave crocuses by now. They would have been covered by snow, and uncovered again, and I'd marvel at their tenacity in the grip of late winter. As it is, I look elsewhere for signs of change, and the promise of spring.

The magnitude of change we've experienced over the past twelve months is immeasurable, the effect different for everyone. We can't help longing for what was, but feel in our bones that what *was* will be no more. We feel angst in our imaginings about what the future will hold and wonder how history will remember these times. This is change like we never could have imagined.

As I write this, I'm watching the morning sky grow lighter. It's still dark, but there's a promise of what is to come in the changing hues. The peace I feel in this moment with a sleeping dog on my lap, another curled up on the sofa next to me, and my husband downstairs eating oatmeal, sipping coffee, and reading scripture, will soon be broken as we move into the busyness of the day. But for now, in this moment, I rest easy as I am filled. Enough for this day, that's all I need.

Friday, February 19, 2021

Some weeks drag, others seem to pass by in the blink of a eye. This was one of the latter. (On that note, we seem to be moving through February at an equally swift pace. Strange, for a short month that usually seems so long.) I pause and take the advantage of an early morning opportunity to look back, with gratitude, at the week that was.

Warmer temperatures. The cold snap broke and Gerry is able to get out on the hiking trails again. It's good for him—and me!

Fresh bread and homemade soup. Gone are the days when baking bread was an all-day thing and soup had to simmer for hours on the stove. Enter no-knead bread recipes and the Instant Pot. Now homemade soup and warm, fresh bread is an easy supper time meal.

Virtual medical appointments. There are some things that can be handled quickly and easily over the phone. I give two thumbs up to this new way of doing things.

Zoom. Around here, we Zoom regularly. Whether it's one-on-one conversation with my spiritual advisor, our Bible study groups, or Sunday morning church, Zoom helps keep us connected in this time where connection is a challenge.

Watercolour. I've got a lot to learn, and I'm still trying to decide where I want to put my focus, but I'm enjoying the process of washing pigment on paper and letting it play. I'm leaning toward abstract but enjoy dabbling with landscapes too.

Saturday, February 20, 2021

It's noticeable. Dawn comes earlier and dusk, later. We're on the other side of the recent cold snap, tiptoeing ever closer to spring. There's still a way to go, and spring fever hasn't kicked in yet, but there's a sense of coming through that's undeniable. Meanwhile, we're still jigsaw-ing and enjoying multiple daily chess games. I win a respectable number of matches these days—testimony to perseverance and a desire to, if not master, at least improve my chess playing skill.

I'm hungry to wrap my arms around my granddaughter. It's been six months—that's longer than we've ever gone without seeing one another. Recent photos confirm that she's grown and changed. Life's too short for this. The low-grade hum of world events still grates, but I'm learning to limit exposure and tune it out in favour of the better thing. The edifying and uplifting thing. The voice of truth and love.

Writing? Not so much. Watercolour painting? More so, but just dabbling. Reading? Always. Somehow days pass by, the necessary things get done, and we rinse and repeat and repeat and repeat. I lean in to established routine. I create new routines. I ignore other routines in favour of moment by moment. Every day, one foot in front of the other, eyes open for magic. It's the best I can do.

Deer tracks in the yard.

A subtle pink in the morning sky.

The glitter of sunshine on fresh snow.

Joy sparkers. They're there if I look for them. Even now.

It's been 346 days since the World Health Organization declared COVID-19 a global pandemic and so much has changed. But not everything. Nowhere near everything.

Tuesday, February 23, 2021

We think about taking the dogs for a walk in the sunshine but the wind kicks up. Instead, we leave the pups at home and go for a drive. We stop by the community garden for the first time this year and see nothing reaching through the straw covered area where we planted garlic last fall, but spy a row of tender green (spinach, I suspect) in another gardener's plot. The dichotomy between the wilderness of these past months and the new growth is stark. Later we sit in the car in the sunshine in the park and talk about nothing much at all but just enjoy the time we carved out to be together. Funny, because we're together a LOT these days, but there's something different about sitting in a park in the afternoon with no distractions.

In past years, by this time, I'd be in garden dreaming and planning mode. Spring fever would be tiptoeing in on the edges of my winter-weary mind. Not so this year. Maybe it's enough just to lean in to the ordinariness of every day. Maybe spring, the season of new growth and rebirth, will work her magic in due time but, for now, there are still things to work out in the desert. Maybe there's still wisdom to be mined in this winter. Who knows?

Saturday, February 27, 2021

I peer out the window over top of the blind in the den and see a cul de sac bathed in light. It's not the artificial light of streetlights, (They're off. I've never been able to figure out the schedule they operate on.) but the ethereal glow of moonlight.

I knew the moon was full when I went to bed last night in a room filled with a similar light. Now I move and twist and try to catch a glimpse of the orb offering such light, but see can see only the slightest sliver over the top of the garage. If I went outside and stood on the front lawn, I'd see the fullness of the moon, but the magic of the glow it washes the morning in is enough for me today.

So, I sit with on the sofa with my dogs and my coffee and reach for my Bible where I read about blessings and other things evident but not always visible and I am reminded that walking by faith is preferred over walking by sight. It's the better way. The best way.

Sitting here, in the artificial light of a lamp, I can no longer tell that my corner of the world is awash in the glow of the moon because I'm sitting under another light. An artificial light. A light I need in order to navigate my way in a world where my senses have limits. But the moonlight's still there.

Somewhere else someone wakes and stands at their window filled with wonder at the moonglow and pauses just to take it all in. Maybe they'll carry some magic with them into the day. Maybe I'll carry some magic of what I couldn't quite see with me into the day. But, you know, these days get away from us and, even now, we get distracted. It's so easy for things like this to slip from our minds. So, we return. Morning after morning. Full moon after full moon. Season after season. And we are filled, so we can pour out.

This is the way of the kingdom.

MARCH 2021

On March 1, 2020, B.C. Premier John Horgan announces that those living and working in independent living centers and seniors' housing as well as home-care support clients and staff are eligible to receive the first-dose COVID-19 immunization.

Beginning on March 8, 2021, seniors born in or before 1931 (90 years+) and Indigenous people born in or before 1956 (65 years+) will be eligible. Beginning on March 15, 2021, seniors born in or before 1936 (85 years+) will be eligible. Beginning March 22, 2021, seniors born in or before 1941 (80 years+) will be eligible. [47]

Tuesday, March 2, 2021

Long before dawn I stand at the window in the den and look up at the moon. It seems especially bright and beautiful in the south west sky. My imagination flits about, and I think about the ancients and the superstition and stories they crafted around this light in the night.

By now twelve of us have walked on the surface of the moon. We've all

---

[47] https://news.gov.bc.ca/releases/2021PREM0015-000355

seen pictures. When I was ten-years-old, Dad roused my sister and I from sleep so we could huddle around the screen of our black and white television and watch man take the first steps on the moon. (Dad was well intentioned, wanting his daughters to experience the monumental event. My recollection is that I was grumpy-tired and just wanted to go back to bed.) So now we have conquered the moon, stood on its surface and examined its geology. I suppose we have learned a few things. But as I stand at the window and look up, I think of none of these things.

Rather, my thoughts are about people who lived long before space travel was even remotely a possibility, those who looked up in awe at the mysteries of a night sky unaffected by artificial ambient light. The awe they must have felt. The sense of their own smallness. And yes, surely there were some among them who dreamed of somehow traveling to the cosmos, but I wonder if there were more who simply looked up in wonder, pondered the magnificence of creation, and could do nothing but worship the One who created. Maybe in our drive to conquer everything we lost something. I don't know. It's something I think about as I look up and then take my first sip of morning coffee.

Tuesday, March 9, 2021

Man, I am tired. Weary, yes, of the din of news cycles and media of all kinds, but the weary in my mind has morphed into something physical. I wake unrefreshed after a full night's sleep. My body aches with pain I struggle to identify. It's there, but where? Everywhere? Nowhere? What kind of pain? Sharp? Dull? Burning? I can't describe it. Can you point to it? No. I'm unable to find words to describe the feeling of the physical manifestation of whatever it is that's struggling to make itself known, other than to say it's familiar. I remember you. I know you. We've wrestled before.

When I rise shortly after four, feeling like I haven't slept and carrying a weight, I look out the window and see lights on in a house across the way. Every window is lit. When I return, a few minutes later, with a mug of soy milky frothy coffee in one hand and a tiny Yorkie in the other, the house is dark again, leaving me to speculate. Did those who inhabit it pack luggage and snacks, climb into their car, and head off on an early morning junket toward somewhere far away? Was someone ill? Had they received a phone call that roused them from their sleep? We're they off on vacation? (Like anyone takes vacation these days.) I'll never know, and it doesn't matter, but as I settle in under a blanket on the sofa I still wonder.

Maybe this morning was one of those defining ones between the Before and After for whoever lives in that house. Or maybe whoever was awake was just getting a glass of water and going to the bathroom and is now sleeping peacefully again. Sometimes defining days come suddenly, other times they creep up and jump out at us. Sometimes we don't see them until we look back, having already arrived on a new shore.

All of this to say . . . what?

That I'm tired, and you're tired, and maybe the weight is getting harder to carry? That maybe your house lights are on in the wee hours for reasons unwanted? Or perhaps the ebb and flow of day to day continues with a familiar cadence while you wait for the next wave to come crashing? I don't know. My ability to concentrate one any one thing for a prolonged period of time has taken a hit. These days, I'm prone to wander. Maybe you too?

I think about the world that was twelve months ago and the world we were tiptoeing into. It's been a long haul, hasn't it? But we're here and we hope and we've learned some things about what's important. Meanwhile, lights come on in the middle of the night and bone-weary women stand at windows and wonder. And the moon glows, and clouds cover it, and we wait for it to reappear without realizing that we're waiting. And winter winds down, and purple crocuses welcome spring, and hope reigns. Even when we're tired.

Wednesday, March 10, 2021

With an empty coffee mug in one hand and a sleepy Yorkie in the other, I turn toward the window. Then my jaw drops. Literally.

"Are you kidding?" I mumble to no one.

Fat white feather-like snowflakes are falling. The roofs of the houses in our cul de sac and the street is white. *Oh, hello, winter. I thought you were gone.* Wasn't it just yesterday I declared that it felt like spring? Didn't I see people out and about wearing shorts? Wasn't I planning on wearing Capri pants this morning to go for a pedicure? Snow? Really? But as quickly as shock overtook me it melts into amusement. This won't last. The white will probably be gone before lunchtime. And it is kind of pretty after all.

Choice made. Give in to the first feeling of "ugh" and let it set a tone for the day or look for delight and go with what flows. This time I choose the latter. It's a beautiful world even when it seems upside down.

On March 11, 2021, Dr. Henry announces that the order restricting all gatherings and events is amended to allow outdoor gatherings of up to 10 people. [48]

---

[48] https://news.gov.bc.ca/releases/2021HLTH0020-000457

Friday, March 12, 2021

We did it. We survived something we never dreamed possible: lived through a year like none other in our lifetime, one fraught with deep potholes and crazy things we couldn't have imagined if we tried. We come to the one-year mark of upside down living somewhat battered. Weary and worn out. More cynical maybe? Stronger, perhaps? Wiser, hopefully. When I look back in my journal one year ago when the topsy-turvyness began, I see a naïveté. We've come through something utterly unimaginable to our relatively comfortable mindsets and we're not on the other side yet.

Forgive me if I'm not marking the milestone. I'm worn out and still trying to regain my equilibrium. Yes, I cling to hope and believe in possibility, but I also believe there's wisdom found in lament. So, instead, I'm lingering. Staying quiet. And working on regaining my balance in a world that keeps jolting. That's enough for now.

Tuesday, March 16, 2021

I wake, for the first time in a long time, with a spark of hope in my spirit. Not a lot, but a glimmer, and a sense of new beginning. Spring arrives next week, maybe that's part of it. Or maybe the time change caused something to shift in a *Back-To-The-Future*-ish manner. I don't know, but I'll take it. A glimmer is enough for today.

Life carries on as we inch toward spring. Backyard project planning is in full swing and, predictably, I'm feeling stress in the planning. I remind myself how nice it will be in summer when outdoor projects are done and we can spend all day outside if we choose.

Gerry and I go out for an afternoon date to the grocery store to buy fresh bright yellow daffodils to replace the withered, crispy ones on the dining table. He surprises me by taking a detour on the way home, stopping for an ice cream cone and a visit to my favourite park where we sit in the sunshine and chat about ordinary things. In the woman cave I play with paint, creating an image of the crispy daffodils. They inspire, even as they've reached the limit of their splendour.

And so, hope. I'm starting to feel it. Limiting my exposure to the news and being disciplined in what I choose to allow into my mind is helping. That, and embracing creativity, stepping back, giving back, allowing myself to be quiet with no explanation. Accepting. Appreciating.

I write these things even as I'm aware of tension in my shoulders and a low-grade headache reminding me it hasn't gone anywhere. There's still a pit in my stomach and concern for things over which I have no control. And the overwhelm. It takes very little to push me into the land of overwhelm. I no longer do some things. Now, I do other things. I set things aside and pick others up. That's the way it's always been but it seems more intentional now. More important. The way I'll make it through.

It's Tuesday, the 16th of March. The last Tuesday of winter. Hope springs.

On March 23, 2021, Dr. Henry amends the ban on all gathering and events to allow outdoor faith gatherings as long as COVID-19 safety protocols are in place. [49]

On March 25, 2021, Dr. Henry announces that indoor religious gatherings will be permitted between March 28 to May 13. Faith leaders can choose four days within this timeframe in which indoor gatherings limited to 50 people or 10% capacity (whichever is less). [50]

Friday, March 26, 2021

Our daughter and granddaughter are here this week! We haven't been together since last summer and, let me tell you, the reunion is so, so sweet. It's tough to pick just five Friday favourites but I'll give it a whirl.

Hugs. From those first hugs when they arrived, to hugs in random moments throughout the day, holding my girls in my arms again is simply priceless.

Words. We're a wordy bunch who love to debate whether or not it's appropriate to start a sentence with a preposition, play word games, and discuss subtle nuances in words and the challenge of choosing precisely the right one to describe something.

Food. I take advantage of having the girls here to stock the pantry with special things and to cook and serve other treat-like things. Nourishment for our bodies while being together nourishes our souls.

Smiles and laughter. I catch myself just looking at these smiling faces I love so much and my heart overflows. When we curl up under blankets to watch a movie, snacking on potato chips and ice cream, making random

---

[49] https://www.cbc.ca/news/canada/british-columbia/covid-march-23-update-1.5960952
[50] https://www.cbc.ca/news/canada/british-columbia/religious-gatherings-bc-spring-2021-1.5964491

comments and laughing, I steal glances at my loves snuggled together and think there's nowhere I would rather be.

Hugs. Did I mention hugs?

> *On March 29, 2021, new and amended orders are announced suspending the earlier variance allowing indoor religious gatherings, restricting restaurants and pubs to delivery or take-out service, and pausing all indoor adult fitness activities.* [51]

Monday, March 29, 2021

My girls return home, a freak snowstorm blows through, and it's Monday again—the last one in March and the start of Holy Week. This morning I'm pondering taxes (ugh) and watercolour and words and books and dogs and the general topsy-turvyness that is 2021. Those, and a week like none other. And, in the midst of it all, Love.

I should start tomato seeds, but I've little motivation to do so. Maybe warmer temperatures later this week will give me the boost I need to pull out my gardening supplies. I should do a number of things and maybe I will, or perhaps not. These are hard days, but there are glimmers of hope. It is spring, after all, the season of rebirth and new beginning. Yet there's a part of me that wants to stay sequestered. There's that push-pull between wanting to move and be still. To speak and remain silent. To laugh and to cry. So, Monday. Here we go. We're all stumbling through and doing the best that we can.

---

[51] https://news.gov.bc.ca/releases/2021PREM0023-000578

APRIL 2021

Monday, April 5, 2021
In my laundry room, in tiny pots fashioned into greenhouses by way of plastic wrap and a heat mat, the first spindly tendrils of tomato plants reach up from the soil. If I were to gently pull one from the soil, I'd find the start of whisper-thin roots. Buds on the lilac bush in our back yard are fat, and the grass grows greener every day. In the garden, green shoots of garlic reach up from the straw under which fall-planted cloves spent the winter. It is spring.

We attend the Easter church service at home for the second year in a row, and afterward drive up the hill to where worshipers gathered at sunrise to put flowers on a wooden cross. We stop, and I stand in the cold wind to capture a photo. If this doesn't look like a beautiful combination of promise, hope, and love, I don't know what does.

Now, we enter the season of Eastertide—50 days leading up to Pentecost—and I'm struck again at the wisdom of observing the liturgical calendar. In this we have opportunity both to go deep and to reach, like the tomato shoots on the washing machine in my laundry room. To linger. And ponder. To see things we might otherwise miss.

We continue to climb out of a long winter and shake off remnants that stubbornly cling. At least, that's how it feels to me. Some days it feels like two steps forward and one back, but there's progress nonetheless. Slow and steady wins the race, my mom used to say. She was right, of course. So, we reach and root and, like Julian of Norwich, trust that all shall be well, and all shall be well, and all manner of things shall be well.

Thursday, April 8, 2021
We wake to snow. Just a dusting on the hills and the rooftops, but snow, nonetheless. We were warned by the evening weather forecast so it's not a complete surprise. It won't stick around so there's nothing to grumble about.

It's amusing, more than anything.

I look up at the pale blue sky that's dotted with clouds but promises sunshine later, and my eyes are drawn to a tiny area of golden hue that takes my breath away. Surprise! it says. Here's a little gift for you. And another day ripe with pockets of wonder and delight begins.

Friday, April 9, 2021

Friday morning, and it's a gray one. The light is on in the kitchen where I'm working in silence, chopping hard-boiled eggs into a bowl, adding them to diced green onions. When I'm finished, I'll add a dash of salt and pepper and Miracle Whip salad dressing, and spread the mixture on buttered slices of sourdough bread. Lunch for today and tomorrow.

The sound of the washing machine humming in the laundry room provides the only background noise. I'm washing towels and a couple of facemasks—it's the standard Friday morning chore. It's amusing to call it a chore, really. All I do is gather towels from the various rooms in the house and toss them in the washer along with others I've been saving throughout the week. The dogs wander in and out of the kitchen to check on what's going on in case a morsel of something has fallen to the floor. Sorry, pups. Not today,

Gerry's gone to get the oil changed in the car and, more than likely, have coffee with a crony. I asked him to pick up a tub of margarine while he was out. Margarine, not butter because suddenly butter started staying too hard to spread even after being left out on the countertop overnight. I'll probably go back to butter when the whole thing is sorted out—I'm trusting that it will be sorted out—or maybe not. Perhaps the convenience of soft margarine will become a mainstay. They told us at the Vascular Improvement Clinic we attended a few years ago when Gerry had his heart incident that it was better for us anyway. I'm not necessarily buying it, but there is something to be said for ease of use.

Once, I saw a meme that said something about remembering that the things we have now are the same things we once dreamed about having and I think that is true. A peaceful Friday morning spent at home making egg salad sandwiches and doing laundry is certainly something I longed for during the busy years when I was still working. The world is still in chaos, the news disturbing, but here, in my kitchen where I'm lulled by the sound of my washing machine, as I side-step around dogs, and make sandwiches we'll enjoy over a game or two of chess, I am nothing but content.

Monday, April 12, 2021

Where is the wisdom we have lost in knowledge?

Where is the knowledge we have lost in information?[52]

I heard these words in a television program we watched a few days ago and they stuck with me. Written close to a century ago, they speak clearly to the state of the world today, and to a trap I'm prone to get caught in.

I was in college studying computer programming when I first heard the term "information age". The arrival of internet access for all made it a certainty. When we first got access to the internet at work, we had to get special permission to go online and were expected to only be online during our lunch hour for the purpose of learning how to use it.

Today, there's nothing we can't research. The accuracy of such research might be questionable, and the volume of information we have to wade through to get to the facts can make us lazy. Or gullible. Overwhelmed. Scattered. All of the above. Information will shout at me all day long if I allow it. It will keep me from my better work. I don't need 24/7 world news, constant commentary, or to fall into the addiction of checking for notifications. In fact, wisdom tells me these things are detrimental to my well-being.

I've intentionally checked out of following everything all the time (not that I was literally doing that, but you get the picture). One might even say that, to some extent, I'm uninformed on some world events. Know what? I'm okay with that. I'm cultivating other things. Simple and quiet things. I'm working on listening for wisdom more than allowing myself to become overwhelmed with information.

And so today is Monday in mid-April and the weather forecast for this week is stellar. I have things to tend to for Story Circle Network. It's time to toss some seeds in the ground at my community garden plot. I've got a float booked. Watercolour beckons. The backyard invites. My goal for the week is simple: to let moments drop like pearls, one at a time, each one precious. Simple happy.

Friday, April 16, 2021

Friday morning. Before my first sip of soy milky frothy coffee, I watch in wonder as the first golden rays of the sun rising kiss the world where we live. I stand at the window transfixed by the grace of a deer wandering in our front yard. My eyes are drawn up as two Canada geese fly across a cloudless sky. It is a perfect start to the day. This week has been beautiful. After a dark and difficult winter, the change of seasons comes like a long expected, and perhaps slightly tardy, saviour. Surely, if I lived in permanent winter,

---

[52] T.S. Eliot, *The Rock*, 1934

especially like the one just passed, I would expire. But spring.

Five favourite things from this week . . .

The garden. The truth is I've had little real motivation to get started in the garden, but we spent a pocket of time preparing the plot, I tossed a few seeds in the ground (spinach, lettuce, radishes, and marigolds), and the garden seems like an old friend again.

Floating. Ninety minutes floating in a sensory deprivation chamber? Pure bliss. Every float is different. This week was the best yet. I'm still basking in post float glow.

Capris. I pulled on a pair of capri pants and a new t-shirt and felt like myself again. Buh bye for now, long pants, sweaters, socks, and black everything. It's time for a touch of colour.

Green. Gerry and I dropped Murphy off at the groomer, picked up a few groceries, then went to my favourite park where we sat in the sunshine and chatted. The green of the budding trees was simply stunning. I thought about taking a photo but it would have been a poor facsimile, so I just enjoyed it in the moment.

Our backyard. We cordoned off an area where Murphy can run free (Maya's always been able to go out there with us, but tiny Murphy is not yet trained to stay in our area and is too attractive to hawks and other wildlife to allow the same freedom). Gerry is working on a landscaping project carried over from last year, and I'm considering what to plant in the large flower pots and little potager garden. It feels so good to have my attention drawn outdoors where we'll spend a good part of the next few months.

So, there you have it. A spring list filled with peace and all good simple things.

> *On April 23, 2021, all non-essential travel for B.C. residents between three regional health authority zones is banned. The zones are Vancouver Coastal and Fraser Health, Island Health, and Interior and Northern Health.*
>
> *Road checks are put in place.*[53]

---

[53] https://news.gov.bc.ca/releases/2021PSSG0029-000758

Tuesday, April 27, 2021

It's not yet dawn when I stand at our living room window, mug of soy milky frothy coffee in hand, and look to the east. The sky above the distant mountains is pink and, with subtle brilliance, growing ever more mesmerizing. I know, having watched countless sunrises, that the brilliance will reach a peak, then fade, and a whisper of something quiet will precede the rising of the sun—the main event, the thing we wait for. But this morning I think about the liminal time between the pre-dawn glorious eastern sky and the moment the first red sun rays kiss the world. The pause. Surely there is something to glean from that slice of time.

Sometimes I focus too much on things that are loud and in my face. It seems unavoidable. Coincidentally, I have just woken from a dream in which I was assaulted by noise and activity, in which I tried unsuccessfully to escape, until I woke, shaken, the residual of that familiar sense of assault clinging and unwanted. Now I stand at the window appreciating the beauty of pre-dawn but also anticipating the peace of the gift of liminal. I'm convinced wisdom lives there. It's a place I feel a call to linger. Without the cacophony of Before and the urgency of After, the liminal offers space in which to ponder. To ask questions and, rather than tossing them up and hoping magic will happen and they'll return with answers, sit with them. To step back and gain perspective. To listen. To change course, if necessary.

I take another sip of coffee and let my eyes linger a moment longer on the increasingly brilliant sky. I listen to the wind. Then I turn, and return to the space I've set apart in my home in which I prepare for the day by reading, writing, praying, and pondering. My personal liminal time. It doesn't always look the same, but it is a necessary precursor to getting on with the business of living another day. The sun will rise and activity will resume, seasons will change, hardship will fall, and joy will return whether I embrace the liminal or not, but I will see it all through a different lens having lingered, and I will influence the course of my path—and that of those whose life I touch—through the wisdom I glean there. I could live without spending time in the liminal. But I wouldn't want to.

Thursday, April 29, 2021

There is something different about the green in this season. Ever since the first trees started budding, even before young leaves began to uncurl, I noticed a shade of green such as I have never seen before. I look at trees in wonder these days. What is it about the green? Does it seem more brilliant after enduring a long winter and dark night of the soul? Is there something different about the light? Or the trees themselves? I am tempted to research. Am I the only one seeing colour in a fresh way this year? Is there an environmental reason for such brilliance? Is there something happening with my vision? My brain?

But no. I choose not to be distracted by the why and, instead, embrace the wonder. I'm convinced I will learn something as I take in the beauty of such green with my eyes and allow it to touch me. Occasionally, I've thought about trying to capture the green with my camera—either my phone or big girl Canon—but I resist. Any photograph I capture won't have the same impact as looking through my own eyes in any given moment.

Go outside and look for yourself. Maybe you'll see it or maybe you won't. Perhaps your eyes and your heart will be drawn to rough bark, smooth stones, or something else in this beautiful creation. Linger a while. Listen. Let go of things that burden your thoughts and just be still. Just be loved.

MAY 2021

Tuesday, May 4, 2021

Some unexpectedly busy days over the past week or so, now I'm hungry for quiet time. Soon. I carve out pockets of time that leave me grateful for quiet moments, but with the need for deeper pockets in which to roll around. I practice appreciating what *is* rather than what could be.

My backyard garden is planted. I've started tossing seeds in the ground at my community garden plot and delight in the green already appearing. I will sow more rows before this week is over. In stolen moments, I splash watercolour paint on paper, playing and practicing. This is a creative pursuit that calls for a measure of both discipline and freedom—a fine balance. I fulfill commitments, cross things off lists, tick boxes, organize papers, tidy areas in my woman cave, and never quite get everything accomplished I intend.

I started a writing group! I always intended to have another group after we retired and returned to Canada but never got around to it. Circumstances aligned and it happened almost effortlessly, with a cross section of women, both local and afar (thanks to the wonder of technology), including some dear ones who were part of the group in Washington.

Days unfold, some with surprises, others with work to be done. Lilacs are in bloom, the garden is waking up, and birds aplenty entertain in the backyard. It is spring. Despite the noise of current events, there is peace in the pockets of simple things.

Friday, May 7, 2021

I'm feeling the weight of many things this week but there have been simple delights, nonetheless.

Spring colours. I continue to be mesmerized by different shades of green as tender young leaves fill out trees. I'm not sure why, but it all seems absolutely brilliant this year.

Iced caramel macchiatos. 'Tis the season to enjoy a cold drink now and then.

Deliveries. Jigsaw puzzles, summer footwear, and art supplies. Ingredients for quiet days spent at home—and there are a lot of them again this year.

A talking crow. Yes. Really. For the second time in as many weeks I conversed with a crow who was standing on my neighbour's chimney calling "hello!". I haven't lost my mind. It's a real thing.

Float therapy. It's one of my favourite things, and in the little arrangement Gerry and I worked out where he brings home dinner on float days and it's a double delight.

Hope your week has been pleasant. We're heading into a weekend of power outages on both Saturday and Sunday while B.C. Hydro does maintenance work. I don't need electricity to read, garden, paint, or write, so I'm good.

Monday, May 10, 2021

We were without electricity for a good chunk of the weekend. On Saturday and Sunday from 9 a.m. to 5 p.m., the power was off in our neighborhood. We anticipate the same next weekend. Other than having to go to the bathroom in the dark (with a tiny Yorkie scratching at the door left open a couple of inches to allow a titch of light in the room), it was no hardship. With books, watercolour paint, and reasonably good weather to go outside, the days passed quietly and pleasantly. We, of course, missed attending online church, but spent the time at the garden instead. Gerry took his camera and photographed owls in a nearby tree, and I pondered, planned, and planted.

At home, I repotted succulents I keep on my kitchen windowsill, I started cucumbers and pattypan squash seeds indoors, we topped up the big flowerpots outside with fresh soil, and I tucked a few cold hardy pansies into some of them. It's still too cold at night to plant the rest of my flowers. We sat outside and surveyed the backyard—newly fenced to keep Murphy safe—remembered summers past and looked forward to this summer. We played chess and read books; I splashed watercolour on paper, and the time passed pleasantly. Not all that much different than days with electricity, in fact.

Now it's Monday. We face challenges this week and, truth be told, I'm not eager for this day to begin. There's a sense of wanting to linger in the vestiges of the powerless, peaceful weekend, but life doesn't work like that, does it? Time passes, the electricity comes back on, and we face whatever comes next.

Many years ago, I attended Al Anon, a twelve-step recovery group for those living with someone with an addiction. The first step—and it's the same in all twelve step groups—is admitting our powerlessness over _____ (insert problem here). Be it a loved one's substance abuse, or the inevitability of trials, I'm powerless to prevent it and I'm powerless to control it. As the first step goes on to say, life becomes unmanageable at times.

Came to believe that a power greater than ourselves could restore us to sanity. That's the second step. The first step is letting go of something and the second is picking something else up. There's so much packed in the words of this step.

Came to believe. It's far from a one-and-done event. Lord, I believe, help my unbelief. No person with faith of any measure hasn't wrestled with this (If they tell you they haven't . . . well, I'd run.) We come to believe again and again. We struggle. Ask questions. What do we believe? Who do we believe? Who can we trust enough to admit our powerlessness to?

I'm not exactly sure how I got here from where I started this post talking about our simple, electricity-less weekend. It's just another example of how, for me (and maybe for you), life presents lessons when we pay attention. In reflecting on my literal powerlessness, I'm reminded of other areas in which I don't have the control I might wish for. And I'm drawn again to the work of coming to believe. So, Monday, here we go. Another week of learning to let go and coming to believe.

Friday, May 14, 2021

Good morning. It's Friday. I love waking up early and starting the day in wonder. It sets a tone. This morning I watched the changing colours of the pre-dawn sky and thought of a haiku.

Pink kisses soft clouds

Sun rises, day begins.

Promise and peace reign.

We've enjoyed a mixture of rain and sun this week, it's good for the gardens. My little backyard garden is planted and is a source of delight when I stand watering it. (I know, all the rage is for drip irrigation but I get such satisfaction from the meditation of hand watering, I'm not likely to jump on board.)

Almost everything's planted in the community garden (The first sowing, that is. I will continue to tuck tiny seeds in the ground all season as things grow and are harvested.) Today, I'll put my tomatoes and basil in the ground. That will leave cucumbers and a pattypan squash and I'll tend those tiny seedlings at home for a while longer.

It's going to be warm this weekend. Hot, even. We'll be without electricity again, but no matter. The world is still groaning and I'm still waiting and watching. Seeking wisdom above knowledge, faith over fear, and love over indignation. Working on those things, at least. I'm not perfect. Who among us is?

At this very moment there's a tiny three-pound Yorkie on my lap with dark eyes as big as saucers looking up at me. (Figuratively, of course. They're more the size of dimes. Remember dimes? Once I could purchase a candy bar with one. I haven't held a dime in my hand for years, preferring cards over cash. Shops prefer it that way now anyway, I hear.) Anyway, back to my pup's eyes. Oh, too late. They're closed now. In perfect peace and total trust, he's fallen back asleep. I think there's something there for me to glean.

So, another Friday, and where the temptation was once to grab it full on, rushing through to make it to the weekend, now I linger. One day is much like the other so there's so need to rush and there's such richness in simply being present. That's my goal for this day.

Saturday, May 15, 2021

The heat mat and lights are tucked away for another year. There are no more plants left in my laundry room. No more toting them outside in the morning and bringing them in at night. Everything's planted and gardening season is in full swing. We're anticipating a hot, summer-like weekend, the second one without electricity. No matter. We'll manage quite nicely without it.

Gerry's going hiking today and, aside for a trip to the community garden to water, I'll settle in at home for a quiet and creative day to write, read, and paint. I'll spend a good chunk of time out in the yard with the dogs. I'll bask in solitude and silence and refill my well.

Sunday, May 16, 2021

We prepare for another day without electricity. Gerry backs the cars out of the garage (the automatic garage door won't open with no power), I think about what to take out of the refrigerator so we won't have to open it while it's off, fill water bottles (yeah, I know we could drink tap water, but we've grown accustomed to the cold filtered water our fridge dispenses), and make sure our Kindles and phones are charged. Gerry heads out to hike with a small group, and I settle in for a quiet day. There are many things I could do, but I elect to get lost in a book. The dogs and I sit outside in the sunshine, moving to the shade when it feels too warm, and into the house once or twice, mostly because Maya wants to go in. It's a lovely, leisurely day.

Gerry arrives home, hot and tired, but with energy enough to wash the car and clean the hot tub. I don't know how he does it. I chop red onion and peppers and, when the power comes on early, boil pasta to make a cold salad. We sit outside chatting while the dogs provide entertainment, enjoy a light supper of leftovers, and watch an episode of a British detective series we like. The day ends early with books. It's been a good one.

Monday, May 17, 2021

"Here, hold this for a sec," I hand the watering wand to Gerry and step into the garden toward the spot where I planted radishes a few weeks ago.

"You're dreaming," he says as I bend and move leaves aside to get a better look.

The bright red radish I pull from the ground may be a dream in terms of something I held in my mind when I tucked the first tiny seeds in a trench, but it's very real. I step out of the garden and hold the radish under spraying water to rinse off dirt then reach for my phone to capture an image to mark the occasion. The first radish of the season. The first food the garden has gifted us with. After checking that I got a reasonable photo, I offer the orb to Gerry, giving him the honour of enjoying the first one. There will be many more. The winter that once seemed endless has officially passed. It is a new season—arguably, the best season. A season in which hope manifests in red radishes.

On May 20, 2021, Dr. Henry announces that B.C. youth aged 12 – 17 can begin registering to receive their COVID-19 vaccine.[54]

Friday, May 21, 2021

It's been a good week. An up-and-down one, but one rich with good things.

Grandchildren. At the top of the list is an afternoon spent with two of our grandchildren. They live in another province and we haven't seen them since before the pandemic was declared. We enjoyed a good, good, long overdue visit.

Lattice. Over two months this ago we started the process of getting HOA/strata approval, deciding on an approach, and finding someone to install lattice on our back deck where tall cedars once provided privacy. It's finally up and I'm thrilled with how it looks. I'm going to grow fragrant sweet peas on it and expect it will look (and smell!) so pretty!

A radish. Or two or three or more. The harvest began this week! I'm eyeing the spinach and expecting we'll enjoy the first spring salad this weekend. Let the season of garden feasting commence!

Good news. Maya had a surgical procedure last week and we received the pathology results this week. Benign. What a sweet, sweet word.

---

[54] https://news.gov.bc.ca/releases/2021PREM0037-000986

Egg salad sandwiches for supper. Why not? They're a favourite around here and, since Gerry started bringing home farm fresh eggs courtesy of one of his hiking friends, we enjoy them often.

We're heading into a long weekend here in Canada. It's the Victoria Day weekend, known casually as "May long", and the unofficial start to summer. The weather is warming up, our yard projects are finished, and it's backyard time.

Sunday, May 23, 2021

We hold the first Zoom of our new writing group gathering in which we get to know one another and establish norms, and I come away from the time walking on air.

From seeing familiar faces who were in my WA group, those of newer friends, and my daughter.

From the sense of camaraderie that bubbles as we identify things we have in common.

From smiles and laughter and the first tentative steps of risking vulnerability for the sake of sharing our stories.

From the sheer power of women's stories waiting to be told and the wisdom we carry.

From a prompt that rattles around in my mind for the rest of the day.

We have a writing group.

And it's a sweet thing.

On May 25, 2021, B.C. Premier John Horgan introduces the four-step plan to lift restrictions and announces the province is entering the first step of the plan.

Maximum of five visitors or one household allowed for indoor personal gatherings

Maximum of 10 people for outdoor personal gatherings

Maximum of 10 people for seated indoor organized gatherings with safety protocols

Maximum of 50 people for seated outdoor organized gatherings with safety protocols

Recreational travel only within travel region (travel restrictions extended)

Indoor and outdoor dining for up to six people with safety protocols

Resume outdoor sports (games) with no spectators, low-intensity fitness with safety protocols

Start gradual return to workplaces

Provincewide mask mandate, business safety protocols and physical distancing measures remain in place

Return of indoor in-person faith-based gatherings (reduced capacity) based on consultation with public health.

The Premier says the earliest dates for entering the next steps are:

Step 2 – Mid-June (June 15 – earliest date)

Step 3 – Early July (July 1 – earliest date)

Step 4 – Early September (September 7 – earliest date)[55]

Dr. Henry says she doesn't expect B.C. will institute a vaccine passport system. "This virus has shown us that there are inequities in our society that have been exacerbated by this pandemic, and there is no way that we will recommend inequities be increased by the use of

---

[55] https://news.gov.bc.ca/releases/2021PREM0037-001008

things like vaccine passports for services with public access here in British Columbia." [56]

Wednesday, May 26, 2021

The day starts out gray, which is perfect because I'm planning to write and there's no siren call of the outdoors to distract me. I decide to work in the den, and settle the dogs first—which turns out to be a challenge because the littlest one, Murphy, wants to claim the spot on my lap where my MacBook is. We come to an understanding and he curls up beside me while Maya is already happy on the cushion next to him. I open a new document and consider the prompt I gave our writing group on Saturday. *Place*. Ideas have danced in my head for days and I finally have an opportunity to release them. Words flow from my mind through my fingers and I tap out an SFD (shitty first draft). I spend hours revising: cutting and pasting; adding and deleting: choosing precisely the right word, then changing my mind and using a different one. Doing what I love. I won't finish the piece until just before the group meets again in a few weeks, but I'll have such fun between now and then wrangling words. I might even learn something about myself in the process. I'm sure I will. It's been a long time since I danced with words like this, and I've missed it. I feel like my true self as I see something take shape on the page where there was nothing before. There are many reasons why I write but this is the truest one: it's who I am.

Sometimes it takes us a long time to own the characteristics that make up the wonderfully complex and fascinating people we are at our core. We feel pressure to conform and, while it may be true that a measure of conformity is necessary to fit in in civilized society lest there be chaos, there's still that true self looking for a creative outlet.

I'm convinced that creativity is far more important than I realized. Whether it's writing, painting, singing, sewing, gardening, playing a musical instrument, or something else, whatever the outlet, we need one to express the deep things that otherwise remain hidden and, sometimes, eat away at us. Through our creative expression we acknowledge our belovedness by our willingness to share a piece of ourselves. We worship the Creator by using what we're given to create and, in effect, to worship.

On May 26, 2021, B.C. residents over the age of 70

---

[56] https://infotel.ca/newsitem/no-vaccine-passports-in-bcs-future-dr-bonnie-henry/it83237

> *and those considered medically vulnerable become eligible to register for the second dose of their COVID-19 vaccine.*
>
> *On May 27, 2021, Dr. Henry announces that faith-based groups can begin holding indoor services for up to 50 people with COVID-19 safety protocols in place.*[57]

Thursday, May 27, 2021

I have three large flower pots near the front door with dark purple, black, and white petunias and potato vines; two in the back yard and one on the deck with geraniums and pansies; a hanging basket filled with a variety of multi-coloured blooms on the upper deck; two rectangular planters with sweet peas already reaching for the newly installed lattice and a big pot where I planted morning glory yesterday between them. In the morning I fill a plastic watering can and visit each one. Deadheading as required, as I pour water I am at peace in the moment. The practice becomes a morning meditation.

Later, I'll stand at my little backyard garden aiming a gentle spray at growing radishes, salad turnip, carrots, and tall garlic, and I'll do the same at my community garden plot where growth increases day by day. Maybe I'll pluck spinach and a few radishes for dinner, pull a few weeds, get lost in my thoughts. Soon, I'll have to go early in the day, before the heat makes it uncomfortable, for now I go when opportunity presents. I've grown accustomed to staying home and need a good reason to leave the sanctuary since the world turned upside down early last year. The garden is one of the few things that lures me into the world beyond my home. I've always been this way—a homebody—and felt a need to explain myself. No more.

Today, I'll create something: a painting, a paragraph, or something else. Maybe I'll pull out my camera and shoot flowers. I'll read and putter and tend to things I once only dreamed of having time to unhurriedly tend to. It's a good life. I'm grateful for it.

Saturday, May 29, 2021

It's a busy day.

---

[57] https://www.cbc.ca/news/canada/british-columbia/bc-restart-faith-based-gatherings-1.6040354

I get many things done, but not everything intended. The world doesn't end.

I take a break to put pieces in a jigsaw puzzle, read a few pages, and finish the book I'm reading.

These, knowing I'm leaving other things undone. But the world doesn't end.

I eat half an egg salad sandwich for lunch
While folding towels.
Not the wisest choice.
But I'm still learning
That haste isn't always the wisest course.
I didn't appreciate one single bite of that sandwich.
I could have taken five or fifteen minutes
To sit in the backyard
Watch the dogs sniff around
Listen to birds
Taste egg and chives and radishes and salt and pepper and Miracle Whip
On sourdough bread
And those might have been the most important moments of the day.
But I didn't.
And the world didn't end.

Sunday, May 30, 2021

My girls are here for the weekend and it's such a joy to have them here. We're not doing anything specific other than enjoying our time together. Gerry and Laurinda are planning a hike today; Makiya and I will take a pass and do a bit of shopping instead. Then the four of us will come together and—well, I'm not sure what we'll do but it doesn't matter in the least.

Laughter, hugs, and conversation: it's practically perfect in every way.

Monday, May 31, 2021

Conversation, camaraderie, laughter, hugs. Lots of hugs. It's hard to say what aspect of the weekend is most precious.

Three girls in the hot tub, being eaten by mosquitoes, but enjoying themselves nonetheless.

Grandmother-granddaughter trip to the, heartbreakingly empty, bookstore.

Mother and daughter working together in the kitchen.
Movie night.
Deep discussion.
Light-hearted banter.
Did I mention hugs?
Time passes too quickly, but we're oh so grateful for what we've had.

At some point today, they'll head home—all of us wishing they could stay a bit longer.

The cadence of everyday will return until next time.

JUNE 2021

Tuesday, June 1, 2021

It's going to be another discombobulated week. Our girls left for home late yesterday morning, and today is another Tuesday that feels like Monday. I'm covered in mosquito bites as a result of girl's hot tub time on Sunday evening, and sporting an impressive purple bruise the size of a large grapefruit that remains a cautionary tale about why you don't step over the dog fence but use the gate instead.

It's going to be a hot one. I'll switch on the air conditioner for the first time this year. The garden is in need of mulching and I want to plant more lettuce and other salad things in the spots where we've already harvested, but that will have to wait until tomorrow. I have things to do this morning and a coffee date this afternoon.

This week will seem like another short one and I've got commitments most days. I'm already looking forward to next weekend! Funny that. Meanwhile, we carry on.

Wednesday, June 2, 2021

I carve out time to sit in the park in the shade of a magnificent tree, and look up. I find peace in the strong trunk and branches, leaves, still in the heat of the afternoon, the sun's rays barely peeking through. I watch a man wearing a red shirt climb out of his red F-150 and pull a bicycle from the cargo bed. He takes time to wrap his hands in black tape, then climbs on the bike and pedals down the road. A curious marmot climbs over the riverbank as walkers pass by, seeking treats, most likely, but he is disappointed today. People in an unmotorized boat float down the river. Teenagers congregate in groups in the shade. A group of older folks have arranged their camp chairs in a circle on the grass to visit.

I chat on the phone with my daughter (there's still so much to talk about, despite having just spent the weekend together), and look up into the peace of this tree. When our conversation is finished, I linger, reluctant to get back on the hamster wheel that is sometimes this life.

I wonder if, as life hints at returning to something more "normal", we will forget lessons learned in the quiet? Will we take deep pockets of inactivity with us into whatever comes next? Have we come to appreciate the wisdom of not always doing? Are we comfortable with less? Or frantic for more?

I rise from my spot in the shade of this beautiful tree and heat heats me like a blast from a furnace as I climb into my Escape. Peace comes with, and moments like this make up, the kind of life I want to cultivate.

Thursday, June 3, 2021

Outside my kitchen window, the surprise brightness of a crescent moon high in the east gives me pause in my morning coffee making routine, and I whisper an involuntary "oh!".

Later, with my hands wrapped around a warm mug, I stand at the living room window and look to the east to see what kind of show the pre-dawn is putting on. Every day is different, uniquely spectacular, and equally praiseworthy. You have to live life at a certain cadence to appreciate moments like these. For a long time, I didn't. Now I see the Divine in the sky and the changing of the seasons, in sweet pea tendrils clinging to lattice on my deck, in the rhythmic breathing of a tiny dog sleeping on my lap—these, all, the handiwork of the Creator.

Thank you for the quiet and the stillness of early morning, the muffled sense of winding down at the end of the day, and the joy sparking moments hidden in plain sight in between.

Thank you for this life with all its beautiful and terrible things, and a faith that turns my heart toward you in the midst of both.

Thank you for dark nights when I've felt alone; drawn sometimes to go deeper, other times to despair.

For mornings that always come. For spring driving out winter with miracles at every turn.

For the embrace of a loved one. For good conversation. For seeing eye-to-eye or agreeing to disagree.

For grace received and granted.

For the gift of a new day.

Amen and amen.

Friday June 4, 2021

It's been a busy lots-to-be-thankful-for week. Here's a handful of favourite things from this week.

Family. It was just a couple of days, but the quality of time spent with my girls far outweighed the quantity. We're counting down days until our next visit.

HOT weather. We love the heat around here—grateful, at the same time, for the option to find respite as needed during the day, and sleep comfortably at night in our air-conditioned home.

Summer haircuts for the dogs. They were both looking far too shaggy. I love their summertime look.

Salad days. It's a joy to shop for groceries at the garden again. Right now, we're harvesting spinach like mad before it bolts and trying to stay on top of the radish harvest. It's time to do another sowing to fill in the bare spots where I've picked the gardens gifts.

Eyes wide open. Our community, indeed our country, is still reeling following the discovery of the graves of 215 children at the Kamloops Indian Residential School. There is a big part of Canadian history I've been blind to—as have many of us. This horrific discovery alludes to only part of the story. Now is the time to listen, seek to understand, and challenge ourselves. The "favourite" part of this is that we're doing that.

Saturday, June 5, 2021

It's a blustery morning. I have things to do in the garden but likely won't do them today. It's more likely I'll catch up on a handful of administrative items in the woman cave, then settle in with a book, the dogs, and another cup of coffee. Maybe I'll put a few pieces in the jigsaw puzzle, or break out my watercolour paints. No complaints here. Gerry is scheduled to go on a bike hike but I'm guessing it will be cancelled. I could be wrong. Those hikers are a hardy bunch! We got a call last evening that the strawberries have arrived at the green grocer, so Gerry will head over and pick up a case. They'll be strawberries and vanilla ice cream on the menu later, which presents a dilemma for Gerry who's doing a "no desert June."

So, it's a home day, not all that much different from any other day. Even though I don't need one, I appreciate the excuse to curl up under a blanket with a book for a good chunk of it.

Sunday, June 6, 2021

I hear horns honking in the distance when I'm tucking tiny seeds into the earth at my community garden plot. On the way home, we encounter an endless line of trucks and busses that have come from nearby communities to show support for the indigenous community at the local former Indian Residential School where the unmarked graves of 215 children were recently discovered. People on the side of the road wave and take photos.

"Thank you for seeing us," they seem to say.

Back home, in my backyard, where I'm outside with the pups, I can still hear horns honking in the distance. The outpouring warms my heart. And breaks it. Did we know about the atrocities committed against a people before the news broke about these unmarked graves? Did we consider the effects of generational trauma? Did we turn a blind eye? *Did I?* It's been a long time since I was in school, but my recollection is having been taught a whitewashed version of history. Is that an excuse? Are we better at truth telling now? Will my grandchildren's generation see things different than I have for most of my life?

Check yourself, Linda.

I challenge my preconceived opinions and my judgemental perspective about these people—and all people. I don't have the answers, but I'm pretty sure they start when I look in the mirror. Assigning blame won't change the past. Demanding apologies where none is forthcoming won't take away trauma that's passed from generation to generation. Throwing resources might help in the short term, but healing comes from a far deeper place than anything tangible can touch. Alone, I can't fix it. It's far bigger than my influence, but I play a part. I have played a part.

Check yourself, Linda.

I haven't always acted with compassion or sought to understand. I've looked through my own filter and forgotten that we live life through different lenses. I've considered generational trauma without realizing tha magnitude of racial generational trauma. I've talked far more than listened. This immediate situation tugs at my heartstrings because it involves abused and forgotten children. It makes me think of horrific, unimaginable things. I have trouble believing there's such evil in human hearts, though history tells me otherwise.

Check your heart.

I struggle with the two most important things: to love God and love people. There, I've said it. I'm not all that good at either one. All the indignation, blaming, and shaming I can muster won't change that.

Look in the mirror, Linda. Check yourself.

The indigenous people, and all people, need light to shine on things that were—and are—not as they should be, and a collective listening is a good place to start. Slogans and protests and ceremony raise our common awareness and show respect, but I dare not stop there. Mine is to figure out what it means to love God and all people—and do it. And when I fail—because I will fail—get back up, make amends, and do it again. That is how I do my part in changing the world. One kindness, one person at a time.

Tuesday, June 8, 2021

It's that magical time of year when every day I see new growth in the garden. We're eating beautiful and delicious lettuce now. I'm going to pull the rest of the spinach before it bolts and use some of it in a lasagne. I thinned the carrots, and am doing the same with the Hakurei turnips, using the small orbs in salads. I picked half a row of beautiful English Breakfast radishes from the backyard garden yesterday and used some in a salad. Laurinda and

I talked about roasting radishes. She tried it for supper last night, deemed them delicious, so I'm going to do the same tonight.

My garden mojo hasn't been what it usually is so far this year and a residual melancholy lingers after the long, dark winter. I expect some good old fashioned Kamloops summertime heat will do wonders for all of that when it finally shows up to stay for a while. Summers aren't what they used to be around here. Nothing is, really, is it? So, I look for wonder in different places and in different forms and, sure as anything, it's there if I pay attention. I remind myself of that when things feel heavy.

Today I'm looking forward to a pedi, watering the gardens, and harvesting the spinach—gingerly, so as not to ruin the pretty toes. There's leftover casserole for supper, and I'll served it with roasted radishes. The sky is blue and the sun is shining and earlier I saw the prettiest soft haze in the valley. Murphy is sleeping on my lap and I'm thinking of moving him so I can get a second cup of coffee. Gerry and Maya are still sleeping. The house is silent and still.

My mind is occupied with coming up with a prompt for my writing group. I think I've landed on something, now I just need to come up with words to frame it for the group. I'm thinking ahead to the story I might write for the prompt. It's something big and I've never written nor spoken about it before. I'm not sure I'll have the courage.

Another day begins unwinding as it will. My thoughts are somewhat scattered (as you can tell by this post).

Friday, June 11, 2021

I vacillate between the mostly-unspoken message I learned as a child (there are some things we just don't talk about—politics and religion being the two most important) and the call from Jesus to be a peacemaker (not a peace keeper, the two are distinctly different). I don't like conflict and my tendency is to be quiet so as not to stir the pot. I keep my thoughts to myself. But as I age, I'm beginning to see wisdom in doing less of that, and more of speaking truth in love.

Will I ever be a radical? Not likely. Will I ever be comfortable with sharing an opposing opinion? Maybe not. But if I believe what I say about the wisdom in listening to differing schools of thought, shouldn't I also be willing to speak of my own? Despite what we see too much of, disagreement can be respectful. It's wise to disagree with an intention to listen and consider another opinion, as opposed to listening with the intent of speaking and changing the others mind. I—we—have much to learn about the value of healthy disagreement. The older I get the more believe that peace for the sake of peace isn't the wisest course. Peacemaking involves discomfort. That's just how it works.

Saturday, June 12, 2021

I finally get some time to play with paint and create a first wash for the latest project. Today, I'll introduce the main subjects into the work. Depending on how it turns out, I might go a step farther and craft something for our home. Either way, it feels good to let creativity flow.

I'm reading about a culture of strong women, a place, and events I've known nothing about. Yesterday, a scene in the story took my breath away by its depiction of cruelty. I haven't been able to get it out of my mind.

History teaches us that the human heart can be unimaginably dark and cruel; paradoxically, kindness, compassion, and self-sacrifice shine lights in even the darkest times. I worry at our modern propensity to attempt to erase or ignore history. Without such lessons, are we doomed to repeat atrocities? Here, in Kamloops, we're giving space for our indigenous neighbours to grieve lives lost and cruelty inflicted. Again, it's hard to fathom the heart of humans believing they were doing the right thing by these people, but I best not become too self-righteous in my musing.

My place in the world, and the influence I have is relatively small. Or is it? If I make a positive difference in the life of one person on one day and they, in turn, go on to do the same, isn't that changing the world? Or at least influencing it? I continue looking in the mirror this week, asking questions and pondering truth, making choices and setting intentions. Looking for beauty in creation, and remembering to look for it in the faces of those I encounter day by day. Because if don't see it there, I'm not really seeing it elsewhere.

Monday, June 14, 2021

I stand at the living room window, while my coffee brews and my soy milk heats, downcast at the gray. I'm hungry for sunshine and heat. Resigned to another cloudy day, I wander into the den. Outside the window in the den/snug, the most exquisite fog bank is rolling by. We used to get fog when we lived in another part of the city many years ago, but I haven't seen rolling fog like this for a long, long time, and never here. I stand transfixed as it undulates and think about grabbing my phone to take a video, but wisdom reminds me to simply be still and enjoy the gift.

On June 15, 2021, B.C. the province moves into the second step of the restart plan.

B.C. recreational travel – non-essential travel ban

lifted. Out-of-province non-essential travel advisory continues

Maximum of 50 people for outdoor personal gatherings

Maximum of 50 people for indoor seated organized gatherings (e.g., movie theatres, live theatre, banquet halls) with safety plans

Indoor faith gatherings – a maximum of 50 people, or 10% of a place of worship's total capacity, whichever number is greater – with safety plans

Maximum of 50 spectators for outdoor sports

Liquor service at restaurants, bars and pubs extended until midnight

Indoor sports games (no spectators) and high-intensity fitness with safety plans[58]

Tuesday, June 15, 2021

My thoughts these days center around the horrors of residential schools, and my country's attempt to eradicate the culture of its indigenous people. The ripple effects of atrocities committed go wide and deep. Generations of trauma manifest in ways no financial restitution, government or religious institution apology can touch. I don't know enough to say much—and that is part of the problem. We didn't know. This isn't a time for righteous indignation on the part of those of us who are seeing history in a new light. It's time to listen. To seek to understand. To look in the mirror and challenge ourselves and our assumptions. To see our indigenous neighbours not as "other", but as fellow human beings who carry the burden of generational racial trauma. I don't know the answers to how healing can begin to take

---

[58] https://news.gov.bc.ca/releases/2021PREM0041-001155

place, but I'm listening.

> On June 16, 2021, the George Road wildfire is discovered 7 kilometers south of Lytton, B.C. The status of this fire will change to "being held" on September 1, 2021.[59]

Thursday, June 17, 2021

I started keeping fresh flowers on the table last March when we started experiencing life through a COVID filter. Daffodils, tulips, roses, lilies, lilacs, peonies, lavender and many more that I don't know the name of have taken a place of honour in the middle of the table. The varieties and colours change with the seasons. It's become standard practice to move a vase of blossoms to the side to make room for daily games of chess. The flowers give back tenfold what I spend on them by brightening up the space, reminding me to hold on to hope when I am low, and countless other unrealized gifts they offer. This week I picked up a colourful bouquet at the grocery store, trimmed stems, and arranged them in a pleasing way in a large glass vase. It's a bright and happy bunch adorning the table right now.

Yesterday, I was moved to take photos (with my phone—big girl camera is still on hiatus) of the flowers in my yard, and decided to capture an image of the ones in the house too. I don't know what prompted me, but I decided to climb up on a chair and shoot one top down and, looking at that image later, I realized that I did a terrible job of arranging the flowers. The arrangement isn't balanced at all. And you know, I don't care. I kind of like the perfectly imperfect look from above, and it's not noticeable from the side—which is the way I usually look at the arrangement anyway.

It's the colour that makes me happy. That, and looking at the different and oh-so interesting shapes of the flowers and watching them change as they peak, then fade. It's removing stems past their prime and creating new arrangements. It's their subtle aroma (except for lilies whose scent is strong and bold and sometimes cloying.) It's an intangible *something* that the flowers being to our home. It's a habit I intend to bring with me as we move past this strange and unsettling time into other strange and unsettling times.

Saturday, June 19, 2021

---

[59] http://bcfireinfo.for.gov.bc.ca/hprScripts/WildfireNews/OneFire.asp?ID=810

We're gathering for our first writing group Zoom meeting this morning (we met once before to introduce ourselves and set group norms). I'm excited to hear the stories women have written for the prompt, PLACE. Writing group is a wonderful sanctuary where stories are shared and listened to, friendships are formed, and we find a spark of something within ourselves that comes when we risk vulnerability by reading our own words aloud. It will be different Zooming rather than sitting across a table from one another, but the technology means we're able to meet with women from across the country and even in different countries.

Being part of a writing group makes us accountable—to ourselves and the other women in the group. It's easy to get caught up in the stuff of life and let our writing practice fall to the bottom of the pile. When we're part of a group, we have unspoken permission to make it a priority. We state our intention—that writing is important to us—by joining a group. Then, we nourish that intention, in the weeks between meetings, by writing. Finally, we face whatever fear or hesitation we feel, allow ourselves to be vulnerable, and read our work to the group.

And there we find support. Acceptance. Validation. All of the above.

We grow stronger as we write and read our truth.

We develop empathy for the stories other tell.

Our writing skills improve.

We work things out in our mind as we wrangle words.

And we repeat the cycle month after month.

It's a sweet thing.

Sunday, June 20, 2021

It's the first day of summer and it's going to be a warm one. The forecast for the rest of the month is hot. Kamloops summer hot, peaking at 39C / 102F later this week. I love it, but I'm exceedingly grateful for air conditioning. Gardening will happen in the morning while it's still cool enough. Afternoons—well, what better way to spend a hot summer afternoon than on the deck with a with a cup of cold tea and a good book, or in the back yard tapping out words on my MacBook. This is what I waited for during the long, cold, dark and dreary months. Maybe my *self* will return.

I spend a lot of time thinking these days. Deep thoughts, trying to figure out things that are mostly un-figure-out-able. Remember back in March 2020 when the world changed? I think back to what it was like then, who I was, what I hoped for. Fast forward to today, when we see a glimmer of light at the end of this dark tunnel, and I think about things I let go of and things I picked up. Things I'm okay with leaving behind and others I might want to return to. Mostly, I'm happy with leaving things behind. I think about why, as human beings, we do some of the things we do and how I don't have the first clue of how to set things right that have gone wrong.

I look at the morning sky and green growing things and see something of the Divine. I challenge myself to look hard for the same in people I encounter. It's harder, but I think it's my better work in this season. I think about time passed and time passing, the present and the future, and how there's no guarantee of tomorrow. I try not to get caught up in melancholy, longing, and regret. I project, and try to let that stuff go. I think about today and what plans I have on my calendar. Commitments I've made, how far behind I am in getting things done, and whether I can put something off for one more day. I think about the timelessness of childhood summers and what it would take to recapture it. I wonder why every moment seems relative to how much longer it is until I have to tend to laundry or lunch or something other thing.

Should I stop drinking soy milk?
Do I need to be concerned about this thing?
Should I pay more attention to the news?
Do I have my ducks in a tidy row?
What if this happens? What if it doesn't?
Why do I feel as if I've hit a wall in this area?
Am I overthinking and under feeling? Or vice versa?

There are always more questions than answers. I think that's okay. The trick is to ask the right questions, listen for answers, and let go of the rest. Summer seems like a good time to do this.

Monday, June 21, 2021

I cut scapes from the garlic in my community garden plot yesterday and, along with fresh cut basil, made pesto, flash freezing it in dollops and tossing the frozen nuggets in a freezer bag. We're at the start of a heat wave (temperatures are forecasted to hit 40C / 104F later this week) and Gerry was amused that I was turning the oven on while the air conditioning was running. I see no problem with this. That's why we have air conditioning, isn't it?

My thoughts returned to days gone by (pre air conditioning) when I'd boil potatoes and eggs early in the morning to make salad and fry chicken for a cold supper later. We kept curtains and blinds drawn in the heat of the day, To this day there's something comforting about a darkened house in the middle of a hot afternoon.

I remembered the torture of trying to sleep on nights when it didn't cool down, sitting outside long into the evening because it was too hot in the house, kids getting cranky (adults too), the noisy *brrrr* of water coolers and fans, and feeling flat-out exhausted by the heat.

Sometimes I'd pack up the kids and we'd go to the mall, not to shop but to cool down. In later years, I was thankful for the gift of spending the day in an air-conditioned office—even if I had to wear a sweater because it was just too cold.

One summer, I drove alone from Saskatchewan back home to B.C. in the middle of a heatwave after the air conditioner in my car stopped working. Windows wide open, I drank bottle after bottle of water, purposely pouring some over myself in the process.

Now we have air conditioning and I don't begrudge it. I'm okay with turning the oven on because the temperature inside is a comfortable 24C. I'm okay with spending hours outside until the heat becomes too much and I have to go in the house to cool down. I'm okay with making a choice between cold suppers and turning the oven on to cook. Whoever invented AC, I tip my hat to you. Air conditioning made Kamloops summers bearable. I didn't have the pleasure of it until soon after Gerry and I were married and he insisted upon it. I'm glad he did.

Tuesday, June 22, 2021

I'm at the garden to water. I've just come from the hairdresser, arguably my least favourite place to leave the house for. I'm wearing contact lenses, because it's just easier than dealing with glasses at the salon, and a pair of sunglasses. It's hot, but not unpleasantly so, and I'm lost in thought as I move my watering wand from place to place, bending to pull a weed or pull a sucker off a tomato plant, inspecting the vegetables and making note of now much they've grown overnight.

I spy a tiny cucumber on the vine, make a note to thin the Swiss chard and look forward to enjoying a first taste in a couple of days, remind myself I still have lettuce in the fridge. I don't need to pick any today. Wait. The lettuce. It's beautiful! And it is, as always, but there's something magical about the way the Merlot lettuce glistens. I lower my sunglasses, and there's the lettuce I'm used to seeing—still pretty and quite striking. I push my sunglasses back up and there, once more, is that almost other-worldly gorgeous lettuce. Same plant. Same eyes. Different filter. The life application is loud and clear. I drench the lettuce a little longer than need be as I continue to feast my eyes on the red gorgeous leaves and ponder truth seen in a new way.

Wednesday, June 23, 2021

3:53. That's what time the birds woke up this morning. I know this because I was awake, trying to sort out the details of a disturbing and convoluted dream I had just escaped from. The sound of birdsong wiped the dream from my thoughts and I just listened while one loud bird announced daybreak to his avian friends. Except it wasn't quite yet. We were still an hour away from sunrise. This bird was happy. He sounded strong and healthy. Just so full of joy that he just had to let it out. His song made me happy. If that early morning birdsong turns out to be the highlight of his bird life today, it's a day worth living. He made a difference in someone's life for a few precious moments. That's a worthy goal for anyone at the start of another day.

When he stopped singing, I rolled over and went back to sleep for an hour. Now I'm sitting here with a mug of soy milky frothy coffee, Murphy snoozing on my lap, remembering that sweet song. Thanks, bird, whoever you are.

Saturday, June 26, 2021

What can I say? It's hot. Very hot. Today, it's 40C / 102F and the forecast is hotter every day until it peaks on Tuesday at 46C / 114F.

Today	Sun 27	Mon 28	Tue 29	Wed
102°	108°	112°	114°	108
70°	72°	76°	76°	70°
☀	☀	☀	☀	☀
1%	0%	0%	0%	19%

Today	Sun 27	Mon 28	Tue 29	Wed
40°	43°	45°	46°	43°
22°	23°	25°	25°	22°
☀	☀	☀	☀	☀
1%	0%	0%	0%	22%

Laurinda and I were talking about the altered state during a heat wave that brings with it nostalgia for simpler, not necessarily easier, days. It's a perfect time to get lost in a book and that's exactly what I'm doing. That, and not much else.

I'm happy to go through this heat wave with the option to come inside and cool off as needed, but I'd rather be outside. I spent a lot of years without AC here in Kamloops. Heat stroke is a very real thing. Ask me how I know. It's too hot for the pups, so we'll spend more time indoors over the next few days. We'll sneak out to the shade in the backyard now and then and maybe we'll linger. Maya would be content in the house while I stayed outside, but Murphy and I are joined at the metaphorical hip. He wouldn't tolerate the separation for long.

Gerry and I will survive on salad, ice cream, and cold tea and water the gardens early. We'll work on the jigsaw puzzle and read and write and read and read. Sounds pretty sweet to me.

Sunday, June 27, 2021

This morning it was the moon, so bright just above the thick-with-evergreens hill to the south. It seemed as though, if I was standing on top of that hill, I would be able to reach up and touch it. An involuntary "oh!" escaped from between my lips when I saw it. I have grown accustomed to seeing such delights, though they are made no less wonderful by their frequency, since I started to pay attention.

I see the Divine at every turn in this created world—in the turning of the seasons, in trees, and vegetables growing in the garden, even in persistent weeds that have no business there. I am not fanatical about eradicating them from my plot. My garden isn't perfect. I don't think enough, weed enough, cultivate enough, but I still see perfection in the imperfection. Lately, I've been challenging myself. As an image-bearer of the Creator, I long held the unspoken (and ofttimes spoken) belief that with such wonder came great and heavy responsibility. To be more. To do more. And I always fell short. I don't believe that any more.

What I need to do is learn to love God and people—and do it. Imperfectly, to be sure, but it's as simple and complicated as that. Pulling weeds and cultivating the metaphorical soil, all that's important. Doing these things from a place of continual transformation into one who is learning to love, step by stumbling step, is far different than doing so from a legalistic judgemental place of rules and laws. The challenge I set before myself is to look beyond the mystery and magic I see in creation, and look for it in people—those who bear the image of God's hand upon them—that's all of them. This is not as easy for me.

As created beings we are God's image bearers. That isn't a burden meant to drive me to do more and be better. It's an invitation to look at the person in front of me and see that image, and love that image the way I'm able to in that moment. And to do it again and again and learn to do it well according to how I was created, not to follow a formula or hit a mark someone sets for me. Maybe one day I'll get to a place where that's my default.

On June 28, 2021, the Sparks Lake fire, approximately 15 kilometers north of Kamloops Lake, ignites and is believed to be human caused. It will turn out to be the largest fire in the province this year in terms of area burned. The status of this fire will change to "under control" on August 26, 2021."[60]

60

Monday, June 28, 2021

It seems a bit like winter in reverse. It's far too hot to spend much time outside so we hunker down inside working on a jigsaw puzzle, playing chess, and reading. Yesterday, suffering from Zoom fatigue after church and a great Story Circle Network board meeting, I suggested popcorn and Prime. We're currently trying to sort out the mysteries in the *Bancroft* series. We munched popcorn, and later salad and Jello, following it all up with a dish of frozen yogurt. With breaks to take the dogs outside—where it was too hot to linger, though the heat felt good for a short time—the day and early evening passed gently.

We're breaking temperature records, and expect more to fall this week. I like the heat, but this is extreme even for me. Today, after early morning watering, another mostly-indoors day. It's kind of a shame, but that's the way it is for now. I'm grateful for air conditioning that's running all day and night, hoping we don't put too much stress on B.C. Hydro which is already reporting outages in the city.

On June 29, 2021, B.C. Premier John Horgan announces that the province will move into step three of the restart plan on July 1. [61]

Return to normal for indoor and outdoor personal gatherings

Maximum capacity for indoor organized gatherings of 50 people or up to 50% of a venue's total capacity, whichever is greater

Maximum capacity for outdoor organized gatherings of 5,000 people or up to 50% of a venue's total capacity, whichever is greater

---

https://www.for.gov.bc.ca/ftp/!Project/WildfireNews/7292021~100347_21%20K21001%20Sparks%20Lake%20Fire%20Community%20Bulletin%20July%2028.pdf

[61] https://news.gov.bc.ca/releases/2021PREM0043-001268

Return to normal for fairs, festivals and trade shows, with communicable disease plans

Return to Canada-wide recreational travel

Reopening of casinos, with reduced capacity and ~50% of gaming stations permitted to open

Reopening of nightclubs, with up to 10 people seated at tables, no socializing between tables and no dancing

Return to normal hours for liquor service at restaurants, bars and pubs with table limits to be determined by venue and no socializing between tables

Return to normal for sports and exercise facilities, with communicable disease plans

Mask wearing recommended in indoor public spaces for all people 12 and older who are not yet fully vaccinated.

Tuesday, June 29, 2021

We broke another heat record yesterday with the temperature reaching 45.8C / 114 F. Worse, a forest fire broke out just northwest of our city that is now 180 hectares and burning out of control. It's hard to believe it's only June. So, of course, it'll be another mostly indoor day. I'm planning on hunkering down and getting things done in the woman cave.

In other news, I received photos from our granddaughter's end-of-year school party. Love them. Love her. And I can't believe how quickly the years go by. She looks so much like her mama. Got to peek at her report card and my favourite comment was "In Makiya's spare time she writes stories." Of course, she does. That's my girl.

I wish I had something more to write about this morning but, really, it's all about the heat these days.

On June 30, 2021, The Lytton Creek fire spreads rapidly toward the village of Lytton, B.C. Within minutes, the entire village is engulfed in flames and two residents die. It will burn out of control until the status changes to "under control" on September 4, 2021.[62]

On June 30, 2021, the Young Lake Fire is discovered approximately 35 kilometers southeast of 70 Mile House, B.C. and is believed to be lightening caused. The status will change to "under control" on August 24, 2021 [63]

Wednesday, June 30, 2021

Here we go heading into another blistering day. The forecast high is a toasty 46C / 115F. That, and maybe thunder and lightning which will be bad news for our tinder dry province. Wildfires are already burning out of control nearby. Last evening, when it was still 47C / 117F, I cooked an egg in a pan outside just to see if I could. It turned into an inedible lump of something weird, but now I know it is possible to cook an egg outside in these temperatures.

Yesterday we learned there will be no raspberries available at the local green grocer at this time because the heat has ruined them. Fingers crossed for a second harvest because I'm itching to make jam. I'm seeing reports of all manner of vegetation being negatively impacted by the relentless heat. So far, my gardens are still relatively happy and, incredibly and thanks to shade from my neighbour, I'm still harvesting lettuce, though it won't be much longer before it bolts. So, again, I've got nothing much to say that doesn't

---

[62] https://www.cbc.ca/news/canada/british-columbia/bc-wildfires-june-30-2021-1.6085919

[63] http://bcfireinfo.for.gov.bc.ca/hprScripts/WildfireNews/OneFire.asp?ID=849

have to do with the heat. It's just all-encompassing right now.

> *On June 30, 2021, the COVID-19 provincial state of emergency declared under the Emergency Program Act, originally declared on March 18, 2020, ends, making it the longest provincial state of emergency in B.C.'s history.[64]*

---

[64] https://www2.gov.bc.ca/gov/content/covid-19/info/state-of-emergency-ends#:~:text=The%20COVID%2D19%20provincial%20state,pm%20on%20June%2030%2C%202021.

JULY 2021

Thursday, July 1, 2021

Waking with a heavy heart after last evening's reports of Lytton, B.C., a nearby village and Canadian hotspot, suffering catastrophic damage from fire. Reports say residents had about ten minutes to get out after the fire started. The videos I've seen this morning are heartbreaking. Record-breaking heat, tinder dry forests, lightning strikes, and now heavy wind. These things don't bode well for this year's fire season. Already, the skies are smoky. I expect it's going to get much, much worse.

Here in Kamloops, they're forecasting a high of 38C / 100F today. I wonder if it will seem refreshing after this week's extreme heat. The wind is wild—and that is not good. Today is Canada Day. There is a shadow this year given the growing number of unmarked graves being discovered on the grounds of former Indian Residential Schools and a collective eye-opening of our past. I am still proud to be Canadian. We are not perfect but we can't change what's happened in the past. The way forward is through listening, seeking to understand, and doing better now that we know better. There's lots to reflect on today.

Saturday, July 3, 2021

The wildfire season has barely started and we've already experienced unprecedented record-breaking heat. A provincial campfire ban is in place until October. City parks are closed. The village of Lytton, B.C. has been 90% lost to fire. The Kamloops Fire Chief says that "We are at risk here and are asking everyone in Kamloops to take extreme care. We haven't seen conditions like this in Kamloops ever before. I want citizens to know that the fire conditions are beyond dangerous." We remember the smoky-filled slides and high anxiety of 2017 and 2018, the worst wildfire seasons in our province's history. So, Gerry and I take a few hours and put an evacuation plan into place.

We gather important papers and set aside an area in our basement for "go bins" that we can grab at a moment's notice. As we walk through the house, I'm surprised at how few things we deem as irreplaceable. We make a list of last-minute things to grab like medications, dog leashes, and other paraphernalia and tape it to one of the bins. Later that night when we're in bed—I've already put my book down but Gerry is still reading—the doorbell rings. It wakes me up and, when Gerry returns to the bedroom, I mumble "who was that?"

"It was Mike," he says tersely. "There's a fire."

I'm awake and out of bed in an instant and we go to the bedroom window as see a fire raging below us. We're thinking about leaving when there's pounding on the door. The doorbell repeatedly rings. It's the RCMP. They're going door to door telling everyone to get out. We're relatively calm as we execute our hours-old evacuation plan, gathering last-minute things, and loading the cars. I post a request on social media for prayer, field text messages and phone calls from family, and make a quick phone call: "There's a fire. We're being evacuated. Can we come?"

We join the long line of cars heading for the one road out of our community. The going is slow but steady. Later, we'll hear reports of it taking over an hour for some people to get out. It's an issue that will need to be addressed but for now we just keep going. It's surreal. It's storming. Heavy rain (a very good thing), booming thunder, and, worst of all, lightening. That's what started this fire and others in the city this night.

Sometime later, once we're safely at a friend's home, still a bit shell-shocked and riding an adrenaline high, the news reports that the evacuation order has been rescinded. We're relieved and in slight disbelief, but a double check of the city website confirms it, so we reload the cars and head home. We don't unload, but grab only immediate necessities and head, tired and grateful, back into the house where we stand on our deck in the wind and the rain watching the fire still burn, surprised they rescinded the order but trusting they know what they're doing. Eventually, Gerry opens the blinds in the bedroom and we crawl into bed. He can see the fire from his side of the bed.

Time takes on a strange property in times like this and I'm not sure how long it is before there's pounding at the door and the incessant ringing of the doorbell again. It's the RCMP again. The evacuation order is back on. We're confused, because the flames have died down from our vantage point but, again, we trust those who know what they're doing, reload the car, and head out.

The rest of the night passes in a blur. In the early morning hours we finally fall into bed, exhausted. Firefighters battle the fire for the whole of the following day aided by helicopters and water bombers. The skies remain smoky. We are tired, beyond grateful, and on edge knowing we're heading into what promises to be a very, very scary season.

Monday, July 5, 2021

We score a flat of raspberries. They're a little burnt from the record-breaking heat, but fine for making jam. It's a little dream come true, working side by side in the kitchen with Laurinda and Makiya, teaching them how easy it is to make jam. I make the first batch, offering tips while I go, then turn over the figurative keys to my kitchen and let the girls have a go.

While my jars are cooling on the counter, I notice the fruit has separated slightly in the jars and remark on it. Laurinda's competitive streak rises up as she draws a line in the sand.

"Ours won't do that." Ah ha! A jam-making challenge! And, sure enough, her jars come out of the canner looking like jewels and she kicks her heels up and gives an enthusiastic fist pump. "Yes!" I'm thrilled she "won."

We spend the rest of the afternoon doing nothing much in particular. The smoke clears enough to allow us to sit outside where we talk and talk about everything and nothing. Gerry joins us and Laurinda introduces us to something called The Mandela Effect and we exclaim "no way" again and again as she reads examples to us. Gerry barbecues burgers and after we eat, the girls head out for a short drive to visit a few of their favourite Kamloops spots. When they return, we grab snacks and settle in to watch the first episode of the latest season of *America's Got Talent*. All in all, it's a quiet and deeply satisfying day.

Thursday, July 8, 2021

It's become a summertime tradition ever since I was blessed to enjoy the Mennonite treat with cousins for the first time a few years ago. Roll kuchen. It's made with a simple dough, deep fried, and served with watermelon and Rogers Golden Syrup. The recipe I use is written on an index card that says "from cousin Ruth" on it. It's a treasure. Something passed to me from the family I didn't know until recently. It's a thread of where I came from connecting to the present.

This time, Makiya makes the dough and I deep fry it. The thought of my granddaughter picking up the thread of our heritage and taking it with her into the future gives me such deep joy. Threads connecting and threads continuing through the simplicity of roll kuchen. Priceless.

On July 9, 2021, the Embleton Mountain wildfire is

> discovered 7 kilometers west of Sun Peaks. The cause is undetermined. The status of this fire changes to "being held" on August 1, 2021 at which time it is no longer classified as a "wildfire of note." [65]

> On July 10, 2021, the Crazy Creek Gorge fire is discovered 29 kilometers north of Sicamous believed to be lightening caused. The status of this fire changes to "being held" on August 26, 2021. [66]

Saturday, July 10, 2021

I'm tired in a good way after a busy Saturday with Gerry and the girls. To start the day, Laurinda and I went to the park to walk and enjoy mother-daughter conversation. Then the four of us went bowling—and I was excruciatingly bad. We went to a nearby lake where the girls had a swim, Murphy decided lake swimming isn't for him after his first encounter, and we were surprised to see our neighbours there also enjoying the beautiful day. Chinese take-out for supper, another episode of *America's Got Talent*, and these grandparents were done in. The girls will head home today. The grandparents may take a nap. Hearts full. Cherishing memories until next time.

Sunday, July 11, 2021

Now we watch the weather forecast for signs of much-needed rain or, worse, lightning. We check the news to see the status of existing fires and how many have started since we last checked. We watch planes and helicopters fly overhead, fighting war against fires burning all over the province. We lift our eyes to the skies and the smoke and appreciate times when it's clear enough to go outside—which isn't often.

Sometimes our eyes and throats burn. Sometimes the smoke is so thick we

---

[65] http://bcfireinfo.for.gov.bc.ca/hprScripts/WildfireNews/OneFire.asp?ID=836
[66] https://www.saobserver.net/news/crazy-creek-gorge-wildfire-north-of-sicamous-being-held/

can smell it inside the house. We pray for those fighting fires, those who have lost their homes and community, and those who are evacuated, who wait and wonder. Our eyes scan the horizon and we are on edge. This, the latest in a long string of things with the power steal our peace.

I think, often, of these words attributed to Julian of Norwich.

All shall be well, and all shall be well and all manner of thing shall be well.

And of Jesus.

I am leaving you with a gift—peace of mind and heart. And the peace I give is a gift the world cannot give. So don't be troubled or afraid. (John 14:27 NLT)

And of my old friend, Frederick Buechner.

The grace of God means something like: "Here is your life. You might never have been, but you are, because the party wouldn't have been complete without you. Here is the world. Beautiful and terrible things will happen. Don't be afraid. I am with you. Nothing can ever separate us. It's for you I created the universe. I love you.

There's only one catch. Like any other gift, the gift of grace can be yours only if you'll reach out and take it.

Maybe being able to reach out and take it is a gift too.

As the heat and the drought and the fires rage on, to the extent that we're able, let's choose peace. And when this storm passes, let's hold on to it. When we drop it, let's reach out and pick it up. If we see someone else who has dropped it and is fumbling around trying to find it, let's pick it up and offer it to them. Whether the storm comes in the form of fire or sickness or any of the other insidious forms storms can take, let's remember the principles we need to weather them are the same.

All shall be well.

In the midst of both the beautiful and terrible.

On July 12, 2021 the Tremont Creek fire ignites 8.5 kilometers southeast of Ashcroft, B.C. The cause is undetermined. The status of this wildfire will change to "under control" on August 26, 2021.[67]

On July 13, 2021, the July Mountain fire is discovered

---

[67] http://bcfireinfo.for.gov.bc.ca/hprScripts/WildfireNews/OneFire.asp?ID=843

45 kilometers southwest of Merritt, B.C. It eventually merges with the Brook Creek wildfire which begins on August 14, 2021. On September 7, 2021 the status of this fire changes to "being held". [68]

On July 13, 2021 the Chasm fire ignites north of Chasm park and south of 70 Mile, B.C. It is lightening caused. The status changes to "under control" on August 1, 2021. [69]

On July 13, 2021, the White Rock Lake fire ignites between Kamloops and Vernon as a result of lightening. The status changes to "being held" on September 2 but fire officials say it may continue to burn all winter. It will destroy at least 29 residences or businesses in Monte Lake, 70 in Ewings Landing and Killiney, and 11 on Okanagan Indian Band land. [70]

---

[68] http://bcfireinfo.for.gov.bc.ca/hprScripts/WildfireNews/OneFire.asp?ID=859
[69] http://bcfireinfo.for.gov.bc.ca/hprScripts/WildfireNews/OneFire.asp?ID=848
[70] https://en.wikipedia.org/wiki/White_Rock_Lake_fire

Journal Entry – July 13, 2021

Depression

It's been a long time

Because I lost a piece of myself in the depression

That slipped in

And lingered

That took medication to give me the strength to open the door

And invite it to leave.

I assured the darkness
That it had done the work it came to accomplish
That I understood the message
That I was ready to do a new thing
Even as I stumbled around
picking up and putting down.

But I was wrong.

Maybe I'm no longer depressed

Or perhaps depression has taken on a different form.

All I know is that I have been holding close something I need to release.

Journal Entry – July 14, 2021

I check the news first thing to see what new fires have started and the status of existing ones. I look out the window to see how much smoke is in the area. This morning it's not too bad. Yesterday was horrific.

Thursday, July 15, 2021

The smoke is so thick we can't see the hills on the other side of the valley. After being outside for a while, my head aches and my eyes burn. We take the dogs out for one last sniff around the backyard before bed and I am struck by the brilliance of the sun in the smoky western sky.

This morning, I wake later than usual and after putting coffee on go to the living room window to see how much smoke we're under today. The sun is brilliant red behind the smoke. I suppose that means it's a clear and sunny day. I hope the smoke clears enough so we can see it.

And, you know, it's heavy, this burden of a bad fire season coming on the heels of what 2020 ushered in.

And I think I need to do less reading and watching and thinking and more putting into practice. While praying for rain.

And those fighting these beasts.

And those who have already lost their homes—or their town—and those who are under evacuation alerts or orders and those who will be or already have been.

It's only mid-July but I'm already kind of done with this summer. I have to look harder for sparks of joy (Oh, wait. Best not to say spark.) Today we're going to the community garden early to harvest the garlic.

And a salad for supper.

I'm going to escape the smoke this afternoon by going for a float.

Gerry's in charge of supper.

Just another day here in British Columbia where our province is on fire.

Friday, July 16, 2021

It's felt like a heavy week with the concern about fires and the oppressive smoke blanketing our city. I need to be intentional about finding joy sparkers.

Blueberries, my favourite summer fruit, are in season and, unlike raspberries which were burned by the extreme heat, they are sweet and delicious. We're filling the freezer with them and I'm filling my stomach and making sure to brush my teeth well before leaving the house.

We harvested 40 bulbs of garlic in the community garden yesterday and had a pungent ride home. Later, when I went out, the car still reeked. A choice had to be made. Open the windows and smell smoke or keep them closed and breathe garlic. I chose the latter.

One day, I received a message from my granddaughter. "I miss youuuuuuuuuu!" Oh, I miss you too, sweet girl.

Saturday, July 17, 2021

In the afternoon the smoke clears and we go outside in the backyard just because we can. Murphy walks the perimeter of the fenced area again and again. Maya does her best to encourage us to go inside because her belly tells her it's dinner time. And I take a few photos in the sunshine just to mark the occasion. And quite glorious. And so, it goes.

Sunday, July 18, 2021

I tucked bean seeds in the ground where we harvested the garlic a few days ago. There's still plenty of growing season ahead for a second crop. Meanwhile, I'm picking yellow, green, and purple beans from the first sowing. I tried something different by planting a mixture all together. I won't do this again because they're coming ready at different paces which isn't necessarily a bad thing, but I'm finding the harvest more scattered. I returned to my trusty Blue Lake bush beans for the second sowing.

What with the extreme heat and heavy smoke, I don't have my usual gardening mojo and I'm already thinking ahead to what I might do differently next year. Some days, it seems like a chore to drive down the hill to the community garden. Gerry's going to enlarge my backyard garden so I can do more up here, though I'll still keep my community garden plot for things that are too tempting for the deer up here.

Yesterday, my writing group met on Zoom. How I love the opportunity to gather with women to share our stories. Our prompt was "unexpected" this month. One could write about unexpected things again and again and come up with a different story every time. The stories were rich and evocative.

Today, we're looking forward to spending a family day with Gerry's siblings and spouses. It's been a long time and it will be good to gather. The sky, right now, is clear and blue. I hope it holds.

And so, time passes.

On July 20, 2021, the B.C. government declares a provincial state of emergency to support the provincewide response to the ongoing wildfire situation and based upon the recommendation from the BC Wildfire Service and Emergency Management BC. [71]

Wednesday, July 21, 2021

After a couple of games of chess, we go to the community garden. Gerry drags out the hose to water while I head to the basil and start cutting. The sweet, fresh aroma wafts up—so fresh! —and a woman working in another plot calls over that she can smell it from there. I fill a large oversized reusable bag with it. It's pesto making day.

Next, I move to the Swiss chard and cut enough for supper. I'll stir fry it in a bit of olive oil with pumpkin seeds and top it off with a titch of feta.

I hunt around in the cucumber vines and pull the largest one I can find. We eat a cucumber a day now.

Next, I move to the beans. They're coming in slower this year, but I find enough to freeze when we get home. The 2021 Restock the Freezer effort continues.

I survey the Black Krim tomatoes and find one that's nearly ripe and I can almost taste the first tomato sandwich of the season. It'll happen soon. Maybe later this week.

By the time Gerry winds up the hose and I tote three full bags of produce to the car, it's heating up. Thank goodness for air conditioning. Man, I appreciate it this year not only because it's hot and dry, but also because we can't open the windows most days due to the smoke.

At home, Gerry gets to work finishing up a project on the deck and I water the backyard garden and flower pots. Next, I set to work in the kitchen washing, chopping, and blanching. By the time lunch (and another chess game) rolls around, we've both done a productive morning's work.

After lunch, Gerry heads out to run some errands. I plan to settle in with my book but, instead, have a short chat with Laurinda and tend to other things here and there and never find an opportunity. The afternoon goes quickly, and Gerry arrives home in time for a webinar we signed up for on macro photography—something I love.

I set my camera aside when I was focusing on writing and birthing *The Presence of Absence*, and haven't picked it up again. The webinar inspires me, making me hungry to make photographic art again.

And now, this morning, on a day in which I planned to dust off my camera and macro lens and spend some time in the yard photographing flowers, it's windy. Very windy. This isn't good news for the fires or the photographer. Macro photography + wind = blurry images. Perhaps I'll pick a blossom or

---

[71] https://news.gov.bc.ca/releases/2021PSSG0047-001404

two and work in my woman cave instead. Or maybe the wind will die down enough to make taking photographs outside possible. Either way, I'm going to shoot flowers today.

Thursday, July 22, 2021

It's windy, so shooting outside isn't an option for the kind of photography I'm hungry for. Fortunately, there's a pretty bunch of pink alstroemerias on the dining table that will do nicely. In the past, when I shoot indoors, I've liked to work in the woman cave using the natural light from the big north-facing window. That space has been taken over by watercolour paint paraphernalia, so I decide to work upstairs near the west-facing window instead. I pull out my camera and check the battery, attach my 60mm macro lens, riffle through my bag for the remote timer, grab my tripod and head upstairs.

I'm rusty, there's no doubt. But I fall into the peace of playing with aperture, shutter speed, and ISO while composing and shooting again and again. I work in silence, as I usually do, and aside from Murphy underfoot and demanding to know what I'm doing, the quiet, meditative time is like balm.

I see something I would never have noticed if I wasn't focusing on the smallest parts of the flowers: the tiniest water droplet on one of the stamens. I switch my lens to manual focus and capture some images, run downstairs for my extension tubes and capture a few more. It's magical, this tiny droplet.

When I'm satisfied that I have enough to work with, I take the card out of my camera and head down to the woman cave to play. I love post processing almost as much as taking photos.

As is sometimes the case and after such a long time away, expected, I don't have much I can work with. Like I said, I'm rusty. But I dabble with sliders and crop a couple images and it's still time we'll spent.

Later, the wind dies down for a pocket of time and I take my camera out to the deck to photograph flowers in pots. I'm captivated by the geraniums and, there, in the hidden places I would pay little mind to on an ordinary day, I find something that looks like magic.

I remember why I love the style of flower photography I like to shoot. It shows me things I would otherwise miss, and in these things, I see the hand of the Creator and my faith deepens. For me, this kind of photography is prayer sure as anything.

So yes, I'm rusty. But after a long, parched time, I'm ready to resume practice.

Friday, July 23, 2021

Whoever described summer days as "lazy" wasn't a gardener. I am, and this time of year is far from lazy around here. Yesterday, after an early trip to the garden to water, weed, and harvest, I spent the rest of the morning washing, chopping, and bagging while I sent Gerry out to foist some cucumbers off on our neighbours. Then I made blueberry freezer jam.

We enjoyed the first Black Krim tomato on sandwiches for lunch (accompanied by handfuls of blueberries and cherries and a thoughtful chess game) and then I busied myself in the woman cave tending to Story Circle Network things. At one point Gerry came in an suggested a drive to the rose garden to take photos. Yes please! It's been ages since we went on a photo-taking junket. (By the way, did you know that the old-fashioned milk-based custard called junket is also known as curds and whey? Me either! Thanks Google.)

It wasn't the best time of day to shoot roses because the sun was visible enough through the smoke to cast a shadow (for a brief time that also happened to coincide with our little adventure), but I shaded the flowers with my body and got a handful of images I was satisfied with.

By the time we got home, I barely had time to download my photos before the pups wanted dinner and it was time to cook those veggies I harvested earlier for Gerry and me. I stole a few minutes with my Kindle while the beets were boiling but that was the extent of my reading time for the day (until we climbed into bed later).

Today, I'm reading. Yesterday, I tasted the first few pages of a new book and am hungry to get lost in it in between watering and weeding and harvesting. Now, if only the smoke would clear so I could read outside. That's the best of summer for me.

Journal Entry - July 26, 2021

I feel the tentacles of depression reaching toward me. The invitingness of the darkness entices me to fall into it. The wrestling it takes to keep it at bay is exhausting.

The smoke. The smoke. The smoke.

Tuesday, July 27, 2021

I'm heading out this morning for an overnight trip to see my girls and take in some Shakespeare. It's opening night for *The Tempest*, the play Makiya's been working on at theatre camp.

I enjoy solitary road trips. I load up on podcasts and find a perfect balance between listening to them and basking in silence. Inspiration finds me and I hear Divine whispers.

It's just a short trip (five or six hours each way), but I'm hoping for big things from it. Aside for a short visit with my girls and seeing the play, I'm seeking a much-needed reset and mental health boost and relief from the smoke. Yesterday, it was raining in Prince George. Sounds like pure bliss compared to here in Kamloops where we can't spend much time outside and ash falls from the sky.

Thursday, July 29, 2021

It's the morning after opening night of Shakespeare's *The Tempest* in which Makiya played Sebastian. I'm tired, and more than a little uncomfortable after a restless night and a flare up of a health issue. She's tired too, after weeks of rehearsals and now, long days, culminating with a performance, but when Laurinda heads off to work we settle in for a granddaughter-grandmother visit.

It's a rich and priceless time, when it's just the two of us. Conversation meanders, intimacies are shared, and our bond is strengthened. She drops some of the tween facade she feels compelled to wear, and I bask in the wonder of this growing young woman who captured my heart the moment I saw her, already wide-eyed and curious, moments after she was born.

Hours pass gently, full of nothing but "us", and too soon it's time for me to leave. She has to get ready for another full day, her mama will be home before long to deliver her to the theatre, and I've got hours of driving ahead of me. We stroll out to my car arm in arm, I toss my water bottle and purse on the passenger seat and push the door shut. I wrap both arms around her, and she does the same. "Grandma is the only person who is allowed to hug me," she declared in a moment of independence a month or so ago. I'll take it. As often and for as long as I can.

"I love you."

"Love you."

"I'll miss you."

"Me too."

And finally, I pull myself away.

"Good luck with your performance tonight," I tell her. "Break a leg!"

"Text me when you get home," she says.

And time stops.

Six words that are not extraordinary yet fat with other things beneath the surface. They say the things we've already spoken—I love you, I'll miss you—and more. "I'm growing up." "Time is shifting." "I've seen some of the danger in the world and I want to know that you're safe."

Once, a lifetime ago when I left my parent's home the words it was "phone me when you get home." Young, and somewhat contrary in my wrestling for independence, I'd pick up the phone and make the call begrudgingly. I'm home. I'm safe. With my children, it became text messages. Progress reports long the way. One word. *Clinton. Quesnel.* And finally, *Home.*

But this one, this girl of my heart, while she's been the deliverer of such progress reports, texting from the passenger seat while her mama is driving, has never been in the position of bidding farewell by herself, but, still, she knows how. Maybe it's a combination of politeness and growing-up-ness, but it's still wrapped in a blanket of care.

On the drive up the day prior I was contemplating the many ways the world is groaning and how I'm weary—so, so weary. I was thinking about how, just when it seemed like the COVID mess was starting to fade, the summer of forest fires began, and how I haven't regained whatever energy and enthusiasm I had before 2020 sucked it out of me. Now, I'm getting ready to leave the clear, clean air and blue skies of Prince George for the thick-with-smoke-and-ash-falling skies of Kamloops and I'll be forced to spend most of my time indoors again to wrestle with dark things.

The world—and my life—has shifted and it is shifting. I think that's how it's supposed to be, in a sense. I could, for sure, do without much of what we've just come through and the kicking and pushing as we try find our way to the light at the end, but there are transitions I treasure too.

Like my granddaughter asking me to send her a text when I get home.

Watching her turn and walk toward her house as I buckle my seatbelt.

Her life flashing before my eyes, and awe at the gift of watching her become.

Yes, it's still a beautiful and magical world

Summer, 2021

The smoky ghost of summer present settles in,

looking like it wants to linger.

Unbidden, unwanted,

stealer of things we longed for during the bleak mid-winter of 2020.

Gray dawn,

apocalyptic sunset

pretty in one sense,

tragic in another.

Ash on green beans
and unused patio chairs
and geraniums I water every day
and enjoy through a window.

Sore throats.
Burning eyes.
Headaches.

Consuming fire.
Lost homes, lost dreams,
lost towns.
Rage, in the name of
lost children, lost dignity,
lost lives.

We either know it all or nothing
depending on which side of the fence we stand
and who we stand with.

Evacuation alerts and orders.
"Go bags" packed and plans in place.

The cacophony of late-night banging on doors

and ringing doorbells.

Gas tanks full.

Eyes scanning the horizon (when the horizon can be seen).

We pray for rain, but no lightening

wind, but not too much.

Firefighters. First responders. Helicopter pilots. Evacuees.

Our mental health.

We smell it in our cars and in our homes.

It clings to our clothes like a codependent phantom.

Housebound again. Held hostage by a haint.

AUGUST 2021

Whiteboard

To tell you the truth I've lost track
of what's burning,
what's out,
what's under control,
and what's growing;
of evacuation alerts and orders
and which of these have been rescinded.

Here's what I know.

A whiteboard hangs on the wall in our laundry room
between the clothes dryer and the pantry cupboard.
We use it to keep track of our weekly commitments.

On the week of June 21st,

in place of scheduled hikes and coffee visits,

my husband scrawled these words:

Too hot.

I never heard of a heat dome

until one settled over us

driving us indoors behind closed windows and doors

with air conditioning labouring all day and night

to keep us comfortable

and safe.

We ventured out to water parched gardens

and for our dogs to tend to canine business,

not lingering,

because the heat was in the danger zone.

Then the dome moved on and the fires came

and my husband updated the whiteboard:

Too smoky.

We've had bad fire years before.

They say this will be the worst ever.

So, we stay indoors behind closed windows and doors

with the air conditioning labouring all day and night

so we can breathe.

We keep our eyes trained on the horizon

ever-alert for signs of new fires

until we can no longer see the horizon

for the smoke.

Now it's the first day of August.
For six weeks the whiteboard has announced nothing but heat and smoke.

I step outside with my blue plastic watering can

and give thirsty purple petunias a drink.

Washing ash off their leaves

ignoring the need to deadhead

suffocated by silence

and breathing smoke.

Inside, I stand at the window and squint

to see if there's anything of the hills in the distance

I can see through the smoke,

but there isn't.

The lights are on in the house in the middle of the day.

British Columbia is burning.

The world is groaning.

We need rain.

That's all I know.

Tuesday, August 3, 2021

Gerry arrives home from a three-day backpacking trip and I emerge from a weekend of solitude, looking forward to the return of a measure of routine. The garden calls. There are things to harvest, things to prune, things to pull, and, perhaps, things to plant. My gardening mojo is absent this year but we plod along, picking and puttering (Well, not really much puttering. It's been too smoky for that.)

I'm eying the beets and thinking pickles, Black Krim tomatoes are ripening, Swiss chard is plentiful, the freezer is filling with beans and there's more to come. And cucumbers? We're overrun.

Yesterday was a holiday (B.C. Day in these parts) and, while holidays don't mean much in retirement, they do seem to set the week askew somehow. I'll be confused until the upcoming weekend causes a reset. The holiday marks the halfway point of summer. It's been a smoky and strange one and I'm trying not to look too forward to autumn. It's hard though. Clear, crisp, smokeless air is a powerful lure.

Meanwhile, life goes on. Words get written. Books get read. Gardens get watered. Dogs get bathed. Salads get eaten.

Wednesday, August 4, 2021

It's the kind of morning that, a few months ago, would have had me saying "man, it's smoky out there." This morning I celebrate the joy of seeing distant hills through a smoky haze because it's been impossible to see much of anything for weeks. Everything's relative, isn't it?

I step out on the deck to take a quick photo with my phone and the air smells clean. Clean enough that I think I might sweep the ash from the deck and the patio later and spend some time out there with a book. That's after I harvest the garlic (it's ready later up here than it is down at my community garden) and tidy up the backyard garden. The fact that I'm considering either is cause to celebrate after week upon week of staying mostly indoors. All things pass. Sometimes, in the thick of it, I struggle to remember this. The many cycles of creation remind me again and again.

I don't know how long we'll have this clear-ish air, but I know we better get out and enjoy it while we can.

> *The White Rock Lake fire jumps Highway 97 about 40 kilometers southeast of Kamloops and tears through the community of Monte Lake. Thousands of people are ordered to evacuate the area.*

Thursday, August 5, 2021

I leave the house in good time for a scheduled coffee date with a new friend downtown. When I get in the car, I see the bags we use for vegetables harvested at the community garden in their space in the console and realize Gerry, who is down there working and harvesting, has nothing to put squash, cucumbers, and beans in. I look at the time. The garden's on the way. I have time to stop and give him the bags.

So, I do, but he's been resourceful and has bags of his own that are already filled. (See, the fact that he's down there working and watering without me overseeing the operation is evidence of my lackluster garden mojo and, perhaps, also a lesson in learning to let go.)

I glance at the clock as I pull out of the garden parking lot, comfortable that I'll be on time at the coffee shop, but as I near the intersection at the library I see the road is blocked off. It's farmer's market day. No worries. I make a left, thinking I'll maneuver close enough to the coffee shop to park and—surprise! —road construction and a detour. Okay. Think.

Long story made short, I take the detour and circle back, find a parking place relatively close to the coffeeshop and set off walking a couple of blocks, pausing at a parking meter to pay. The street noise seems especially loud. It's a sharp contrast to the silence of home. And I think if it wasn't for the opportunity of meeting with friends for coffee now and then I'd be tempted to become a hermit.

Anyway, I make it. With time to spare. And settle in for a couple hours of coffee and good conversation about life and writing (what a joy it is to have someone to talk about writing with!) and other random things. It's time very well spent.

By the time I get home, Gerry's left bags of vegetables on the kitchen counter. I wash and select which things to keep and which things to offer to neighbours. The day carries on with gratitude and thoughtful introspection as a result of the visit with my friend. Perhaps I'm not quite ready for the hermit life just yet.

It's Hard to Rest Easy

We wake to news

of evacuation alerts and orders

and reports of what hungry fires consumed while we rested.

It's hard to rest easy.

With daylight comes updated reports

of the monsters

consuming our forests and communities.

We don't want to look, but we have too.

'We're glad for wind that cleared smoke from our skies

so we can go outside

and do summer.

But not too glad.

Because we know the wind is partly to blame

for new alerts and orders.

Destruction.

Lives altered.

To celebrate clearer skies seems selfish.

Our hearts ache

for those who have lost,

for those who don't yet know what they've lost,

and for those on edge, with go bags ready.

We check district and city websites

that are slow,

stretched to their limit.

And the news, though we've grown disenchanted by the news.

And it's hard to rest easy.

Saturday, August 7, 2021

Like my gardening mojo, my canning mojo is in short supply this year too. Nevertheless, there are things to do, and this weekend it's tomato soup time. Other than jam, this will be the first canning I've done this summer. Crazy, when I think about previous years, but there it is. This year is different.

The world is different. This season is different, and if we expect life to return to what it was before 2020, the harder it is on us and the more likely it is that we'll miss lessons and opportunities. I try to remind myself of that when it all seems especially heavy.

Yesterday morning, I was out watering the petunias and potato vine in my front flower pots, observing the ash covering them that is especially apparent on the dark flowers and leaves I chose this year, and thinking about how the simple task of pouring water from a vessel to nourish pretty flowers enriches the few minutes it takes to do so every day. I did the same on the back deck for pots of pink geraniums, purple morning glory, brilliant mandevilla, and a multi-colored assortment in a hanging pot, and made a mental note to write an actual note to myself to plant a larger assortment of brightly coloured flowers on the deck next year. They're visible from inside the house and, if we're driven indoors like we are this year, provide an element of cheer. It's a simple adjustment that could make a big difference.

As always, I had such hope of spending copious amounts of time on the deck with books and my laptop, doing what I love: reading and writing. The heat dome, then the smoke, forced those plans to change. There's still time. I haven't lost hope. Meanwhile, the dogs and I curl up in the den when opportunity presents to lose myself in a good book or the sweetness of wrangling words for a blog post or essay. We adjust to change, not without lament, but with intention to find new ways to be in a changing world. This is just a small example, but I believe the principle scales up.

So, I'm canning tomato soup this weekend, and starting with 25 pounds of tomatoes rather than the customary 50 (I'll do more in the days and weeks to come, but I'm not killing myself to do as much in a day as I used to do). And I'm toying with the idea of not canning dozens of jars of tomatoes, but buying cases of tinned tomatoes for the winter (I know. Radical.) and, instead, taking the easier path of slow roasting Roma's with garlic and herbs and freezing the delicious result. (They are delicious done this way. I did it for the first time last year and got a bit fanatical about them.) I'm not canning dill pickles (but I am making beet pickles, just as soon as I get around to harvesting the beets), or coleslaw, or vegetable soup, or meatballs, or relish, or any of the other myriad of things I've put in jars in the past, but our freezer is filling with fruit, green beans, and pesto—and soon, roasted tomatoes.

Seasons change, the world changes, and (to borrow a mantra from my working days) we try, test, and adjust our intentions. Some wise person once said that the only constant is change and, surely, we must know that to be true by now.

Monday, August 9, 2021

I transform 25 pounds of field tomatoes into a dozen beautiful jars of tomato soup and roast two trays of Black Krims and I am exhausted. Absolutely spent. Once upon a time I could easily can 50 pounds of tomatoes in one day and, aside from a sore back and feet, still have a measure of energy left. Those days are behind me.

At one point during the afternoon, Gerry comes into the kitchen and hands me a beautiful salmon our neighbour just gave him.

"Dinner!" he says.

"You're joking," I tell him.

I'm grateful for the remnants of a quinoa salad in the fridge because there's no way I have energy to make anything for dinner, much less cook a beautiful fresh salmon. Tomorrow is another day.

When the last jars have been lifted from the pressure canner and are cooling on a kitchen towel, I feed the pups and we head down to the community garden to water and pick (still more) cucumbers. I eye the beets, and think about beet pickles that are up next on the canning roster. I'll need a couple days of rest before I tackle them. The mad canner has left the building. It's a new season. I don't need to can cucumber relish that nobody likes except me or watermelon rind pickles just to see what they're like. The freezer is my friend now. Wash, blanch, flash freeze, and bag—or, in the case of my favourite roasted tomatoes, wash, chop, sprinkle, drizzle, slow roast, bag—is a whole lot easier.

To everything there is a season.

Friday, August 13, 2021

We weren't sure it was going to happen this year because of the forest fires, and the weeks leading up to it seemed like a roller coaster ride of "it's happening" and "it's not happening", but it came together in the end and Gerry headed out yesterday morning. I'm on a solitary writing and reading retreat until he returns.

Watering

By the time I finish watering the garden

my head aches

my eyes burn

and my throat is sore.

It's not the pleasure it once was

before viruses and fires and smoke

changed the landscape.

This is not a poem

as much as lament

for summer past.

Saturday, August 14, 2021

By the time I finish watering the garden, my head aches, my eyes are sore, and there's that irritation in the back of my throat again. It is a hasty watering. I look past the odd weed and ignore the pruning and thinning and general tidying up I should tend to. Just enough. That's become my mantra in the garden this year—in pretty much everything, really.

The smoke is bad this morning. A woman arrives at the garden wearing a facemask. She lives in the condominium complex down the street—as do many others who garden here. I watch as she stops at a handful of plots and turns on the drip irrigation. She must have drawn the short straw today. At the tennis courts across the street from the community garden, two men wearing facemasks hit a tennis ball back and forth. Driving up the hill toward our neighbourhood, I spy an older man wearing headphones. I see him out walking often and wonder what he listens to. Books, I imagine. Mysteries or detective stories. Today he's wearing a facemask too.

The *Baroque and Beyond* program is on the *Symphony Hall* channel on Sirius XM, and there's a folk song playing. Folk music is not my usual cup of tea, but this morning it makes me think about people sitting around in a rustic cabin singing and, in the process, lifting one another's mood and taking their attention away from whatever outside forces threaten their safety and peace of mind. Maybe we could all use a little folk music right about now.

At home, the smell of slow-roasting tomatoes, garlic, and herbs greets me when I open the door from the garage into the laundry room. The dogs too—and we lumber down the stairs to make a quick trip out to the backyard to tend to some canine business. I roll an essential oil synergy on the back of my neck, around my forehead and temples to ease the headache, grab my MacBook, and settle in to wrangle words. But first, I gather my Bluetooth speaker and tune my phone to the *Symphony Hall* channel. The folk music is over, and there's a delightful piano concerto playing instead. Much more my style. Usually, when I'm home alone and on a self-imposed retreat, I favour silence, but this morning seems to need background music. So, I check on the roasting tomatoes, brew a mug of coffee, settle in with little Murphy on my side, open my journal, and the day unfolds.

What if?

What if the birds

put the word out

that three of the past five

summers

have been different

around here?

Nests burned

fledglings perished

and cries from fleeing fauna

and flaming flora

left indelible impressions

on avian brains.

So, they put the word out.

To those who migrate:

don't return. Find another, safer place to summer.

To natives: move on. It's impossible to breathe here in the smoke.

What if bossy, noisy stellar jays stopped coming?

What if robins no longer heralded spring?

What if the red feeders we hang in front of our windows

became barren decorations

that we took down

washed

and put away?

Journal Entry – August 17, 2021

It. Is. Raining.

Praise the Lord!

Tuesday, August 17, 2021

We're taking the pups outside to the ash-covered backyard. Maya and Murphy race past me and, thinking Gerry's right behind me, I leave the door open. We can't leave the door open for long or smoke creeps in, so I quickly look behind me and see he's not there.

"I thought you were right behind me," I call as I pull the sliding door closed.

A few minutes later, while I'm watching the dogs take care of business, he comes out.

"I heard you say something, but I couldn't make it out. It sounded like you said there's a tiger in the backyard."

I laugh because by now, it wouldn't surprise me. A tiger? Sure. Why not? Because a pandemic and a heat dome and drought and a province on fire and grasshoppers and apocalyptic skies and endless ash and charred pine needles falling aren't enough. Let's add a tiger to the mix. Nothing surprises me anymore. We watch the dogs and I lean into his arms, weary, so weary of it all.

"It feels like it's the end of the world," I say.

It does. And it doesn't. Until it does again. And I know, faith, but I trust you'll forgive me a moment (or more) of despair, because it's all getting a bit heavy.

Later, Gerry uses the power washer to wash the ash from the front sidewalk and the leaf blower to move ash from the lower patio, and when he comes in we're startled by thunder. And lightening. No one wants to see lightening around here right now. More thunder, more lightening, and—hallelujah! —a few drops of rain!

This morning, it's raining. It's still dark as I write this, but I can hear it in the downspout. It's a sweet, sweet sound. There are reports of mudslides, and I'm wary of what the day's news will bring. For now, I'm just rejoicing in the rain and praying for more.

Wednesday, August 18, 2021

Yesterday, I pulled on a long-sleeved shirt and put a little t-shirt on Murphy before we went out. The hottest days of summer are behind us. We're into a cooling trend (it was 10C / 50F when I got up this morning) and we enjoyed a smattering of rain the other day (please, oh please, send more). Late yesterday afternoon, the skies cleared and we took a breath (literally) of relief. Clear skies. It's been so long. After a number of very tense days, there was optimism on the forest fire scene. Rather than new evacuation orders, there were reports of alerts being rescinded. British Columbia is a long way from being out of the woods (pun unintended) on the forest fire front, but the slight respite yesterday was a welcome relief.

Still, I'm ready to call it. Buh bye summer. You were no friend of mine this year. I'm ready for crisp and colourful falling leaves, pumpkin spice lattes, flannel sheets, warm apple pie, fall mums, rain, rain, and more rain. I'm ready to say goodbye to never ending cucumbers on the vine, Swiss chard (that, again, I planted too much of), tomatoes (hurry up and ripen so I can roast you), the second crop of beans, beets (okay, I'm not ready to say goodbye to beets), and lettuce and radishes for salad that I don't really want anymore. I'm ready to put away flower pots fat with petunias that I never deadheaded because it was too smoky to spend that much time outside; to sweep ash and charred pine needles from the deck I barely spent time on; and to put away cushions for lawn furniture we didn't use. It's time to move on. Bring on fall.

On August 20, 2021, Dr. Henry hints that the province won't enter the fourth step of the restart plan in early September as planned. "It's very likely that we won't be seeing a move to any more loosening of restrictions in the near term." [72]

Friday, August 20, 2021

I'm in the living room at my daughter's house. It's early, and Daughter and Granddaughter are still sleeping. The only sound is that of the refrigerator running and my fingers tapping on the keyboard. I'm enjoying the first quiet moments of the day to gather my thoughts and offer prayer while I wait for Starbucks to open. (Laurinda doesn't drink coffee and the shop is just around the corner so what's a woman to do?)

We enjoyed watching Makiya and the rest of her theatre group perform in *How To Survive Being in a Shakespeare Play* last evening. It was a fun and rollicking production that kept us in stitches from start to finish. Man, it felt good just to laugh! I have no photos because it was an evening just to be present.

We'll spend time visiting this morning before I head toward home. Laurinda's officially on vacation starting today, so the girls will follow in a few days for the last visit of summer.

Summer's winding down. Can you feel it? There's a definite something in the air these days. Makiya will perform once more this evening, then that's it for summer theater camp. I saw on social media yesterday that the iconic pumpkin spice latte is returning to the menu at Starbucks next week. It might be a tad early to partake, but it's just another sign of changing seasons. Bring it. I'm beyond ready.

When I get home, we'll harvest the beets (Assuming they're still there. There are reports of widespread theft in the community garden again.) and I'll make pickles and freeze greens. Aside from that, we'll continue to wait for, and roast as they ripen, Black Krim tomatoes; pick cucumbers and give them away; freeze basil, and do something with the mountain (again, this year) of Swiss chard that I'm ending up with. I'm about ready to wind down the community garden plot. There are still carrots in the backyard garden—I look at them and think soup. Yes, we're definitely on the cusp of autumn. I've got a long drive ahead. I'm loaded up with podcasts though I feel more drawn to listen to classical music this trip. Podcasts inspire deep thinking and I'm more in need of something else as I head toward home and a changing season.

Sunday, August 22, 2021

I'm sitting here listening to the sweet sound of rain. RAIN! At long last!

---

[72] https://www.cbc.ca/news/canada/british-columbia/covid-19-bc-update-aug-20-1.6147651

The heavy weight of fire season is still with us but with many alerts and orders being rescinded and fires being brought under control, there is an easing of the burden. Skies, though not completely smoke free, are clear enough to enjoy spending time outside. The respite comes just as I felt close to crumbling. Of course, there are other things; there are always other things. But I look up at clouds that are finally visible without the cloak of oppressive smoke hiding them, and see hope. In the backyard, Gerry is laying out supplies and preparing to enlarge the footprint of our garden. Already, I am anticipating next year's planting. And, today, I am looking forward to my girls arriving later for one last summer visit.

Without such glimmers of hope, life becomes difficult to muddle through. Days grow long and dark when there seems little to look forward to. My faith helps with that, but let's be real, some days it's just not enough. Some days it's more difficult to find joy sparkers. That's one reason I started keeping a vase of fresh flowers on my dining table last when the madness started in 2020. It's a simple thing, but it helps. With all the big things prone to steal my peace, it's often the little things that restore it.

Like the blue sky I just noticed out the window.

Or the deep and regular breathing of my dogs when they sleep.

Or the box of beets on my washing machine that I'll cook and pickle today.

Or a moment of prayer.

Thank you.

Today promises to be a busy one despite it being the sabbath. We'll take time for Zoom church, then I'll get busy in the canning kitchen and Gerry will work in the yard and our girls will arrive later and somewhere along the way I'll figure out what to make for dinner. There will be hugs and laughter and the heaviness that tries so hard to claw its way in will be kept at bay.

On August 23, 2021, Dr. Henry announces implementation of the B.C. Vaccination Card program. A "vaccine passport."

"Starting Sept. 13, 2021, proof of vaccination will be required in B.C. for people attending certain social and recreational settings and events [requiring] individuals to provide proof of vaccination to access a broad range of social, recreational, and discretionary events and businesses throughout the province. As of Sept. 13, one dose of vaccine will be

> *required for entry to these settings. By Oct. 24, entry to these settings will require people to be fully vaccinated at least seven days after receiving both doses. To enter certain spaces, including indoor ticketed sporting events, indoor and patio dining in restaurants, fitness centres, casinos and indoor organized events, like conferences and weddings, people aged 12 and older will be required to show their proof of vaccination."* [73]

Monday, August 23, 2021

A local news source often prefixes its early morning social media posts with "what you need to know". It gets my back up. I don't like the news media telling me what I need to know for many reasons, none of which I'll go into here. Rather, I scroll past and think about what I do need to know on this beautiful August morning. Here are a few things.

My girls arrived safely yesterday afternoon and are fast asleep downstairs.

Everyone in this house is safe and healthy.

Gerry is heading out early this morning to get soil for my new raised garden beds.

I have to tend to some Story Circle Network business this morning.

Six beautiful jars of beet pickles rest on the kitchen counter and need to be taken downstairs and put on the shelf.

There's a big bag of beet greens in the laundry room that I will blanch and freeze today.

Today, the four people in this house will work and play and enjoy hugs and laughter and good conversation. We don't have to agree on every single jot and tittle in order to get along, be respectful, and love one another.

Tuesday, August 24, 2021

We talk almost daily, but the opportunity to chat face-to-face for hours with my daughter about light and heavy things, things we agree on and others we don't, is simply priceless. These are trying times. Having safe places to talk about hard things is more important than ever. So, we do. And there is silly laughter and tears but, mostly, there is love.

These are hard days. We need safe places and safe people and respite from the cacophony. I want these things for myself and I want to create a haven

---

[73] https://news.gov.bc.ca/releases/2021HLTH0053-001659

for those in my sphere. It's not easy. We get distracted—I get distracted. But we begin again to seek peace and reason wisely.

This morning, the sky is blue and the air is clear. It will be a good day to go outside, spend time in nature, and focus on the natural world rather than the abnormal and slippery slope we find ourselves living on.

> *On August 25, 2021, Dr. Henry announces a new order mandating the wearing of non-medical facemasks in all indoor public spaces in the province, including for school children in Grade 4 and up.* [74]

Wednesday, August 25, 2021

Suddenly, I am alone. The girls are behind searching for rocks along the river, and Gerry is resting with his eyes closed at the car. I am struck by the silence and the peace of this place and stop to breathe prayer. For a moment, all that is, is here and now. I hold a stone my daughter gave me in my hand. There's a special little thing about it that she pointed out when she gave it to me. It initiated a short conversation about natural gifts, and I thought about a little piece of twig I have in my office. My granddaughter gave it to me when she was three years old. Sometimes I pick it up and think back the moment she handed it to me. Maybe this stone will serve, in a similar way, as a marker of an afternoon when we three went into nature to escape the madness of the world.

"Listen," I say to my daughter when she catches up to me.

She stops, closes her eyes, and takes in the sound of silence that punctuates water sounds of the river we have just come from.

Peace.

Selah.

Friday, August 27, 2021

I thought by now life would have resumed much of its pre-2020 look and feel. That's what the provincial "restart plan" told us, anyway. Instead, I feel like I'm in an old movie where the walls are slowly closing in around me. It's heavy and it's getting heavier and now we're heading into the dark months. I don't know about you, but as much as I'm looking forward to fall, I recognize the need to prepare for the changing season by intentionally putting into place practices to strengthen and support my emotional and physical self.

---

[74] https://news.gov.bc.ca/releases/2021HLTH0053-001665

Mine will be grounded in faith. I will stumble, but I'll get back up.

I'll make intentional choices.

Embrace the power of the written word.

Keep my eyes and heart open to simple, ordinary joy sparkers that will maintain focus on what matters.

Figure out how much is just enough of the news, and be mindful of where I get it.

Keep my home as a sanctuary.

Make no apologies for saying no. Or yes.

Eat healthy. Stay hydrated. Up my intake of Vitamin D. Be mindful of my carbohydrate intake (this one is tough).

Go outside to quiet places where I can hear myself think.

Establish a new routine and allow it to flex as needed.

Pray and keep watch.

Sunday, August 29, 2021

I'm not canning as much as I have in recent years. Rather, I'm relying more on my freezer to preserve the harvest and the bounty we get from the green grocer. This morning there's a container of chocolate cupcakes Makiya made on my counter instead of canning jars. Seasons change. I'm going to roast the rest of the tomatoes from my garden, and buy a case or two of Roma's and roast them too. Then, I'm calling it done.

This week we'll pull the cucumber vines and decide whether to pick the rest of the tomatoes and let them ripen indoors. I often do this as a safeguard against theft, I'm sorry to have to say. There's still lots of Swiss chard that will see us through until frost, same with carrots. It's turning into soup time, and these will fit the bill nicely. I'm weary of gardening and canning and ready for change. We'll enjoy this week with Makiya and then settle into fall regardless of what the calendar says.

Lord, it's already heavy. Help us keep our focus on what truly matters in the coming months.

What did we talk about?

What did we talk about

Before?

When we went about our days

too busy

or not busy enough

carrying burdens

big and small

with enough left over

to take weight

for a time

from those whose load was too heavy.

What did we talk about
Then?

Before we became
Us and Them.

When we listened
and debated with honour
or remained silent.

When we granted grace,
knowing we didn't see the full picture
of anything.

When we didn't need to know your position

on A, B, and Z

to decide if you were of Us or Them.

And when,

if we caught a whiff of disagreement,

we wouldn't cut you out of our life.

What on earth

did we talk about

before the world's groaning grew audible

and the noise deafened us

and we formed warring tribes?

Tuesday, August 31, 2021

After a busy morning out and about that included a trip to Costco because I wanted to get some pretty fall mums (of course, we came away with more than two pots of flowers), we settle in at home. Gerry heads downstairs to check his hiking schedule and make plans, Makiya reaches for my MacBook to write, and I put my feet up to browse through a flyer that arrived in the mail earlier.

I glance over at my granddaughter's furrowed brow as she ponders her story. Maya snoozes on the sofa next to her; Murphy is asleep on my lap. The only sound is Makiya tapping on the keyboard. There's nowhere I'd rather be, and nothing I'd rather be doing.

SEPTEMBER 2021

On September 1, 2021, the availability of booster doses of the COVID-19 vaccine in B.C. is announced beginning with the elderly in long term care homes.

Wednesday, September 1, 2021
 A long and lovely drive along country roads refreshes. Leaves are just barely hinting they're soon to don their autumn cloaks. We drive past farms and fields and imagine how peaceful it would be to live out here. Gerry reminisces about driving this road with his dad when he first got his learner driver's license. We enjoy a beautiful afternoon walking along a boardwalk, chatting with people who were smitten with our tiny pocket dog and wondering if he is full grown, and just enjoying one another's company. Grandfather, Grandmother, Granddaughter, Maya, and Murphy. We make a grand team. After our walk, we stop at a candy store and load up with a ridiculous amount of fudge. We take the slow way back home favouring country roads over highways. It's a good choice. We arrive, weary but rested at the same time. Seems strange, but it's true. A simple choice, like which road to take, made a world of difference. Food for thought, yes?

Thursday, September 2, 2021
 I bake bread and serve it fresh from the oven with homemade soup.
 "This is one of my favourite suppers," Gerry says.
 "Mine too," responds Makiya, munching on another piece of bread

snitched from my plate after she asked, with a cheeky grin, if I was going to eat it. This is the richest moment of my day.

Saturday, September 4, 2021

I canned the last of the beets from my garden yesterday. Gerry's going to head to the local green grocer early this morning to snag 25 pounds of Roma tomatoes (they go fast, so one has to be there early) and I've asked him to get beets so I can process a few more jars. I'm going to slow roast the tomatoes and will go through a few more boxes before the season is over. My kitchen will be a fragrant place today.

We're making adjustments downstairs and I'm doing a long-overdue purge of the closet in my woman cave in preparation for our daughter and granddaughter coming to stay with us for an extended time. That's the big news around here. Laurinda's work is transferring her here to Kamloops. Makiya is already here and will start school on Tuesday. Laurinda will follow in a few weeks. They will both stay with us until Laurinda finds a place of their own.

This is a grandma's dream come true and an answer to many, many prayers. We are thrilled to be able to help ease the burden of solo parenting that weighs heavy on Laurinda. More grand days with Makiya? Sign me up! There are adjustments to be made, but we'll figure them out along the way. Meanwhile, after many years, I'm thinking ahead to school lunches and homework and after school activities.

Sunday, September 5, 2021

I am not as young as I once was. It doesn't trouble me, in fact, I embrace this season of my life full on. I wouldn't trade these years for anything, but occasionally unexpected things look me in the face and say "you're not a young woman anymore." Yesterday, I canned one last batch of beets and, with that, I'm declaring canning season over. I wrote before about how I'm paring down my canning activities this year. I have mixed feelings about the decision, but I'm sticking with it.

Thinking about school lunches, I also baked oatmeal cookies and bran muffins (Gerry did a happy dance when I announced that I was going to bake), and chopped raw veggies to have on hand for the week. I realized early on that baking while babysitting a pressure canner wasn't the wisest choice, but carried on nonetheless. There's more I intended to do, but by the time I pulled the last tray of muffins out of the oven I was done and seriously thinking about a nap, but we had other things to tend to. I begged off cooking dinner by declaring family pizza and movie night, and by the time I climbed into bed I was too tired to read more than a page.

This morning I slept late. Waking around 7 a.m. doesn't allow for the anywhere near the amount of quiet morning time I like, so that was disappointing. It reinforced for me that my weariness yesterday was real and that I need to give myself permission to do one thing not ten things at the same time. Isn't it lovely that life continually offers opportunities for us to learn and grow?

Wednesday, September 8, 2021

Makiya rocks her first day of grade seven. After days of her asking to make sure I'll pick her up afterwards, she walks toward me on the sidewalk at the end of the shortened first day with a new buddy.

"This is my friend, Sawyer. Can we walk home together?"

Turns out Sawyer lives at the other end of the street we live on and is also new to the school this year. Two new kids connecting on the first day of school. What's not to love about that?

There's a lot going on. I'm not talking about "out there" (but, yeah, there is still a lot going on out there). There's a lot going on with the three people calling this place home right now. September is going to go by in a whirlwind. It will take slow and steady intention, with a healthy measure of down time, so as not become overwhelmed. (Note to self.)

After supper (newly dubbed Taco Tuesday) we remain at the table and coordinate calendars. I see this becoming a regular practice in the coming weeks. It's a good opportunity to get organized, but also to talk and connect and make plans. A family meeting of sorts, as we figure out new routines. Then Grandfather and Granddaughter do the dishes while I take the dogs out to the backyard. It's partly a ruse to allow the kitchen cleanup crew to finish their work. Maya is ready to go inside long before me, but I'm comfortable sitting in a chair taking in the beauty of my surroundings and breathing clean air, so I make her wait. *Just a little longer, girl.* Murphy is content to stay out as long as possible. Turns out, he's a sun dog.

The day winds down and Gerry and I stay up later than we're used to because an almost thirteen-year-old girl isn't going to go to bed at absurdly-early-thirty. It's all good. Just another adjustment we'll adjust to in the coming weeks. And, we're off and, if not running, sprinting into a new school year, new routines, and a new season.

Friday, September 10, 2021

Makiya is off to school, Gerry just left for a hike, the pups are snoozing and I'm finally taking some time to write this post. The first week of school comes to an end today. It's been a good week—a different week—but one rich with good things.

I'm proud of how well Makiya is adjusting to her new school and the arrangement here at Camp G &G while we wait for Laurinda to join us. It's an adjustment for all concerned, but the biggest one is hers and she's handling it like a champ.

Mornings are quiet in a different way now as my body adjusts to new routines. For the time being, my 4 a.m. quiet time is pushed forward and cut short. I'm quite delighted with the quiet of a house after everyone has left in the morning, though. It's reminiscent of many, many years ago and invites me to nest.

I have such appreciation for clear air and blue skies after the horrific fire season and am taking advantage of every opportunity to go outside and soak them up, even if it's just a few minutes in the afternoon for an after-school chat with Makiya.

On September 11, the Royal Inland Hospital in Kamloops announces it is hiring more nurses as it struggles with understaffing.

Saturday, September 11, 2021

A stellar jay lands on a chair on my deck. I stop chopping tomatoes and watch as he hops from the chair to the railing and back again. They he takes flight, and I lose sight of him through the morning glory growing on the lattice. He is the first of his kind I've seen up close this year. A month ago, when the smoke was thickest, I'd step outside with the dogs into eerie silence. No birds. No nothing. Just suffocating smoke. Now, at random moments in the day, I step out onto the deck or the lower patio and watch an assortment of birds flit from tree to tree and dance glorious and free minuets in the sky.

Things pass. Seasons change. We learn to be grateful for the simplest of things. And all those days in which I prayed for just enough grace/peace/energy for the next twenty-four hours, culminate in a moment where I stand in the kitchen, put down my knife, and watch a blue stellar jay deliver joy.

On September 13, 2021, Dr. Henry announces that two doses of the COVID-19 vaccine will be required for workers in all B.C. health care facilities by October 26, 2021. Those choosing not to be vaccinated will be placed on unpaid leave. Some businesses begin requiring proof of vaccine (aka the vaccine passport) for entry.

Monday, September 13, 2021

These are good days. Different, but good. We are adjusting to new routines that come from having our granddaughter, Makiya, with us and the changes have brought gifts. Just now, I'm sitting in a quiet house (well, except for our Yorkie, Maya, who has spotted someone outside and is letting me know about it). Makiya is at school and Gerry is out hiking. The house smells inviting thanks to the combination of tomatoes, garlic, and herbs I just took out of the oven. I'll tuck the mixture in the freezer once it cools for future dinners. The bowl I mix bread dough in is sitting on the counter, waiting for me to finish this post. I've left an apple on the counter to remind me to mix up an apple crisp later this afternoon for dessert this evening. These small things make me content.

Earlier, Gerry and I took a second cup of coffee out to the backyard where, as the dogs wandered and enjoyed the sunshine, we sat and chatted about this-and-that. It's moments like that I once dreamed about when I was still working. We talked about what it's like having our granddaughter with us and agreed—it's nothing but good.

I love the cooler September weather. Mostly, I love the clean air. The little sanctuary I created on my deck that got hardly any use this summer, is autumn-pretty and inviting. I sit out there for a few minutes in random minutes throughout the day watching birds and enjoying the flowers. We attended church yesterday—in person! —and came away feeling like we had been well fed on many levels. Like I said, these are good days. Different, but oh-so-good.

On September 14, B.C. lifts the state of emergency enacted to support wildfire support in the province. "While the provincial state of emergency is no longer required, the wildfire season is not over. It is vital that the public remain prepared and follow the continued direction of local authorities.

As of this date "205 wildfires are burning in B.C., with three evacuation orders affecting approximately 223 properties and 12 evacuation alerts affecting approximately 254 properties. Overall this year, 1,585 fires burned 868,619 hectares in the province.

> *"At the height of the summer, 3,631 personnel were helping fight the fires, including support from Mexico, Australia and across Canada. Approximately 32,000 people were displaced, and 19,807 people registered with Emergency Support Services."*[75]

Wednesday, September 15, 2021

September is one of my favourite months and we're midway through it already. In the spirit of embracing this month of transition, I thought I'd consider sensual things it offers.

I see...
leaves on trees hinting of change
the smiling face of our granddaughter
a flock of birds undulating across the sky
a bear strolling by while Gerry and Makiya are in the backyard kicking a soccer ball around
dang fruit flies

I hear...
rain dripping in the downspout (such a sweet, sweet sound!)
"Grandma!"
kids laughing
dogs snoring
the pop of the thing in the middle of the game of *Trouble* that rolls the dice

I smell...
apple pie baking
tomatoes, garlic, and herbs roasting
African sweet potato stew simmering
clean air (i.e. the absence of smoke)
fresh basil

I feel...
the grip of a serrated knife in my hand as I chop tomatoes
spiderwebs cling to me in the garden
the arms of my granddaughter around me when we share hugs
chilly, like it's almost time to put socks and shoes on

---

[75] https://news.gov.bc.ca/releases/2021PSSG0056-001784

I taste . . .
pumpkin spice frappuccinos; they are like drinking pumpkin pie (yum)
warm bread
hot soup
frozen yogurt
just-picked carrots

Saturday, September 18, 2021

I'm in Prince George. Makiya and I drove up yesterday because she has an appointment with her orthodontist today. It'll be the last one here; Laurinda will have to get her hooked up with one in Kamloops going forward.

It's a long drive and it rained the whole way. No complaints about the rain after experiencing the effects of a tinder dry province on fire this summer. The autumn colours were beautiful—more so than we're seeing in Kamloops so far. We enjoyed a balance of good conversation and healthy pockets of silence along the way. Last evening, Laurinda and I watched a movie we've been wanting to see called *Four Good Days*. It was intense. I'm glad we had the opportunity to watch together.

My writing group meets today and, thanks to the magic of Zoom, I can still attend. I'm looking forward to hearing the stories the women have written this month. Just now, I'm sitting up in bed tapping out these words and thinking about coffee. It's time to get moving.

Sunday, September 19, 2021

I'm waking up at my daughter's house this morning. There is a big tree growing outside of her bedroom window. It's beautiful, and a little gnarly. It shelters her sanctuary in a home that has served as a blessing and a place of healing since she moved here a few years ago. She is in transition. Weeks away from packing up everything and moving. In a sense, she is going home, but the magnitude of change is no small thing.

As I look out the window at this tree, I am thinking that one day, in the not-too-distant future, it will no longer fit the role it now plays in providing shelter. It will outgrow this space and, left to itself, will begin to cause harm to the home it now guards. Roots may disturb the foundation of the house and the deck in front of it. Its branches may reach into the newly shingled house and cause damage.

I wonder who planted it, and if they sometimes drive by this house and think about the memories they made here and realize they planted it too close to the front door. The day will come when it is time to cut it down. My daughter will have long since moved on and will call another place home. I don't know who will look out this window at this tree and whether, in their eyes, it will look like shelter or just something blocking their view.

So, I honour it, this home, and my daughter's journey, by pausing to admire a tree that links the past with the future growing in surroundings that are not necessarily conducive to good evergreen health. One day it will be gone. Those who walk past every day will forget about it. Neighbours will change and, one day, there will be no one left who remembers it. The woman—my daughter—who lives in the house that this tree now shelters will have stepped into a new life. Perhaps she'll keep the memory of this tree as a marker of an important stage in her journey that moved her forward.

Wednesday, September 22, 2021

Today I have:
1. prayed
2. laughed
3. enjoyed a quiet cup of coffee when I was the only one awake in the house
4. taken a shower and gotten dressed
5. made the bed
6. talked with Gerry about something important
7. talked with Makiya about other important things
8. blanched and froze green beans
9. offered suggestions on what to take to school for lunch
10. said "no" to a half-hearted ask for a ride to school
11. lost a chess game
12. put dishes in the dishwasher
13. ground coffee and filled reusable Keurig pods
14. cuddled dogs
15. settled the littlest dog in a bed next to where I was working in the kitchen
16. given treats to dogs
17. sent an e-transfer to the dog groomer
18. sent a couple of emails
19. deleted a LOT of emails
20. made inquiries
21. stood at the window captivated by bright yellow fall mums on the back deck
22. hugged my husband
23. decided what to make for dinner
24. firmed up afternoon plans to get the pups to the groomer and back, and Makiya to theatre
25. watered the sunflowers on my dining table
26. fed the dogs
27. given Murphy his meds
28. sipped a lukewarm mug of coffee (still sipping)

29. checked in on the judging for a poetry competition I'm coordinating for Story Circle Network
30. enjoyed the silence
31. enjoyed the noise
32. watch smoke curl out of a neighbour's chimney
33. folded a sweatshirt that I restored to its former white glory and put it on Makiya's bed
34. doled out three sets of vitamins and taken said vitamins
35. tossed laundry in the washer
36. made the bed
37. felt content
38. groaned inwardly when my MacBook told me it needed to be plugged into a power outlet
39. tiptoed from the room to avoid waking a sleeping dog (it didn't work)
40. put a piece of paper on the kitchen counter so I won't forget to take it with me when I take Makiya to theatre
41. written a blog post

Saturday, September 25, 2021

Gerry and I have been retired for seven years and have grown accustomed to every day feeling like Saturday (except for the retirement gift of not having to go to busy places on the weekend like grocery stores and the like), but now, with a granddaughter in residence, Saturday feels like Saturday again.

I'm lingering, and may even enjoy a second cup of coffee before heading to the shower. It's going to be a stellar day and Gerry's going to head off on a hike. I don't know yet what Miss M and I will get up to, though I have a couple of ideas. There are tomatoes to roast and beans to harvest, neither of which is likely to garner much enthusiasm from Makiya. Ah, but these things must be done. We'll fit in some other things like a trip to the library and maybe she'll connect with some friends. Truth be told, I'm tired, and would be happy to spend the day on the deck with a book.

I have been writing mostly about surface things lately and, for the time being, that's okay. It keeps the writing muscles exercised. I want to get back to daily posting but am still trying to figure out new routines. We're still in transition. I find plenty of time for pondering as I go about these days and it's good. Peaceful. I'm content with the cadence. I'm not doing some things, but doing others. Listening and learning.

OCTOBER 2021

Sunday, October 3, 2021

It's a sunny Sunday afternoon and I'm listening to the sweet sound of laughter from my granddaughter and her new friend coming from downstairs. Next to me on the sofa in the den, the Yorkies are sound asleep. Gerry is out hiking. I'm taking a break from kitchen work where I've chopped carrots, onions, and celery for minestrone soup I'm going to make in the Instant Pot for supper. A boule of bread dough is rising next to the stove.

My mind is full of inspiration gleaned at the InScribe Christian Writers' Fellowship Fall Conference I attended virtually this weekend. I'm trying to figure out what comes next in terms of my writing. Do I want to tackle another big project? Focus on the kind of tight writing poetry demands? (I'm dabbling with it in my journal and am having a grand time.) Continue with the kind of posts I've been putting up here lately? Go deeper? Take a break? Branch out? Stick with blogging? Quit blogging? Get serious? Relax?

It's one of those thoughtful-but-scattered afternoons when I'm unlikely to resolve anything. Maybe I'll just pick up my book, put my feet up for a while, and think about it tomorrow.

> *On October 1, 2021, Dr. Henry announces that beginning on October 4 it will be mandatory for all students in B.C. schools, regardless of age, to wear facemasks.*[76]

> *On October 5, the B.C. government announces that all employees must be fully vaccinated (two doses) by November 22 or they will be put on unpaid leave. As of October 26, visitors to acute care hospitals will also be required to have two doses.*[77]

Thursday, October 7, 2021

The gardens are harvested, the sprinklers are blown out, and, today, the landscaper cut the grass for the last time this season. We have pulled out tender annual flowers from pots around the house. The hostas look yellow, and more than a little worse for wear, thanks to the cooler temperatures. This morning, Gerry cleaned the furnace filter and we clicked on the heat for the first time.

The trees are wearing their October finery and we haven't taken an opportunity to go for a drive to capture fall images with our cameras. Gerry and I have wondered if we missed the peak again this year and perhaps, we have. Lord willing, we will see another early autumn and have an opportunity then. This year is different. Then again, they all are, aren't they?

We're seeing things in the world I couldn't have imagined a couple of years ago. I do my best not to focus too much on the insanity and, rather, think about the better things. My mind is a whirlwind these days thinking about different things now that Makiya is with us. Good things, but things I haven't had to think about for a long time, like long division, school lunches, after-school activities, and bedtimes. It's better for me, and those in my household, if I remain balanced with my attention on the people in front of me—the ones I love and have a measure of influence in the lives of. That is my better

---

[76] https://news.gov.bc.ca/releases/2021EDUC0059-001880
[77] https://news.gov.bc.ca/releases/2021FIN0055-001915

work.

A few months ago, when we were in the midst of the worst of the forest fire season and every day seemed smokier than the one before, we were on perpetual high alert. That, on top of the angst of year two of the pandemic, wore me down. I looked forward to autumn and a fresh start and, while some of that has come to fruition, there is still so much that causes me anxiety—most of which I write about only in my private journal.

Just now, I'm looking outside at our back yard where the freshly-mowed grass is still green and the garden is barren. Pots of sunny yellow mums on the deck next to a bright pink mandevilla vine make me smile. The sky is blue, the air blessedly clear, and the temperature is cool but not cold. It's a beautiful October afternoon. I heard the "s" word spoken on the evening newscast but I think we're still a way away from the white stuff. One more week, that's all I ask, at least until we get Laurinda moved down from the north in ten days.

I'm still working on finding a new routine and figuring out what I want to say in this space. For now, I'm okay with just rambling. I hope you are too.

Sunday, October 10, 2021

As I lift my favourite mug toward my mouth the handle breaks, spilling soy milky frothy coffee all over myself. That's a troublesome way to start the day but maybe it reinforces my intention to stop with the soy milky frothy elixir first thing every morning. I'm starting a 16:8 intermittent fasting routine and soy milk in the morning is a cheat. I'm toying with switching to a good, but less satisfying in the morning, cup of peppermint tea. Or maybe maté tea. But, man, I'm going to miss that first cup of coffee. Maybe I'll establish a special routine to enjoy one delicious mug after 1:00pm every afternoon. Anyway, enough about the coffee.

When it gets light, I see a dusting of snow on the hills—the first of the season and a harbinger of what's to come. I snap a quick photo with my phone to mark the occasion.

Then church.

And a quick lunch.

And an afternoon of puttering in the kitchen to prepare a Thanksgiving meal for the three of us. I take an almost-embarrassing number of shortcuts with the menu—no, wait, they're not embarrassing at all. I'm 62-years-old and I've cooked more than my share of turkey dinners the long way. No apologies for taking a simpler route this year.

Makiya initiates the traditional "what are you thankful for?" conversation and when her turn comes around the first thing she says is that she's thankful to be living here in Kamloops. She goes on to name her new school and new friends and my own sense of gratitude grows as she speaks, thankful she's weathering the transition so well.

Tomorrow is officially Thanksgiving but I embrace the tradition of eating turkey on Sunday and enjoying rest and relaxation on Monday. And I need the rest this year. I'm weary. Bone weary. Skin weary. Organ weary. Every-part of me weary. There's much I could do today but I'll probably do very little. That's my plan anyway. We'll see how things unfold with the other two residents of this home who seem to have far more energy than I.

In five days, we'll travel and move Laurinda down from Prince George. There are many things to be thankful for this year. That's one of the biggest ones.

On October 12, Dr. Henry issues an order mandating the wearing of non-medical facemasks in all indoor public spaces by children aged five to 11. [78]

Tuesday, October 12, 2021

Two lonely pots of bright yellow mums are all that's left on the back deck. Gerry is busy outside bringing in pots and mats and outdoor furniture. The season is changing and we're inching toward waking up one morning to white—but not just yet. Please, not just yet. There was a hard frost overnight, and the rooftops in our cul-de-sac were white when I woke this morning. I'm putting on sweaters, pulling on socks, and pushing our feet into shoes after months of flip-flop freedom.

I haven't had coffee this morning and I have a headache. (I'm a little testy too, but we won't get into that.). Instead of coffee, I'm enjoying a second mug of a blend of Yerba maté, black tea, and red rooibos flavoured with bits of sweet cocoa, chocolate and almond, pistachio nuts, macadamia nuts, and coriander rounded off with warm hazelnut and cinnamon.

Here I am on this Tuesday that feels like a Monday morning, sipping my maté tea, looking at these lonely mums on the deck, and waiting. For what, I'm not quite sure, but it feels like a time of anticipation so I might as well embrace it.

Saturday, October 16, 2021

We're in Prince George. It's early. I'm the only one up and relish these moments of quiet before the busy day ahead. Murphy is wrapped in a blanket and snoozing in my arms. I'm surrounded by boxes and things waiting to be loaded into the U-Haul parked in our daughter's driveway. I'm debating

---

[78] https://www.theglobeandmail.com/canada/british-columbia/article-covid-19-vaccine-mandate-now-in-effect-for-long-term-care-assisted/

whether or not I should make a Starbucks run. I've been caffeine free for a couple of days and have a low-grade headache. Coffee now and start the detox all over again? Or take some ibuprofen and brew some tea? Dealing with a headache today doesn't thrill me, and I'm leaning in the direction of Starbucks.

It occurred to me a few minutes ago that, if we get the big things loaded today, we'll have nowhere to sit or sleep later. I'm not sure how all that's going to come together. This time, I'm just a worker bee. I'll let Gerry and Laurinda figure that out.

On the drive up yesterday, I enjoyed the changing fall scenery. We passed through different microclimates and, as a result, saw autumn in different forms. All beautiful. All whispering of winter. I expect I'll drive solo on the return trip (Gerry driving the truck, Laurinda and Makiya in her car) and look forward to podcasts peppered with times of silence. But first, there's a truck to load. It's time to get moving.

Sunday, October 17, 2021

I'm in the drive-thru, behind a long snake of red taillights, waiting to place my order. These days I never know if an establishment is open for dining-in, or if there are other rules in place I've lost track of since I stopped force feeding myself a steady diet of news. The drive-thru is usually the best option, except when an establishment has closed early like the one I stopped at two-and-a-half hours ago when I really needed caffeine.

There's a scrolling marquee on a building across the highway—a pub and restaurant. *Help Wanted.* I see these words on posters tacked to shop windows, on sandwich boards out front of businesses, and now here—in lights. I won't speculate on the reason behind shortages of employees that require businesses to reduce hours and services while, at the same time, people are losing their jobs for choosing bodily autonomy over compliance to government mandates. It's an upside down inside world, and I'm weary.

My car has finally inched to the front of the line and a masked young man extends a device on a long pole through a plexiglass barrier that I tap a plastic card on to pay for my order. Then I wait. It turns out to be one of the longest I've waited for my order in a drive-thru. I watch the scrolling red Help Wanted words and think about the fact that this isn't the same world I grew up in and it's not the same world my children grew up in but it is the world my grandchildren will grow up in. This groaning, changing, confusing world is the one we've got now.

Unbelievably, after nineteen months, we still haven't reached the After. And, man, I'm weary. I'd bet money that you are too. In the early days, we talked about how the world wouldn't be the same after this—and it won't. We asked ourselves how we ourselves might be changed through this trial. Now we challenge ourselves, our behaviour and beliefs, and ask "is this who

I want to be?" We've lost a lot. We're still in the middle and we're grieving. Denial. Anger. Bargaining. Depression. Acceptance. Over and over again like a marble spinning on a roulette wheel we bounce from phase to phase praying we'll land on a space that kicks us out of this cycle of perpetual grief.

Letting go is hard. I think of tears in my granddaughter's eyes as the pressure of the move and the ache of leaving her home took hold. Once we let go, we can extend our reach toward the future, but the letting go part is hard. It hurts. It's scary—terrifying, actually—and we're all in the midst of a long letting go. No wonder we're tired. I don't claim to know a lot but I know for sure that what *was* isn't what *is* or *will be*. I'm kidding myself if I'm still waiting for "things to get back to normal".

The masked man appears at the window and extends his hand through the window with my order.

"Thank you."

"Yup. You have a good evening."

"You too."

We see a lot of discord these days and every encounter we are part of or observe chips away at something within us. Maybe simple pleasantries help counteract the turmoil and in some small way heal something in this broken world. Maybe a butterfly flapping its wings can influence change around the world. Maybe *maybe* is all we've got right now and it has to be enough.

Wednesday, October 20, 2021

In the morning, I catch up on Story Circle Network business while Gerry runs errands, then we spend a chunk of the day organizing and rearranging. I make an apple pie, because that's what you do in October, and while it bakes, I brew a cup of soy milky frothy coffee (my first of the day) and put my feet up. The rest doesn't last, but I enjoy the few minutes I squeeze out.

It's Taco Tuesday, a new and loose tradition we established with Makiya, so supper is easy. Tacos and apple pie. I know, it's a strange combination. What can I say? We play a game of *Clue* while we enjoy desert. Usually, the game confuses me, but this time I win. Maybe weariness is my *Clue* superpower.

At one point during the night, I realized I was awake. It was the strangest thing. Middle of the night waking is usually a gradual awareness of moving into liminality. This time it was different. I simply and suddenly realized I was wide awake. I prayed for a while, rolled over, and returned to sleep easily. Perhaps what was needed was accomplished.

This morning I'm stealing away for a 90-minute float in a sensory deprivation tank. Part of me is afraid I'll fall asleep and miss the experience. Another, perhaps wiser, part of me believes that, like my nighttime wakefulness, what is needed will be accomplished.

Meanwhile, the three adults, one twelve-year-old, two Yorkies, and one cat who live in this house for the time being are settling in and finding our way. We older folks are learning our limits. And so it goes.

Saturday, October 23, 2021

I'm sitting here in the den, cozy under a Sherpa blanket and sipping a mug of Yerba mate tea. The dogs are curled up next to me—also on Sherpa blankets—and have gone back to sleep. We're the only ones up. I glance out the top of the window and see two lights in the sky. One, a twinkling star, the other, I'm almost certain, is a satellite because it's moving ever-so-slowly across the sky. But maybe I'm wrong. Who knows? The point is that I have a moment of doubt when I look up at stars in the sky and wonder what is real and what isn't. This is the world today.

When I was in school studying computer science, there were modules about artificial intelligence. We even designed rudimentary applications using the technology. I thought it was cool. Now, the concept of AI fills me with dread. I find myself paying more attention to what's right in front of me, and less to the elusive "out there" that I can't influence or, increasingly, believe. I lean on my faith and timeless and eternal truth that doesn't change in light of this global groaning—perhaps especially in spite of this global groaning.

Things from yesterday don't necessarily translate to today. I have to let go in order to move forward. I have to release my steely grip on "if only" and "that's the way we've always done things" not because I want to, but because I have to, lest I shatter and be rendered useless. While I might wish to remain safe and comfortable in my Sherpa-safe nest, even here there are unreasonable facsimiles that can easily shake my faith and hinder my ability to focus on that which I was created for. So, I hold close my trust in the Divine. I whisper prayers, find peace in words, and look for wisdom and wonder in creation. I remind myself of my belovedness—and yours—and let the remembering guide me.

I am tired. You're probably tired, in some degree, too. This is a hard slog we're pushing through and it's made even more difficult by paradoxes and deceptions and shifting sand and downright evil. Find your true north. Set a course. And when you drift, be kind to yourself as you work to get back on track. Seek wisdom, be discerning, firm when necessary, and focus on the better thing in front of you. Remind yourself of your purpose. Believe in your belovedness.

Sunday, October 24, 2021

We spend a beautiful afternoon together at the Adams River salmon run. Every school kid in Kamloops visits the salmon run and learns about the incredible life cycle of salmon. The first time I took Laurinda, she was ten days old and tucked in a Snugli on my chest. For Makiya, this is something new. The main event happens once every four years and the next one will happen in 2022. So, while it isn't a significant run, we see enough to explain what happens to Makiya and soak up a healthy measure of family time and the outdoors in the process.

It is impossible for me to spend time in creation without being in awe of the Creator, and this day is no different. I walk on the soft forest floor pausing, now and then, to rest my hands on the bark of tall black cottonwoods. A squirrel scurries along a log, startling a couple trying to photograph the salmon. We stop to examine interesting fungi. Gold leaves dance as they fall toward the ground. The aromatherapy of forest (punctuated with the odd whiff of salmon) does a work. There is laughter, light conversation, and pockets of silence. It's a sweet, sweet time.

Eventually, we make out way to the riverbank and walk along the rocky shore. Laurinda looks for special stones. Makiya is fascinated by the odd salmon that has done its final work and now lies dead, giving the rest of itself to the ecosystem. Gerry trundles ahead, seeking a destination. I pull out my phone and take a few photos. Content. Nothing but content. Wrapped in a Divine embrace and at peace with my family.

Monday, October 25, 2021

I'm having a quiet, albeit busy, Monday morning. With Makiya at school, Laurinda at work, and Gerry out hiking, it's just me, Maya, Murphy (who, incidentally, joined our family one year ago today), and a pretty kitty named Chica who is still adjusting to being a Kamloopsian. Earlier, the dogs and the cat declared a truce, agreeing the living room was a conflict-free zone for the time being, and settled in for morning naps. I had to take photos to capture the occasion. They reflect Maya's disgruntled attitude about the whole cat thing.

Supper boiled over in the oven the other night so one of my tasks today is to clean the oven. I don't know who invented self-cleaning ovens but I tip my hat to them. When the cleaning cycle started, predictably, there was some smoke in the kitchen. I pulled out the air purifier and decided that it was as good a time as any to deal with the garlic harvest that's been taking up space in my laundry room.

Fast forward a few hours and the garlic has been peeled, washed, minced, and tucked away in the freezer. The cleaning cycle is finished and I'm waiting for it to cool down so I can wipe out the oven. I've unloaded the dishwasher. The pets are sleeping again. Soon, Laurinda will arrive home for lunch break (she comes home at lunchtime and we have an opportunity for a few minutes of mother/daughter time in the middle of the day).

Maybe this afternoon I'll get lost in a book or tap out a few words on the piece I'm working on for writing group. It's a good day. It's a good life.

> On October 19, 2021 the City of Kamloops issues a statement requiring employees, contractors, and volunteers to be fully vaccinated by December 15 or be put on unpaid leave. [79]

> The deadline for health care workers to be fully vaccinated is reached and over 4,000 workers in the healthcare system have chosen not to be vaccinated. This includes 7% of employees in Interior Health region where we live—the highest rate in B.C. Non-urgent surgeries are postponed to cope with staffing issues. [80]

Friday, October 29, 2021

It's the kind of day that was the norm at this time of year when we lived in the Pacific Northwest, but that we rarely experience here in arid Kamloops. The sky is gray, clouds are low, and raindrops dance in puddles on the sidewalk. The rain washes away memories of the endless smoky skies, forest fires, and middle-of-the-night evacuations of the past summer. White lights wrapped around the trunks of leafless trees lining the main street give off a festive mood. It's early enough in the season that there's still a soft carpet of gold-coloured leaves underneath the bare branches. I'm walking toward a coffee shop to meet a friend and I'm carrying a burden. Most of us are, and on some days, they feel heavier than others.

A man walking quickly catches up to me on the sidewalk.

"Hello. How are you?" he asks with a friendly lilt.

I look sideways to see if I recognize him. No, he's just a random stranger wearing a smile on his face.

---

[79] https://cfjctoday.com/2021/10/19/kamloops-implements-vaccination-mandate-for-city-employees/
[80] https://bc.ctvnews.ca/thousands-of-b-c-health-care-workers-off-the-job-as-vaccination-deadline-passes-1.5638687

"I'm good. How are you? It's quite the rain we're having, isn't it?"

And in the space of a few feet, we have conversation about how we're both enjoying the weather—and, oh, is that barbershop gone now? —and in less than a minute, he strides ahead of me across the street while I hold back waiting for the walk signal.

It was a brief interaction, but I feel the weight on my shoulder's lift. My mind, clearer now, is grateful for the brief connection. I'm reminded of all that is good and pure and true in the world that has not changed, despite what the news media leads us to believe. We don't see the full picture. When I put the bulk of my attention on that which I see with my limited human eyes and neglect the unseen things, my burden becomes nearly unbearable. Sometimes it takes a simple moment or an encounter such as this one to shift my focus.

I look around. There's a man with tattoos on his head waiting for the streetlight to change. A woman wearing a green rain jacket holds the small hand of a small child wearing a yellow slicker and rubber boots as they cross the street. A tall, well-dressed man carrying an umbrella, strides—almost glides—down the sidewalk; he's got an important destination on his mind. I wonder what their stories are.

I reach the coffee shop, pull open the door, and step inside. It's busy. Guitar strings from background music pluck out a tune I don't recognize. That's okay. It's the hissing from the espresso machine that's the music I'm listening for this morning. I take my frothy mug of caramel macchiato to a table near a window, shrug out of my jacket, and lay it on top of my purse on the chair next to me. I notice that my blue mug has a chip out of it as I lift it and take a first sip of frothy coffee but, of course, that doesn't detract from the deliciousness. I look around to ground myself.

There are two carnations in a glass vase on the table—one white, the other yellow. An umbrella plant in the front window and a spiky sansevieria (aka: mother-in-law's tongue) bring a touch of the outdoors in. There's a man sitting in a wing chair reading the first pages of a library book; a red ribbon page marker hangs from the spine. A cackling laugh from a man wearing a reflective vest at a table in front of me catches my attention. At the table next to him, a young man taps on the keyboard of a laptop while a young woman sits across from him picking pieces off of a muffin and dropping them in her mouth.

No longer do I take lightly the blessing of sitting in a coffee shop. Eighteen months ago, there was a sign in the window of this place that punched me in the gut when I saw it. *See you soon.* One shop of many on a main street that was shut down. There was something about the sign in this window that hurt my heart almost as much as seeing yellow tape around playgrounds. But now, on this gray, wet morning, the comfort of sitting here listening to random ambient noise and sipping coffee is sweeter than ever. In the absence of my laptop, I pull out my phone and tap out some words while I wait for my friend to arrive so I can hold on to these moments and pull them out if I need them again in the future.

Sunday, October 31, 2021

Laurinda and Makiya have run out to the store. Gerry is downstairs—booking hikes or playing solitaire on his computer. Maya and Murphy are munching on their supper. The sun is shining but there's still frost on rooftops where the sun hasn't touched the space today. Makiya reported there was still frost on the ground on the playground when she was there earlier. It's coming. We know it. Before long the ground will be white and I'll happily settle in for the winter at home.

I'm listening to the comforting sound of the clothes dryer. There's something about it that is peaceful. Do you know what I mean? Maybe it's the ordinariness and predictability of warm, clean clothes being readied for the week ahead, or the almost-hypnotic sound of tossing clothes, whatever it is it's soothing, like the sound of the furnace humming on cold mornings or turning the lights on on dark afternoons. The simple, comfort of home. Priceless.

NOVEMBER 2021

Tuesday, November 2, 2021

It's one of our favourite things: an afternoon drive in the country, me with coffee in hand, the littlest Yorkie asleep in my arms, the other perched in her car seat between us, and Gerry at the wheel. We haven't done it for ages. We missed the spectacular colours of fall. It's mostly stick season now, but there's beauty out there in every season.

That comfortable balance between being lost in your own thoughts and sharing conversation that comes when you've been married a couple of decades is a gift. I'm thinking about the Help Wanted sign I spied in the window when we stopped for coffee and how they're showing up everywhere these days. That, and countless other things that are no longer as they were a short time ago.

I used to imagine what my parents, gone almost forty years now, would make of the world today if they could somehow come back and experience it. These days I imagine the astonishment and disorientation of someone returning from living off-grid for just two years. Two short-but-oh-so-long years. I'm disoriented and I've lived through them. Just imagine if all of this smacked you in the face all at once.

Out here, the country seems almost untouched by the madness. It's good to get away and get a taste of what's real and unchanging. Our daughter, Laurinda, is a master at this. Gerry too, with his enjoyment of hiking. I think they may be on to something.

The car climbs higher and we hit a spot of winter. There's no snow where we live, except on distant hills, but it's coming. I both dread and look forward to it. Next weekend we'll turn our clocks back and soon it will snow. Before long we'll be in the darkest weeks, pining for the light. But now, the skiff of snow on the side of the road delights.

We don't drive far before we've dropped down far enough to leave the snow behind. We come upon water and ducks and rogue cows wandering across the road. Gerry stops the car so I can capture a photo. Then, we turn a corner and it's like we're on the prairie. I feel myself relax. "I could live here," I say. But Gerry reminds me that the lack of available water would present significant challenges. Still, the peace and quiet is inviting, especially in light of what we've just come from and what we'll soon head back toward.

By the time the road meets the highway, it's almost like we've transported through three seasons and two lifetimes as we head toward town. The drive has done a good work. We are shored up to make it through the rest of another upside-down day.

Wednesday, November 3, 2021

I finally tended to the carrots we harvested from our backyard garden many weeks ago. They've been resting on the back deck waiting for me to get a burst of energy and turn my attention to them. This morning I brought them in, washed, and chopped some for soup and others for munching, and the rest I tucked in a reusable bag in the crisper drawer of the refrigerator. It feels good to have them done. It also felt good to putter in my kitchen. Odd as it may seem, chopping carrots helps support my mental health.

I feel as if I should be offering you more than just a glimpse into my day with these posts but, on the other hand, I'm nostalgic for the "old days" of blogging when that's pretty much what it was all about. We connected back then, in ways that quick updates on divisive social media platforms never managed to duplicate. I'm getting kinda tired of antisocial media.

Anyway . . .

Chopped vegetables are sitting on the counter ready for me to toss them in the Instant Pot for soup. Bread dough is rising on the countertop. Murphy is sleeping beside me and Maya is doing the same on the floor in front of me. Chica (the cat) is downstairs somewhere. Gerry is hiking. Laurinda is working. Makiya is at school. All are well and accounted for.

Thursday, November 4, 2021

It's almost 2 p.m. as I write this and it's dark. Next week at this time it will be darker because this weekend we turn our clocks back an hour. I wish we'd stop trying to mess with time but, for now at least, we persist. The end of Daylight Saving Time starts our descent into the darkest days of the year and, for some of us, the beginning of a struggle to maintain our mental health. Some years it's more of an effort than others.

These days . . . it's wet and gray and dark and I'm holding my breath for the first snowfall.

These days . . . I drink Yerba maté tea all morning and enjoy one mug of soy milky frothy coffee in the afternoon. The coffee is losing its charm. I hate to admit it, but it's true.

These days . . . there's a backpack on our banister. I retrieve an empty lunch container from it in the afternoon and wipe it out and in the morning, I put it, open, on the kitchen counter to be filled for Makiya's lunch.

These days . . . I am toying with the idea of pulling out my watercolours.

These days . . . I am allowing myself to get lost in books. I've already read eight more than I challenged myself to read this year.

These days . . . I'm tired of all things COVID.

These days . . . I watch very little news and I'm mentally stronger for it.

These days . . . I blog in the afternoon more often than in the morning.

These days . . . I'm thinking I might put up the non-traditional trees after we turn the clocks back.

These days . . . I put four piles of vitamin pills on the kitchen counter first thing in the morning to help my loved ones stay healthy.

Okay, that's it. That's enough. I was going to say "just for today" and I was reminded of a card I used to have on my office wall with a meditation I learned when I was attending AlAnon [81]. Are you familiar with it? There's wisdom in the words and living them out.

Just for Today I will try to live through this day only, not tackling my whole life problems at once. I can do something at this moment that would bother me if I felt that I had to keep it up for a lifetime.

Just for Today I will try to be happy realizing that my happiness does not depend on what others do or say, or what happens around me. Happiness is a result of being at peace with myself.

Just for Today I will try to adjust myself to what is and not force everything to adjust to my own desires. I will accept my family, friends, my business, my circumstances as they come.

Just for Today I will take care of my physical, intellectual, and spiritual health.

Just for Today I will do an act of service for someone else without being found out. If anyone finds out about it, it will not count. I will do at least one thing I do not want to do, and I will perform an act of love for my neighbor.

Just for Today I will try to go out of my way to be kind to someone I meet; I will be friendly and act appropriately, I will dress

---

[81] https://al-anon.org/

becomingly, talk low, be courteous and not critical, I will not try to control situations or other people.

Just for Today I will have a program. I may not follow it perfectly, but I will have it.

Just for Today I will stop saying, "if I had time." I will never "find time" for anything. I will have to take time.

Just for Today I will make time to meditate and seek serenity, truth, and acceptance of myself and others.

Just for Today I shall be unafraid. Particularly, I shall be unafraid to be happy, to enjoy what is beautiful, and what is lovely in life.

Just for Today I will accept myself and live to the best of my ability.

Just for Today I choose to believe that I can live this one day.

Friday, November 5, 2021

It's November. I can hardly believe it. Weeks fly by and yet, in another sense, they drag. This morning I took a look back in the archives of this blog to see what other Novembers were like, and I found a common theme.

One year ago, on this day I was struggling with depression and doing my best to pay attention to the good things.

Two years ago, I was recovering from surgery and struggling with the sense of vulnerability I felt.

Five years ago, my heart was heavy with the burden of things in the world. (It's a good thing I wasn't able to look into the future and see what was coming.)

Ten years ago, I was still working and also feeling the weight of current events and made the wise decision to switch off the news during my morning commute.

Thirteen years ago (which is as far back as my blog goes) I was drowning in work and heeding the call to listen for a still, small voice.

Notice anything? There's always something weighty, be it current events over which I have no control or personal responsibilities and situations that I'm struggling to wade through.

As I reread each of these posts, I noticed something else. I've always known that turning away from some things (the news and busyness) and toward others (paying attention to what's in front of me and leaning into spirituality) is the antidote to whatever is grieving me. I've always known this, which makes sense because that's the way we human beings were created.

For connection: to our Creator and one another. To be still and know. To pay attention so we can see the Divine in the everyday. To be loved and to love. It's folly for me to focus the majority of my time and attention on things over which I have little or no control. I can't know all the answers or foretell the future (thank goodness I didn't see 2020/2021 coming). Paying attention to what and who's in front of me is of far more value than wasting energy on things I have no influence over.

Here's something else. I've struggled. In different seasons, at different times, in varying degrees, it's been a hard slog. But you know what else? There have been times that were glorious and joy-filled. The good and the not-so-good. The beautiful and the terrible. That's how life is for all of us.

I could, having looked back over thirteen years, feel discouraged by the fact that I've carried burdens and haven't yet found the golden ticket to get me out of a life of trials. Or, I could be realistic—even encouraged—knowing that (as M. Scott Peck said so succinctly in *The Road Less Traveled*), "Life is difficult." I'm learning to accept that, and turn my heart and attention toward the better things and trust that, in the end, all will be well.

SOCIAL MEDIA POST.

We're growing weary, aren't we? Of the pandemic, politics, and a myriad of things in between. Maybe we just want to move to an off-grid solitary mountaintop and check out. I get it. Some days I'm right there with you.

But I'm reminded again and again—and again this morning—that I need you. I need the things you bring, that you create, and that you offer. I am richer because of the gift you are in the world.

Yeah, we're all tired and cracked and there are even chunks of us that have been shattered but we need each other. Every crusty, cranky, kinda lost and wandering one of us. We need one another. That's how we were created.

So—say it with me—I won't give up, I'll keep showing

up. I'll contribute more than I consume when I'm full
and be wise and vulnerable enough to reach out to
receive when I'm empty. I'll keep creating and keep
giving in whatever large or small way I can.

Let's do this together. I need you.

Monday, November 8, 2021
Lord, keep me from the propensity to want to be right and certain and puffed up with knowledge.
Meet me in the mystery.
Teach me to love well and live in the grace of you loving me well. Help me to know—really know—that I'm beloved, as is everyone else I will encounter today.
Remind me that my struggles are not with man nor mandates and that your way might not look like the way of the world. Help me to discern the difference.
And meet me in the mystery.

Wednesday, November 10, 2021
Well, I did it. I put up our two non-traditional trees, one in the living room and the other in the den. Later, when the day gets dark too early, the glow of the white LED lights will warm the rooms. Cue the *hygge*. I'll be delighted every morning when it's just me and the lights, and comforted in the evening with this cozy light filling our home.

After I put the trees up, I changed out some throw pillows in the living room and ordered a new duvet cover for the bedroom. Then, because I was on a roll with leaning into something different, I pulled out my watercolours. It's been months since I dabbled, and my woman cave is no longer conducive to being an art studio, so I plunked everything down on the kitchen counter and set about playing. It was fun watching the paint play on the paper and not try to create anything in particular. I think I'll do it more often. Sometimes I need to switch things up a bit. Especially now, as the dark days roll in and it's easy to get overwhelmed by things I can't change. Doing things that spark delight helps, as does creative play and paying attention.

Thursday, November 11, 2021
Gerry and I grab our cameras and head to a park. He's been taking classes and wants to put some of what he's learned about landscape photography and camera settings into practice. I grab my favourite 60mm macro lens and trust I'll find something interesting a little closer to shoot. He crouches down by the water and leans over a bridge, while I'm captivated by crispy leaves and bare branches. It's the in-between time. The glorious colour of fall has given way to stick season. Now we wait, almost holding our breath.

Soon it will snow.

Soon we will enter Advent, the season of waiting and longing and leaning in.

Soon (may it be so) we will learn to live in the After and, while we'll remain nostalgic for the Before, we'll welcome the opportunity to recover from the exhaustion of the During. We'll see who we've become and consider what we've learned.

Crispy, fallen leaves, remind me that all things change, and with every ending, there comes a new beginning. They are beautiful in their letting go—perhaps more beautiful than they were in the newness of spring and during the intensity of summer. Now they just are, taking on character and, yes, somehow even wisdom, as they drop to the ground and give themselves back. *Memento mori.* I remember I will die. One solitary leaf clinging to a branch on a tree that's somehow, in ways I can't see, preparing for the deep freeze that's coming whispers that, for me too, the days ahead are fewer than those behind.

Is the sphere I inhabit better for having me in it? Am I giving more than taking? Contributing more than consuming? Listening? Loving? Being transformed? These are the questions I ask myself when I sit at my desk later processing the images I captured with my camera.

Monday, November 15, 2021

It's been decades since I've had a cat in the house. I'm a dog person—Yorkies, in particular. But this morning, on a foggy, blustery November morning as I was in the kitchen baking oatmeal cookies and bran muffins, I glanced over and saw Chica (Laurinda and Makiya's pretty kitty) sitting on the windowsill and was reminded that there's something special about having a cat in the house too. I don't anticipate going out and getting a cat any time soon—or ever—but it's a treat for the time being to enjoy the coziness of having one in the house. Maya still keeps her distance and doesn't hesitate to voice her displeasure every now and then, but it's just a disgruntled kind of letting us know that she won't be sorry when Chica leaves. For now, she's part of the family and adjustments must be made.

Tuesday, November 16, 2021

We curl up in the living room in the morning—me with a mug of yerba maté and her with a mug of soy milky frothy chocolatey coffee, and enjoy mother-daughter conversation for an hour or so. When we've exhausted every topic (well, almost, and only for the time being) I head to the kitchen to bake oatmeal cookies and bran muffins while she goes downstairs to tend to some things.

Later, I talk her into making banana bread with some of the many overripe bananas in the freezer and sit at the dining table so we can chat while she follows my mom's recipe for the bread. I'm transported back to when my mom and I sipped cinnamon tea and chatted in my kitchen and, in a sense, she's here with us through her recipe. It's a sweet, sweet intergenerational thing.

I've waited decades for a simple afternoon like this. Oh sure, my daughter and I have had plenty of opportunities to sit and visit in our respective homes, but it's different now. She lives here—in Kamloops and, for the time being, with us. There's no rush to cram in as much as we can during a visit. The conversation is easy, though often about difficult things because that's the world we live in these days.

While the banana bread bakes, we break out *Bananagrams* and she beats me again. And again. Makiya arrives home from school and asks "What's that smell?" when she enters the house. (I love giving her the opportunity to come home to the smell of baking.) She grabs a few cookies and tells us a little (very little, because that's the tween way) about her day. Gerry's nose draws him in from the bedroom where he's been lost in a book and suddenly it's pleasantly hectic in the kitchen.

After a supper of African sweet potato stew and naan, Gerry and Makiya take cleanup duty. Later, Gerry and I curl up to watch an episode of a British detective series we're following, Makiya heads downstairs to practice her lines for theatre, and Laurinda goes down to do something (I'm not sure what. And that's as it should be.). Predictably, I fall asleep partway through the TV program because I've been up since before 4 am, and the day winds down—earlier for the retirees than the young folks. It's been a good and rich one and I go to bed content.

....

Mudslides and floods were the news of the day here in British Columbia yesterday with widespread evacuations, communities flooded, and travelers stranded due to record breaking rainfall. (Ironic, as we spent most of the summer praying for rain due to the forest fires.) The main highway connecting us to the coast—and goods—is now closed and will be for weeks or months. In fact, all of the roads connecting us with the coast are now closed due to the situation.

I went to the grocery store this morning to buy a cabbage for something I was planning to make for supper and found empty shelves reminiscent of last year's panic buying at the start of the pandemic. The rollercoaster called life continues to take us on a wild ride of uncertainty. Thank goodness there are days like yesterday to help shore up our reserves to prepare us for whatever is on the horizon.

Many years ago, my doctor sent me to stress management classes and a phrase I've held onto since then is: *The key to stress management is learning to build your physical and emotional reserves to prepare you to meet the next challenge.* If we didn't realize it before, 2020/2021 has taught us that there's always another challenge around the corner. May we learn to cultivate the things that strengthen us physically, emotionally, and spiritually as we navigate our way through these uncertain times.

On November 17, 2021, British Columbia declares a state of emergency due to the impact on transportation of essential supplies caused by severe flooding and landslides in the province.[82]

Wednesday, November 17, 2021

British Columbia declares a state of emergency because of widespread flooding throughout the province past few days because of something called an "atmospheric river." This, after summer's "heat dome" that claimed lives, destroyed an entire town, and contributed to a horrific wildfire season. And oh, like everyone else, we're still stumbling through a global pandemic and everything that means.

From March 2020 to July 1, 2021, we were under a state of emergency due to the COVID-19 pandemic. From July 20, 2021 to September 14, 2021, there was another one declared because of the wildfires. Now, the province has declared a third state of emergency in light of devastating mudslides and flooding. Another state of emergency? Sure. Why not? These, and other unspoken burdens, have me agreeing with Annie. "It's the hard-knocked life."

Here, at home, I turn on the tap and expect potable water to flow. The furnace is running, keeping us warm. We have more than enough food and supplies, so we don't have to worry about grocery store shelves that have emptied due to panic buying as a result of highways being closed indefinitely. Life around here is fairly "normal" (whatever that means anymore), but I feel a push and tug between concern for those who have been displaced or otherwise affected by politics, viruses, floods, and whatever else is wreaking havoc today and focusing my thoughts on that which is good and right and beautiful in the world to preserve my mental health. How on earth does one maintain balance?

And so it is that these things flit around in my mind as I move through my morning routine: showering, dressing, and making myself presentable for the day. With these things done, I pull down the blinds in our bedroom and am

---

[82] https://news.gov.bc.ca/releases/2021PSSG0073-002190

greeted by the loveliest light on the hills. I pause in my rumination, and drink in the view.

Oh my.

I reach for my phone to capture an image that doesn't do the view justice, but taking the photograph marks the moment and reminds me of other moments when the handiwork of the Creator lifted me from a state of overwhelm, and whispered of mysterious things I can neither see nor completely comprehend. I am lost in silent worship.

Another day begins. The news is bad and it's so easy to allow myself to get caught up in it. But instead, I set out four piles of vitamins, pour hot water over a tea ball in my mug, retrieve my granddaughter's lunch kit, and put it on the countertop to be filled. By tending to the everyday and ordinary things that make a life I'll get through today and tomorrow and however many tomorrows I have left. Learning to love well and be loved well with sufficient grace to get through this day alone. And on and on.

Thursday, November 18, 2021

The first fluffy flakes have fallen, and the driveway has been shoveled for the first time this season. Gerry and I, out and about on an early morning errand, encounter a pickup truck coming toward us with its lights flashing, warning us of something ahead. We brake, and slide, and come upon a young man standing on the meridian talking into a phone, the front of his truck wrapped around a street sign.

Now it is white.

I think of those affected in our province by mudslides and floods: those without heat and potable water and those who have been displaced, their homes destroyed or damaged. To them, the snow and freezing temperatures mean something else entirely. With the downstream impact (no pun intended) of rising prices and a broken supply chain and the paradox of labour shortages amid job losses, I wonder how this winter will play itself out for all of us. I don't know, and I'm almost afraid to speculate.

All I know is that now it is white.

Friday, November 19, 2021

It's been a difficult week for British Columbia due to mudslides and floods, and for all of us everywhere because that's just the way it is right now. I feel the burden and, in some respects, it seems frivolous—and perhaps even insensitive—to write about simple things I'm thankful for. On the other hand, setting one's attention on gratitude and simple good things is a way to counteract the chaos and heaviness of the present day.

Sunshine helps, doesn't it? We've got plenty this afternoon and it's so pretty after the snow we had yesterday.

Cabbage too. Getting groceries has been a challenge this week. The disruption in the supply chain as a result of the flooding prompted droves to clear out the grocery store shelves. Supplies are trickling in, and Gerry scored the head of cabbage and package of ground beef I've been wanting all week so I can make a comfort food type of supper.

Community. Stories about people pulling together to help their neighbours in flooded communities abound and counteract the clanging cymbals of discord that get too loud.

A handful of green leaves clings to the lilac bush in our backyard. I keep meaning to go out and take a photo and maybe I will when/if the snow melts in a day or two. The tenacity of a few leaves stubbornly holding on for dear life and trying to remain victorious in a battle they have no chance of winning inspires me some days. One takes it where one can get it.

> *On November 19, 2021 Dr. Henry announces that "Health Canada has approved Pfizer's COVID-19 pediatric vaccine for children aged five to 11."* [83]

Monday, November 22, 2021

This morning I feel like whatever I write will be inadequate. To write something cheery seems an insult to those in British Columbia who are already dealing with loss from mudslides and flooding, and insensitive to those in the north who are waiting for a second atmospheric river to hit the province. It would be easy to slip into despair and yet, that too seems ridiculous writing from the comfort of my home where we have heat and electricity and a pantry full of food. So, I ground myself in what's in front of me.

I'm listening to the wind and the sound of water dripping in the downspouts from snow melting on the roof. The tap-tap of Maya's feet across the floor. The unidentifiable hum of a home where the electricity is on.

I'm sipping lukewarm tea, a blend of yerba maté, hibiscus flower, elderberry, peppermint, and organic blueberry and raspberry flavours. My stomach is telling me it's close to the end of my fasting time and I'm wondering what to have for lunch.

I'm thinking about the book I'm partway through and thinking about picking up my Kobo and getting lost in it for a while. Or maybe tapping out a few more words in my journal. Or putting on headphones and listening to a podcast I've been wanting to sit with about trauma and its effect on us in

---

[83] https://news.gov.bc.ca/releases/2021HLTH0204-002205

light of all that 2020/2021 has brought.

I'm sitting with two Yorkies nearby: Maya, now curled up on the chair beside me and Murphy, asleep in my arms and with his tiny head tucked in the warmth of my neck. I'm wondering about what it must be like for Maya, almost deaf and with failing her eyesight, who has grown skittish in her advancing years.

I'm wondering if I should go out this afternoon, just for the sake of getting out or stay hunkered down at home. I'm leaning toward staying home. I usually lean that way.

It is Monday. Another week begins and I wonder what surprises it will bring. I think it's probably best I don't know.

Wednesday, November 24, 2021

I'm a huge fan of the Christmas classic movie, *It's a Wonderful Life*. Watching it solo is a holiday tradition because Gerry doesn't appreciate it in the same way. I missed seeing it last year because I just couldn't muster my usual enthusiasm. This year? We'll see. Anyway, I was thinking about Uncle Billy this morning and the scene where he leaves the Bailey's home after imbibing in a little too much holiday cheer and offscreen it sounds like he stumbles into garbage cans. Did you know that wasn't planned? The sound we hear is a crew member dropping equipment. The actor who played Uncle Billy ad libbed after the noise.

On one level, I was disappointed when I learned that, on the other, it makes perfect sense. The point, for the purpose of this blog post, is that something unexpected happens and Uncle Billy recovers and keeps moving forward. I can't tell you how often I've thought about the sound of that crash and Uncle Billy's words: "I'm alright. I'm alright." When life pitches a curveball in my direction and I have to do some fancy footwork to dodge it, or the burden of another day feels almost too heavy to shoulder, I think about Uncle Billy and tell myself that I'm alright too. Or, at the very least, I will be alright. Eventually.

But, you know, I'm not always alright and neither are you. By the time we reach a certain age—which is usually younger than expected—we've amassed an array of battle scars and war wounds, some of which are visible and many more that are not and on top of all that, the events of the past two years continue to take a toll on all of us. Lately, I've taken a lighter tone with my posts in this space and there's nothing wrong with that. It's my blog and I write according to my rules, but something is sticking in my craw about my lighter tone in the wake of current events and I'm asking myself if I'm being inauthentic.

Annie Dillard, in her inspiring book, *The Writing Life*, advises the writer to "Write as if you were dying. At the same time, assume you write for an audience consisting solely of terminal patients. That is, after all, the case.

What would you begin writing if you knew you would die soon? What could you say to a dying person that would not enrage by its triviality?"[84]

That's where I'm stuck this morning, and have been for a while. How and what can I write that doesn't risk of enraging the reader by its triviality in the wake of fires and floods and a pandemic and mandates and everything else that causes us shake our heads and ask "what's next?" Who cares about the words I tap out here most days? Is my Pollyanna-ish propensity an insult to those who are wading through very real muck? How much "I'm okay, you're okay" does a person really need? What's the healthy balance between "I'm alright" and "man, I'm struggling?"

The other evening, I stood at the window and watched the moon rise over the northeastern hills. A fog leviathan snaked down the valley this morning. Yesterday, I watched a deer forage for green next to the fence in our backyard. These are real things. Just as real as events reported on the news—maybe even more-so. Creation speaking. The Creator calling. That's as authentic as it gets. So, I suppose I'll keep writing about ordinary things that happen on ordinary days, both when I'm alright and when I'm not, and hope you'll find something that resonates on days when you're alright and others when you're not. It's usually a mixed bag around here and I don't see it changing. Forgive me my triviality . . . Behind the curtain there's more.

Saturday, November 27, 2021

I accidentally watched the local news the other night. Well, "accidentally" may be a misnomer, but it came about because the girls were out at supper time. With just Gerry and me at home, we fell back into our old pattern of tuning in to the local news at 5:00. I had to walk away because, not only was the doom more than I wanted to get caught up in, the commercials were focused on holly jolly buy, buy, buy seasonal consumerism. No thanks. I'll stick with my quiet non-traditional trees, a few thoughtful brown paper wrapped things under them, and a handful of Hallmark movies.

I'm feeling restless these days, and a little wobbly. The dark month is almost upon us and it's time to focus on the light and Advent. I struggled mightily at this time last year and don't want a repeat. I'm hungry for a writing project. Images I captured along the journey to write *The Presence of Absence* brought to mind the pleasures (and tortures!) of having a work in progress. I'm chewing on that and pondering a couple of ideas—even as I wrestle with what to write for the topic my writing group is working on this month. This morning I came upon some words attributed to Ann Voskamp that ring true. "The hurry makes us hurt." I know this, but I also know that inertia contributes to another kind of hurt. Ah, the delicate dance of finding balance.

But, back to the evening news. Watching the commercials was just as

---

[84] Annie Dillard, *The Writing Life* (New York: Harper Collins. 1989), 68.

stress-inducing as the news itself. The pressure to manifest a picture-perfect December is strong. Even now, maybe especially now, having endured 2020, come through more of the same in 2021, and seeing not much improvement as we round the last turn toward 2022. I won't even try. Hurry makes me hurt.

The restlessness whispers that the balm of busy will ease my discomfort, but I'm not falling for that ruse. I've learned that relentless restlessness is actually a call to stillness—not the do-nothing kind, but the lean-in-and-listen kind. The kind that writing invites. The kind that Advent offers.

So, where does that leave things?

Writing project? *Yes.*

Leaning in to Advent? *Yes.*

Leaving room for a little Christmas wonder? *Absolutely yes.*

Evening news? *Hard pass.*

DECEMBER 2021

Friday, December 3, 2021

We're not going back. What *was* is no longer and won't be again. It's difficult to wrap one's mind around it—at least it has been for me—but I'm there now. The sense of being trapped on a rollercoaster I didn't choose to ride, careening on a course into the unknown, is more real today than ever. It's not about what we thought it was about. Lines have been crossed. Words have been said. The train has left the station and we're not going back.

One morning I stand at the kitchen window transfixed by the crescent moon in the sky and think of things that haven't changed. Things I know in my deepest place and see in the sky and sprigs of chamomile and lavender growing in the hydroponic kitchen garden on my kitchen counter. Creation whispers. The Divine speaks. I brew tea and offer prayer. Dip my toe in world events and lift it out again. I play another game of *Bananagrams* with my daughter and chess with my husband. Cook and serve another meal. Set out four piles of vitamins on the kitchen counter. Take the dogs outside. Share a laugh with my granddaughter. Think about next year's garden. Look up at the moon in all its different and glory-giving phases. Everything has changed except that which is most important. The anchor holds.

Thursday, December 9, 2021

It's been almost a week since I posted here. Where on earth has the time gone? Makiya had no school on Monday and that turned the week topsy-turvy. I haven't been overly busy, but there have been things that needed doing and I was out of the house more than I'd like to be getting them done. I've puttered and visited and run errands and just carried on with life this week.

There's snow on the ground and it's here for the season now. The days are short and dark. I'm going to bed early and sleeping later than I like, tangled up in vivid (and not always pleasant) dreams. And reading. Always reading. What a treat it is to crawl under flannel sheets and dive into another good story. This year I allowed myself to unapologetically embrace once again the sheer pleasure of getting lost in good fiction. It's all I've read. I needed the escape words have provided because, you know, the whole world is kinda crazy right now.

This December is different (aside from current events). Right now, for example, three tweenage girls are laughing and having fun in our hot tub. It's good to hear laughter. The world needs more of it. How do we navigate these days when every day it seems like the news offers something different to be concerned about? After struggling mightily in 2020 now, at the end of 2021, I've come to the conclusion that we do so by living and loving as well as we can—not seeing the world through rose-coloured glasses, but through a filter of knowing we all struggle and carry different burdens and, despite evidence to the contrary, it is still a wonder-filled world. As individuals, we can't change everything, but we can change something for someone and that, more often than not, is our better work.

Saturday, December 11, 2021

We spend a pleasant evening with the neighbour's home, sitting around a circle in the living room, nibbling treats, and conversing with one another. I'm not much for social gatherings, but I'm struck by the peace and relative normalcy of people in a similar demographic gathering together. We talk about all manner of things and, maybe most important, I get a tip about where to score a Christmas turkey, as they're in short supply this year. Many things are—I never gave much thought to the "supply chain" before now. Doing so moves me closer toward intention, and need versus want. There's talk of Gerry organizing another Christmas Day gathering like he did last year when we were all sequestered at home with no visitors allowed, and everyone met in the cul de sac (socially distanced) at an appointed time to sing a chorus of *Silent Night* and wish one another Merry Christmas.

I've been chewing on words I posted here a couple of days ago when I was feeling overwhelmed by the impact on people of a pandemic, forest fires, mudslides, floods, and all manner of other things that keep coming as if on a conveyor belt of hardship, while my own life remains relatively unscathed. Sure, there are rising prices, inflation, that pesky supply chain issue, and the never-ending and beyond-wearing pandemic impact; but we're safe in our home with heat and potable water and more than enough to eat.

I can't do everything but I can do something for someone. A kind word or gesture, an unexpected gift, keeping my home a sanctuary, and caring for my own mental, physical, emotional, and spiritual health, so I'm equipped to do the simple, but better, work of caring for another. Quiet things. Peaceful things.

I'm not into grand gestures or loud protest or believing my influence reaches farther than it does. I choose to stand quietly, with intention, and do my best to put people above politics or anything else that causes division (which seems to be almost everything these days). I've come to believe that my role as a change agent is small but equally important, and one I am best suited for. Inadvertently, I have stumbled upon, and chosen, my word for 2022. *Something*. And a phrase. *I can't do everything but I can do something for someone.*

Sunday, December 12, 2021

Wasn't I taught that it's better to give than receive? Didn't I do my best to teach my children to appreciate the joy that comes through giving? Don't I remember the quiet delight of watching someone open a special gift I chose for them and saved up to purchase? And still I am prone to get caught up in the cares of the world that are, in reality, no small things, but that steal my peace to the extent that I focus more on disquiet than what I have to offer.

Isn't it true that being intentional about what I allow to occupy my mind influences what I have to offer another? Doesn't the whirlwind of "what if?" and "if only" and "but this" easily overshadow the truth that I have something worthwhile to offer in the midst of it all? Isn't it robbery to believe otherwise? To withhold the simple thing I have to offer because of overwhelm? Isn't the wiser thing to guard my heart, protect my peace, and look past things that serve to distract from my better work toward that which isn't on shaky, sinking sand?

Do I believe in my belovedness? My worth as a human being? That I have some small thing to offer every day? A gentle word. A listening ear. A kind gesture. Does my purpose have more to do with doing laundry, making meals, and participating in supper time conversation than changing the world? Or are those things part of my contribution to changing the world?

Is sitting in my pajamas, warm and cozy under a Sherpa blanket in my den while the rest of the household still sleeps, with one dog asleep on my lap and the other beside me, reading sacred texts and offering whispered prayers, enough? Is it true that self-care is not all that different from creation care?

When does thinking turn into overthinking? Is there more grey than I thought? Is love enough?

Thursday, December 16, 2021

We are still five days away from the official start of winter, but, for all intents and purposes, it has arrived and settled in. As I write this, Gerry is out front with the snowblower for the first time this season and other neighbours are clearing snow from their driveways. The sound of scraping shovels and noisy blowers disturbs the morning quiet. Makiya is pushing back against wearing her heavy winter coat to school.

"I'm from Prince George," she says. "It's not even cold."

And, yes, it's true that winters are harsher up north than they are here in Kamloops. But still. One can't argue with an almost-teen (she's just weeks away from reaching the milestone) who doesn't feel the cold in the same way as we older folks do so she heads off in the snowy morning wearing a hoodie and no coat.

The pace has been steady, but not busy, for the past couple of weeks. Going out to shop for a few things, having coffee with friends, and taking time for personal pampering (hello pedicure and float) has added cadence to the days. Next week, Makiya will be off school and I'm thinking ahead to slower pajama days spent watching movies, playing games, and munching on treats.

How are you doing with balancing staying informed and not becoming overwhelmed about current events? I'm managing by praying and looking past what I see to focus on what I believe. Still, a sense of foreboding lurks around every corner and one has to be careful not to get caught up in the vortex. Three conversations I had this past week are uppermost in my mind this morning.

One, with a woman who was at the end of herself and felt the freedom to express her frustration about something that sent her over the edge—the snow plow driver who consistently blocks her driveway with a ridge of snow (If you have ever had this happen, you'll understand. Especially if it's just after you've exerted yourself for a half-hour of clearing your driveway so you could get out. Ask my husband.) This woman even cussed while she was telling me about it. It was refreshing. Not necessarily the cussing part, but the letting go and getting real and expressing her frustration. Relating to others from behind a mask of "everything is okay" or "I'm fine" gets old. I appreciate refreshing honesty.

The others were with two different women at different times whose lives and choices over the past two years have also looked different. They each expressed frustration with ongoing restrictions and weariness, with shifting goalposts and the seemingly endless narrative that has changed all of our lives. More importantly, they spoke of how we seem to have forgotten how to be civil and choose, instead, to point fingers and judge those who have different opinions. I am certain that if they were in a room together, they would have the grace to listen to one another. I am equally certain that there are many others who wouldn't, and that is one of the most tragic results of what these years have cost us.

Now it is winter. We don't know what it will be like to shuffle through this dark season but we will come through it. Spring will come—it always does. Meanwhile, wisdom tells me to embrace the season to slow down, turn inward, and rest well.

> On December 17, 2021, Dr. Henry introduces new health orders to be in effect until January 31, 2022. Proof of vaccine (two doses) is required for events of all sizes regardless of the number of people attending. Indoor gatherings are limited to one household plus 10 individuals or one other household. Unvaccinated people are allowed to attend any gatherings. All sports tournaments are cancelled. [85]

Saturday, December 18, 2021

This is what love looked like this week.
Hands held.
Driveways shovelled.
Laughter shared.
A chocolate offered.
A gift given.
A sacrifice made.
A candy bar cut in four pieces.
A serious conversation.
Meals cooked.
Tears.
Hugs.
Prayers.
Clean bath towels in bathrooms.
Notes written.
Dishes washed.
Questions asked.
Mincemeat tarts.
Vegetables chopped.
Ringing bells.
A coffeeshop.
Text messages.
Windshield washer fluid poured into receptacles.

---

[85] https://news.gov.bc.ca/releases/2021HLTH0230-002414

Headlights cleaned.
Vegetables peeled.
Dinner table conversation.
Four sets of vitamins set out on the kitchen counter every morning.
A gift wrapped.
A phone call made.
A thermos filled.
A story shared.
Grace granted.

On December 21, 2021, Dr Henry orders the following to be in effect until January 18, 2022.

No organized indoor social events and gatherings of any size

Concerts, sports games and theatres reduced to 50% seated capacity, regardless of venue size

Closing gyms, fitness centres and dance studios

Closing bars and nightclubs

Limiting table sizes at restaurants, cafes and pubs to a maximum of six people per table with physical distancing or barriers.

Tuesday, December 21, 2021

I dream I'm in the little bungalow I grew up in on 7th Avenue Northwest in Moose Jaw. I'm downstairs in, what we called the rumpus room, but in my dream, I refer to it as the rec room. It hasn't been used for a while and I'm tidying up because I'm hosting a gathering (which, if you know me, is the first thing that confirms it's a dream). The room is much the same as I remember it, only bigger. The steel-backed Willis piano is still there, as are two comfy overstuffed sofas. My little pink toy stove is gone, as are dolls with eyes that close and wooden blocks. I'm rearranging seating and testing out lighting when I discover many lightbulbs are burnt out and I go upstairs in search of more. Mom is in the kitchen making supper and I open the door to the pantry looking for bulbs.

"Isn't this where we keep them," I ask. She says no, and directs me to the top of the cupboard in the hall. There's no way I'll be able to reach the top cupboard but I head there anyway and, surprise of surprises, I have no problem reaching to open the wooden doors and rummage around looking in vain for new lightbulbs.

The only other place I can imagine finding them is the garage, so I head down four steps to the landing and out the side door. Dad is out there, just locking the garage door and I ask him about the bulbs. He hands me the keys so I can have a good look. Meanwhile, my guests are arriving and I am transported back to the rec room with lightbulbs in hand. There's a motley assortment of people there, co-workers from just before I retired and other people I don't recognize but seemed to know in the dream.

The gathering is scheduled to start at 6:30 but Mom told me earlier that we'd be having dinner at 6:30. I excuse myself from the company of my friends and hurry upstairs to join Mom and Dad at the table and wolf down fried chicken and mashed potatoes. I hurry back downstairs after we eat and I'm still tidying and rearranging even while my guests mingle. Someone plucks out a tune on the piano, others form a circle with chairs and wait for something. I do some slip-shod dusting and tidying and find a tiny toy rabbit that a little Dutch girl gave Dad when he was overseas during the war. When the time comes for our gathering to end, I ask everyone to gather together so I can take a photo to commemorate the occasion. Most people are dressed in red and white and I capture festive Christmas-like images. As I shoot one photo after another, the group move their arms and becomes a singing Christmas tree. It's quite magical.

In the liminality of that fuzzy space when sleep gives way to wakefulness, I take one more walk through the house and join Mom and Dad in the kitchen before I'm fully awake. Then I linger, between flannel sheets and under a down duvet, basking in the sense of home.

Wednesday, December 22, 2021

I'm praying as I drive. I often do. Alone in my car, I whisper petitions and, sometimes, speak aloud the longings of my heart for those I love. More often, my prayers are deep and silent, offered in the fugue-likeness of autopilot driving. Today, I'm praying for someone I love who is struggling, reminding the Creator of things done in the past in this person's life, as if my reminders are necessary. Finally, in my mind's eye, I lift my raised cupped hands toward the heavens, imagine this dear one sitting in them, and release into the care of the Divine. Over the course of my life, I've intentionally released concerns countless times this way—again and again, because of my propensity to pick things up and worry them until I remember the wisest choice is prayerful release.

I'm thinking about words I read earlier in a news story that framed the recent mandates in a different way. *Unvaccinated British Columbians are legally not allowed to attend social gatherings outside their household.* It sent a chill through me. Today, it's the unvaccinated, who's next? I can't believe we've come to (or returned to) this place. There must be a balance between prayer and action in this, but it's unclear to me what that is at this moment. There must be lines we dare not cross, and yet we keep crossing them.

I turn off the highway, north toward home, and my eyes are drawn to the west where the sun is just setting. The heavens are glorious. There's something magical about the shades of pink and red and the cloud formations. I turn right, detouring, to get a better view. I circle the block twice, stopping at the side of the road the second time around to take in the majesty. Creation gets me every time. It's often how the Divine speaks to me. I have no words to adequately describe what I see and what I know, and that's okay. Some things are meant to be indescribable.

Later, my social media is flooded with images of the sky captured in those moments all over the city. These are dark days and we are drawn toward the wonder of light. The burdens remain and sometimes anxiety overwhelms, but we worship. Whether we call it that or not, we worship. Finally, I turn toward home and people I love, where my better work awaits. Sometimes loving well is the hardest thing, but it's the thing for which I was created. Sometimes it's soft and easy, other times it pinches. I'm still figuring out how to do it marginally well.

Sometimes current world events seem distant, other times they demand more than prayer. I'm still figuring that out, too. But *(fill in the blank) are legally not allowed to attend social gatherings outside their household* seems to be, at the very least, one worth sitting up and taking notice of.

Friday, December 24, 2021

As we settle in for a few days of quiet celebration peppered with laughter and joy, may the turmoil that has coloured this year and last be overshadowed by peace. Henri Nouwen reminds us that "Optimism and hope are radically different attitudes. Optimism is the expectation that things—the weather, human relationships, the economy, the political situation, and so on—will get better. Hope is the trust that God will fulfill God's promises to us in a way that leads us to true freedom. The optimist speaks about concrete changes in the future. The person of hope lives in the moment with the knowledge and trust that all of life is in good hands."[86]

So, too, while we acknowledge the grief we've all been living with over a world we barely recognize, may we remain people of hope.

Emmanuel. God with us. Hallelujah.

Tuesday, December 28, 2021

Traditionally, I use the last week of the year to clean up loose ends, tidy up, look back, and plan for a fresh start in the coming year. Years ago, when I was still working and many people were out of the office during this week, a reduction in the number of meetings and a quiet office provided a perfect environment in which to do so. In more recent years, I've sequestered myself in my woman cave for hours every day with my heater humming and soft music playing. This year is different again, with Laurinda and Makiya in residence, and my woman cave in use for something else, so I'm stealing pockets of time and spending more time than usual in my head sorting things out. It doesn't necessarily make for good company all the time, but I'm finding balance between solitude-that-doesn't-look-like-solitude and family time.

It's bitterly cold this week, and a perfect week to stay inside. That said, I will have to venture out at some point for an important errand. I'm watching the weather and weighing options. Meanwhile, it's daytime pajama week and I make no apologies for it. I'm sick of turkey and craving something crisp and green. We don't, as a rule, eat salad out of season but I'm considering making an exception. I probably won't. Any greens now would be an unreasonable facsimile of what will available locally in a few short months. Meanwhile, I'm going to mangle the turkey carcass and make soup stock today. One step closer to seeing the end of the bird for good.

We had such hopes for 2021, didn't we? In a short conversation with my granddaughter yesterday she predicted that by mid-2022 we'd return to a semblance of normal, but that true normal (whatever new thing that turns out to be) wouldn't show up until 2023. I think her prediction may turn out to be fairly accurate. Are we up for another year of upside down? What choice do we have? We talk about the unprecedented-ness of 2020 and 2021 but the reality is that global societal upheaval is nothing new. We've been here before. The cloak it wears this time seems more sinister, the pace of change, faster, and the trajectory more apparent, but behind the curtain there's nothing we as a people haven't already encountered.

So, as the hours tick away and the year winds down, my attention returns to taking care of loose ends, tidying up, and shoring up my foundation to be ready for whatever 2022 has in store. These, under the umbrella of hope,

---

[86] https://henrinouwen.org/meditations/living-with-hope/

faith, and love: three small and simple concepts that I will spend the rest of my life unpacking.

> On December 29, the B.C. government announces that return to school after the winter break will be delayed. Staff will return on January 3 at which time they will implement enhanced safety measures in preparation for a full return to school the following week. K-12 students will return on January 10. [87]

Wednesday, December 29, 2021

As we step lightly through these final days of 2021, it occurs that I'm leaving this year with a vastly different mindset than what I entered it with. As was the case for many of us, my emotional well-being took a beating in 2020 and I fell into deep depression. I began 2021 seeking help and withdrawing to reconnect (ironic, yes?) and regain what I thought was lost.

This has been a year of carrot dangling. If A, then B. But C, so D. When E, then F. Until the letters became so scrambled that no one knew anything about anything anymore.

Then came the heat dome and record smashing temperatures that held some of us hostage indoors grateful for air conditioning, while others lost their life due to unrelenting heat. Fires followed. Our province burned and homes and an entire town were lost.

One crazy night we were awakened by a neighbour pounding on our front door. We stood on our deck and saw fire ignited by a lightning strike burning too close. Then the RCMP came and our entire neighbourhood was evacuated. We were lucky. We lost nothing more than a good night's sleep. So many others in British Columbia were not so fortunate this summer.

Finally, the rain we all prayed for came in the form of atmospheric rivers bringing mudslides and widespread flooding. More loss of homes and livelihoods. Part of our province was cut off from the rest and we gave more thought to the supply chain than ever before.

All of this midst the rumble of a pandemic and heavy handed, not entirely rational, government mandates. Political storms. Empty store shelves. A news media we no longer trust. Lost livelihood and, yes, illness. Now it's winter and a deep freeze has us hunkered down at home thankful for heat

---

[87] https://www.vancouverisawesome.com/coronavirus-covid-19-local-news/bc-delays-return-to-school-for-k-12-students-4908085

and water and a stocked pantry, more aware than ever that these are no small things. Our household of two seniors and two Yorkies has expanded for the time being to include a daughter, granddaughter, and a cheeky cat. We are all coming to the end of this year weary. I dare not try to imagine what 2022 will bring us.

Over the past weeks I've been pondering the difference between hope and optimism and have come to the conclusion that it would be foolish to march into the new year with a flag of the latter held high. Am I optimistic that 2022 will fix all the troubles 2020 and 2021 brought us? Not a chance. Truth be told, I expect even greater woes in one form or another in future years. But hope. Now there's something I can put my faith in. Hope, in terms of trusting in the mystery of a Divine hand moving when I don't see it. Hope, turned tangible with every sunrise and changing of the seasons.

When I brew tea, I let my eyes rest on the mint and lavender and chamomile growing in the hydroponic garden on my kitchen counter and see it. It's there in the curl of snow reaching over the edge of our roof, and in my granddaughter's smiling face. I hear it in the sound of a shovel scraping snow from a driveway, in the performance of a composition by Ludovico Einaudi, and in laughter around our dining table when we play a game together at lunchtime. Hope will spur me on to lift a cardboard box filled with seeds from a closet shelf to take inventory in a few months. It will be with me when I drop tiny seeds into pots and imagine the taste of sweet warm-from-the-sun tomatoes. It will remind me to look past the nonsense that clamours for my attention and to find peace in the moment and the One who holds it. No, I'm not optimistic as we head into 2022, but I am hopeful. And that, I believe, is the better thing.

Friday, December 31, 2021

On this the last day of the year, it seems fitting to take a literal look back at some ordinary days of 2021.

We welcomed the start of the year with a mild **January**.
We went outside and took the dogs for walks on balmy afternoons.
We did jigsaw puzzles.
I played with watercolour paint.

Smitten by pre-spring fever, in **February** we visited the garden to see if the garlic we planted the previous fall had sprouted yet. It hadn't, but it wouldn't be long.
We did more jigsaw puzzles.
And played with the pups.
I bought a bunch of pink tulips for the dining table.

The mild weather continued in **March** and we enjoyed the first ice cream cones of the year.

I learned that if I put an empty heart-shaped box of Lindor truffles in my husband's underwear drawer, it reappears on my dresser filled with chocolates.

Gerry was on the evening news talking about tick season.

I painted.

Laurinda and Makiya came for spring break.

In **April**, the gardening season got off to a slow start. I wasn't feeling it.

I started tomato seeds.

We celebrated Easter.

It was warm enough to leave the front door open and let the sun shine in.

On a couple of occasions, we sat in the sunshine in the backyard with the dogs.

In **May**, Gerry bought a bike.

Maya had surgery to have some skin growths removed from her back.

I planted flowers.

I took my MacBook outside to write.

I harvested the first radish from the garden.

In **June**, I harvested the biggest radish I've ever grown and it wasn't woody at all.

It was far, far too hot.

We ate salad with ingredients from the garden.

On the rare day when it wasn't too warm, I sat outside for a short time to read.

I froze blueberries.

I cooked an egg in a frying pan in the backyard just to see if I could because it was so hot.

In **July**, we were awaked by our neighbour hammering on our door to let us know that lightning had ignited a fire just below us.

We prayed for rain.

We stayed indoors because it was too smoky outside.

I made raspberry jam with Laurinda and Makiya.

We had roll kuchen.

We went to the beach.

Gerry, Laurinda, Makiya and I went bowling.

Ash covered everything in **August** and it was too smoky to spend much time outside without feeling ill.

Gerry went salmon fishing.
We harvested and harvested and harvested.
It was still too smoky to spend much time outside.
I went to Prince George to take in Makiya's theatre performance.
Makiya moved in with us.

We finally got rain and the skies cleared in **September** giving us a few days to enjoy the deck that had sat empty for most of the summer.
Back to school!
We harvested tomatoes and more.
I took Makiya to Prince George for her last appointment with the orthodontist there.

We moved Laurinda down in **October** and our little household grew by two and a cat.
I replaced flowers on the back deck with pots of fall mums.
Gerry and Makiya painted her bedroom.
We four went to the salmon run at Adams River.
I chopped and froze a mountain of garlic.
Makiya and Gerry carved a jack-o-lantern.

Gerry celebrated a birthday in **November** and we took advantage of the occasion to enjoy a Tuxedo cake.
A truck backed into me when I was waiting for Makiya at the dentist's office.
Gerry and I went out for a drive and to take photographs.
Laurinda and I played game after game of *Bananagrams*.

In **December**, it snowed.
Gerry and I caught a few hours of alone time.
Makiya did snow-shoveling duty.
Laurinda slipped on the ice and broke her arm.
It was cold. Very, very cold.
Our son popped in for a surprise visit.

And, that's a wrap for another upside-down inside-out topsy-turvy year. There remains a piece of every one of us still grieving for the Before, though we've come to realize it won't return. We wonder how we'll recognize the After when it finally shows up. For now, we continue wait in this liminal space.

As of December 31, 2021, there is still no estimation of when B.C. will enter Step 4 of the restart plan.

The province remains under a state of emergency due to the impact of severe flooding and mudslides.

AFTERWORD

March 11, 2022

Two years ago today, the World Health Organization declared COVID-19 a global pandemic. Here in British Columbia, after countless ups and downs through an assortment of restrictions, Dr. Henry has lifted the mandate requiring everyone to wear a facemask indoors effective today. Proof of COVID-19 vaccination (two doses) for anyone over age 12 is still required to enter restaurants, attend indoor ticketed events, at gym facilities, in post-secondary student housing, and more. On April 9, 2022 the provincial government will no longer mandate the so-called "vaccine passport", however private entities will have the freedom to continue to require them.[88]

Countless British Columbians in both public and private sectors remain on unpaid leave or have had their employment terminated because they made a choice not to receive two doses of the COVID-19 vaccine. Besides losing their paycheque, they were denied access to the employment benefits they were required to pay into. Our healthcare system is crumbling, in part, because of a shortage of workers, while able-bodied medical professionals in the province who want to work can no longer practice the profession in which they are trained. B.C., along with Nova Scotia and Ontario, remain the only provinces who continue to enforce the vaccine mandate for healthcare workers.

March 2023

This chronicle of the events of 2020 and 2021 was a difficult project to and I wasn't sure I would see it through. It has been a labour of love for those who will follow. Mostly, I've stopped paying attention to what's happening in terms of COVID-19. I don't know if we've arrived in the After or if we're still in the uncomfortable In Between.

Late last year, Gerry and I moved to my hometown in Saskatchewan. We seem to be closer to, if not in, the After here, where the provincial health authority dropped the mandate for healthcare and other workers to be double vaccinated for COVID-19 in February 2022, welcoming the unvaccinated back to work. At that time, Premier Scott Moe said "It's time to heal the divisions over vaccination in our families, in our communities and in our province. It's time for proof of vaccination requirements to end."[89]

---

[88] https://news.gov.bc.ca/releases/2022HLTH0081-000324
[89] https://www.saskatchewan.ca/government/news-and-media/2022/february/08/saskatchewan-ending-proof-of-vaccination-requirement

British Columbia, on the other hand, remains firmly in their mandate, [90] while hospitals in Ontario hospitals are considering hiring unvaccinated healthcare workers to ease staff shortages. [91] B.C. and Nova Scotia are the only two provinces where the provincial government mandate for healthcare workers to be double vaccinated remains in place. Calls to "follow the science" seem confusing in the face of such inconsistencies. I've given up trying to make sense of it all.

These were difficult years for all of us but they have taught us things too. We are always in some kind of liminal space. Whether it's a pandemic or a horrific fire season, a diagnosis, relationship challenge, lost employment or one of the countless other ways we are knocked off center, learning to live in the I-don't-know is a skill we be called to cultivate again. Living liminal is not comfortable, but it can be—if we allow it—a time of gaining wisdom and finding truth in fresh ways. It is, by definition, what it means to walk by faith.

---

[90] https://news.gov.bc.ca/releases/2022HLTH0184-001394
[91] https://www.ctvnews.ca/health/ontario-hospital-considers-hiring-unvaccinated-nurses-health-care-workers-to-combat-staffing-shortage-1.6187910

ABOUT THE AUTHOR

Linda Hoye lives in her hometown in Saskatchewan, Canada, with her husband and their doted-upon Yorkshire Terrier. She thought by now she'd have things figured out, but keeps coming up with more questions, and believes that's okay. She is the author of *The Presence of Absence: A Story About Busyness, Brokenness, and Being Beloved* and *Two Hearts: An Adoptee's Journey Through Grief to Gratitude* and *Living Liminal: A Slice of Pandemic Life*. Find her online at www.lindahoye.com where she ponders ordinary days and the thin places where faith intersects.

www.ingramcontent.com/pod-product-compliance
Lightning Source LLC
Chambersburg PA
CBHW010612100526
44584CB00040B/3801